The Mythology of Sleep

The Waking Power of Dreams

Also by the same author:

The Mind's Mirror: Dream Dictionary and Translation Guide
Nothing Bad Happens in Life: Nature's Way of Success
Tao te Ching: The Poetry of Nature

The Mythology of Sleep
The Waking Power of Dreams

By Kari Hohne

Published by Way of Tao Books.
P.O. Box 1753 Carnelian Bay, Ca 96140
PaperBird is a division of Way of Tao Books.
www.wayoftao.com
Printed in the United States of America

ISBN 978-0-9819779-0-4

For Ed, the Armani dressed Master who taught me to walk in two worlds.

CONTENTS

Forward

"For Yahweh speaks in one way, and in two ways,
though people do not perceive it.
In a dream, in a vision of the night,
when deep sleep falls on mortals,
while they slumber on their beds,
then their ears are opened."

Book of Job 32

Since our beginnings, we have wondered about the puzzling nature of our dreams. Sigmund Freud, a pioneer of dream analysis, believed dreams appeared cryptic to allow transformative ideas beyond the defensive walls erected by the mind while we are awake. Rapid eye movement (REM) proves everyone dreams. While we may not remember them, our dreams change us in powerful ways.

Working as a dream therapist, analyzing more than 100 dreams per month, I have observed how dreams offer clues about the pathway before us. Acting as another sensory organ, dreams release us from our habitual way of viewing experience where we can explore existence from a more boundless perspective. The omniscient ability to see our way forward, something beyond our reach during daily life, emerges as the story lines of our dreams.

Like the landscape and hero cycles of our ancient myths, dream settings and themes are constructed of similar plots. Both present the journey of empowerment for heroes who must traverse strange *underworlds* to obtain bizarre clues that will reveal one's identity and therefore, destiny. In this way, dreams portray how some aspect of the psyche appears to know us better than we know ourselves, providing guidance that can activate self knowledge and direction in life.

Both myths and dreams portray beliefs, concepts and a way of questioning and making sense of existence. They convey ideas that transcend reason as a way of moving us beyond the known. Mythology's primordial imagery existed long before written records and similarly, dreaming employs the area of the mind that existed before language.

1

These fantastic adventures awaken the sleeping hero to the prospect of metamorphosis. Utilizing a type of hybridization, a myriad of ideas can be blended into profound morsels meant to teach us about our inner world. Just as myths orchestrate laughter, healing and renewal, dreams too, are often comical, and offer inspirational direction during times of transformation.

We can gain additional insight into the meaning of dreams when we contrast this symbolism against the backdrop of our mythical themes and hero tales. As we follow ancient characters from around the world on a journey of initiation, conquest, and renewal, we observe similar patterns emerging in dreams. It is no wonder, since both myths and dreams present the *exact opposite* of what we believe to be true about existence. In essence, we dream about that which we fail to acknowledge, or repress in daily life.

The Mythology of Sleep explores the transformative landscape reserved for dreaming where *The Waking Power of Dreams* lead us toward a pathway of lasting fulfillment.

Introduction

"My friend, the mountain which you saw
in the dream is Humbaba.
It means we will capture Humbaba and kill him
and throw his corpse into the wasteland."
Epic of Gilgamesh Tablet IV

Each night, we drift off to sleep, believing the trials of the day have ended. Little do we realize we will awaken to a world that is upside down and topsy-turvy. As if we have entered a house of mirrors, nothing is what it appears to be, and everything we encounter becomes a reflection of *us*.

Sleep's mythology spins characters and scenery which personify our *inner setting* or how we are currently moving forward in life. Using the principle of *displacement,* dreams move ideas in covert ways to bring taboo subjects into a neutral space for processing. *Other* characters *displace* the idea of *us* to reflect *personal* characteristics that are emerging and changing over time. Dreaming allows us to remain objective enough to watch, rather than reject any new and emerging information.

Just as Gilgamesh embarks on a journey to confront the frightening beast guarding the Cedar Forest, we are also the hero of a nightly adventure where we must confront *the forest* of our fears. When we ascend the mountain of our beliefs, we look below and can tap dream imagery for its profound guidance. Whatever would block our forward progress must be vanquished, and even the most hideous creatures are meant to teach us about our beautiful nature. Like Gilgamesh, we access its primordial power and "throw the corpse into the wasteland."

Although we may not remember the strange initiation that gives form to our complex inner life, the adventure is every bit as enlightening as every-day experience. We spend *one-third* of our lives accessing this perspective, which Freud called "a peculiar form of thinking, made possible by the condition of sleep." We encounter the bizarre in cryptic ways that present us with a puzzle. Solving this mystery sheds light upon our attempts at transformation. Like the mythical hero, we gain valuable insight that will allow us to continue along the pathway of our destiny.

During the day, we hold tightly to our beliefs, and in the process, are stunted in our growth. While we sleep, our defenses are at ease and this "peculiar form of thinking" has an uncanny way of *tricking* the mind into exploring existence objectively. We spend *two-thirds* of our lives building the belief structures that are disassembled during the time we spend dreaming. In this way, dreaming reinvigorates the inner landscape which can become a wasteland.

When we sleep, the body is regenerating and healing itself at every level. Yet we believe this regenerative process stops at shoulder level. When a solution to a problem appears elusive, I have witnessed how dreams provide uncanny detail and direction for the dreamer, offering pathways of healing. Dreams are more active during times of crisis, and therefore suggest *unhappiness is merely the hunger pain for change.*

Myths and dreams present characters and settings constructed of fantastic scenery, frightening underworlds and forbidden forests. Both reveal symbolism or *metaphors,* which package everyday ideas into a meaningful adventure of *self-*discovery. Emulating our mythical heroes, we are on a journey to understand how light must overcome darkness. Both myths and dreams provide a point of view that is unique and strange, but more importantly, can move us emotionally and inexplicably toward a change in perspective.

I have observed the common symbolism and storylines common to *both* myths and dreams and use these transformative landscapes to coach others toward personal and professional growth. In my book *The Mind's Mirror: Dream Dictionary and Translation Guide* and in my website: *www.wayofdreams.com* the reader will find a comprehensive dream dictionary and additional interpretive tools. My articles have appeared in Medline, Pubmed, OphSource, Journal of Allergy and Immunology and in the Journal of Trauma Nursing.

If we had a common language, it would be the global symbols of empowerment that emerge from myths and dreams. Whether clients are deciphering personal clues from their dreams, or exploring timeless landscapes to discover the myths they live by, these images are powerful mechanisms that can unleash enormous human potential.

We may believe we can remain static in a changing world. Our dreams of rickety structures and landslides reveal just the opposite, because the foundation must forever give way. At the same time, the most hideous and grotesque creatures of our ancient stories shed light on the healing pathway to overcome *dis-ease,* or how guilt, fear and anger can become self-destructive.

There are timeless healing messages hidden in our ancient stories and dreams. *The Mythology of Sleep* is a groundbreaking look at the similar plots and storylines that appear in both. When we compare the two, a reciprocal exchange of information occurs: *mythical characters allow us to uncover additional meaning in dream symbolism; and our understanding of dream interpretation allows us to see myths in a new light.*

The Fundamentals of Dream Analysis

In his first major work, *The Interpretation of Dreams*, Freud described how dreaming condenses complex ideas into digestible and accessible morsels. For example, the complex idea of exploring potential can be symbolized by unknown rooms in a familiar house. Since the house represents our *inner architecture*, the various rooms will symbolize personal aspects as we change over time.

The symbols which appear in dreams are not very different from their everyday meaning. The only difference is that dream imagery presents a more *holistic* representation of our thoughts and feelings. For example, we explore our sexuality in the bedroom. To *dream* of a bedroom however, brings this aspect of our life forward for closer inspection. Since we generally dream about what we are repressing, dreaming of something taking place in the bedroom reveals how we are currently exploring repressed sexual dynamics to allow for a greater sense of freedom.

The kitchen is a place where we find nourishment, although to *dream* of a kitchen suggests the ways in which we are finding nourishment in a broader sense of fulfillment. Therefore, dreams bring forward what we ignore in daily life, at the same time that they lift us high above our lives to understand our way forward.

Entering a hallway can symbolize going into a neutral space where we make choices as we move toward change. Since we are in the *adjoining space* which leads from room to room, or the various aspects of our inner architecture, the hallway embodies how these different areas are fundamentally connected. The furniture symbolizes the attitudes that we *rest upon*, while the windows, doors, and lighting reveal how we *view* the familiar, unfamiliar, dark or hidden aspects of our potential. The garden, roads, and adjoining structures suggest what we cultivate for public view, while the backyard, basement and attic portray what remains hidden. In this way, dreams are a snapshot of the inner workings of our mind as we explore our evolving identity.

Fiction and fantasy mirror the transformative dreamscape because like the dream setting, there is always *one* hero embroiled in conflict. In the end however, the conflict is always resolved.

In my workshops, I use nature as a model for transformation because nature demonstrates the promise of renewal and is always regenerating itself. Using nature as teacher, clients identify a feeling and find something in the natural world which personifies this feeling. When they follow nature through its process of renewal, they discover rejuvenation. Nature is a great teacher of how to discover meaning in difficulty and always offers a transformative pathway that leads to resolution.

I may ask participants to identify a particular story in which they have found a special connection. For the most part, this story will come to them spontaneously. On closer inspection, they are able to see how the plot parallels a type of crisis they are facing. We can be Hamlet with a spiritual message that cannot be validated, or Osiris defeated and lamenting our sad fate. By following the story to its end however, we can explore its deeper relevance to discover additional clues or insight about our condition.

Someone drawn to the story of the ugly duckling, which becomes a beautiful swan, might miss the special nuance of being rejected by the mother. This story offers a healing pathway for anyone who was adopted or overcomes unsupportive early dynamics to discover their *beautiful* and unique nature. *Even within family members,* nature endowed us with unique variations to ensure competition for short supply is always minimized. Against the demands of conformity, dreaming ever reminds us to be the unique creature nature designed us to be.

The reason most people ignore their dreams is because they often view the dream from the perspective used in daily life. Our logical sequence is non-existent during dreaming, which allows us to explore existence from a more holistic perspective. Dream analysis leads to heightened self-awareness once we recognize how *everything* in a dream is a reflection of us.

The dream portrays *inner* dynamics using scenery, objects, and characters which portray the dreamer. This all-inclusive approach is fundamental in understanding *The Mythology of Sleep*. It is always *one* hero's journey of self-discovery. When we approach our ancient stories from this same unified perspective, we can draw deeper insight from their healing messages.

Dreams reveal the exact opposite of what we believe to be true about ourselves and allow unrecognized ideas to come out in the only way the mind will allow. For example, to dream of an *aggressive* animal attacking us will signify the opposite tendency, or how our passionate or "uncivilized" nature may have become *regressive* or repressed. Because we do not express its vitality during the day, we encounter it as something threatening coming from *out there*. Additionally, the most *important* clues will appear as the least charged or *most insignificant* symbols in the dream.

Dreaming gives expression to non-integrated information. It funnels complex issues into an objective format so even the dreamer's ability to shut down emerging information cannot stop the process of integration. In the same profound way our body heals itself *without our conscious input*, dreams heal us when we are unwell *whether or not we remember them*. It is usually a recurring dream, which brings a client into dream work in an effort to understand its meaning. When we are stuck, its guiding message can reveal the way through difficulty.

The mind is the organ most important to our survival and demonstrates the same organic healing processes as our body. The body knows when it is unwell and knows how to heal itself. In the same way, the psyche understands the blockages that lead to crisis, and knows how to resolve it. We accept the idea of psychosomatic illness, but shy away from the belief in psychosomatic healing. Approaching dreams as the hero's journey through a landscape of wellness, we discover a new dimension in the study of dream interpretation.

In the following chapters, we explore how unbalance occurs, and how we are healed through the *Waking Power of Dreams*. Like the mythical hero, abandoned as a child and forced to rediscover his *real* identity, dreaming rehashes the past so we can fertilize the seeds of our future. Our Holy Grail is the treasure we discover once we understand who we really are against the demands of conformity. The story line of our personal adventure can span many years, incorporating the past, present and future in a way which awakens us to our destiny. Dreams offer a perspective we are missing when we are caught up in the habitual mechanics of defending our beliefs.

The Cycles of Myths and Dreams

Myths are called cycles because we are told many tales about the *same* hero undergoing various stages of transformation. Dreams too, come in similar cycles. This pattern can be observed to generally come in threes, meaning a client will describe a dream morphing into three different settings, usually right before waking. Regardless of the setting, it is always the *same* hero in a different landscape of growth and discovery.

Both myths and dreams progress through conflict, discovery and resolution. In dreams, the first cycle or setting reveals symbolism *about* the conflict to be resolved. The second cycle describes the *creation* of this conflict, the move toward resolution, and utilizes past images, which have contributed to the crisis. Oftentimes this second cycle includes family members, close friends or childhood imagery and settings. Finally, the third cycle points to the *new way* which will allow the transformation to occur. This final cycle is often bizarre and most mysterious to the dreamer, yet richest in transformative clues. Although clients have a tendency to dismiss this last portion as nonsense, the third part of the dream is often prophetic and most significant in terms of healing.

Most of my dream work is done online, which allows me to focus on the actual dream content and its guiding message. Just like a doctor who analyzes laboratory tests or listens to the heart to explore wellness in a patient, I use dream imagery to explore wellness in the dreamer. I find the dream not only describes the conflict, it also reveals how to solve it. A client can spend days explaining a current crisis, although the dream will sum it up in a few cryptic landscapes. My website also allows me to analyze common dream searches, and I have identified eight common settings or landscapes where crisis is transformed.

The following dreams of actual clients demonstrate the three-fold cycle of dreams:

The first cycle will portray the conflict to be resolved. "Cathy" is driving a car while her father yells at her for not driving correctly. As children, we often heard messages that play as habitual, yet unconscious "tapes" in the present. The dream shows how her motivation to go forward is being checked by paternal tapes that have left her with an arrested sense of self-worth. Vehicles represent forward movement in life, and in her case, these negative tapes are "driving" her. When we began dream work, she was in a dysfunctional relationship that fed her low self-image. The conflict to be resolved *is how she must break free from the tapes that validate her lack of self-esteem.*

"Maggie" dreams of driving around in the dark, looking for a dorm or a place to live. The dream symbolizes how she is living the transient lifestyle of a college student, while she is in her 30's and would like to settle down. Driving in the *dark* suggests she is not aware of the motivation driving her forward. The conflict to be resolved is *overcoming a feeling of being homeless and lost.*

"John" dreams about a familiar house. Peering out the window, he sees a policeman searching the bushes with a flashlight. Since the house embodies his inner architecture, he is inspecting (flashlight) his public persona (outside bushes) against internal laws and tapes (police). The house represents the familiar structure of ideas rooted in the past, although the police personify the need for further inspection. The dream reflects how his feelings about a recent promotion made him question his recent disciplinary action with a subordinate. The conflict to be resolved is *whether a self-assessment will reveal that he did something wrong.* He must integrate the new persona created by his promotion in a way which is acceptable to his psyche.

The second cycle describes how the conflict was created. Cathy then describes how the dream changes into a setting where she is packing for a trip. In the first cycle, her father was critical about her driving, but now *he drives her* to the airport. On the way, he tells her how he feels bad and apologizes. She said, "I hate fighting with him and feel bad too." The baggage now symbolizes how she packs and carries her father's perspective. In her words: *She feels bad because her father feels bad.* It is interesting how clearly our dreams speak to us, yet we tend to associate the dream with the past and miss its obvious relevance to the present: *she carries self-criticism that she adopted from her father.* When she opens her baggage in the present, she finds herself perpetually in dysfunctional relationships with critical men.

The luggage in the dream offers a treasure: *your present sad state is only baggage.* Since her father is now the driver, she is given an objective view of what is driving her low self-image. She is not in command of her motivation and becomes a passenger. Going to the airport however, reflects her move toward independence, or a place where she can *fly* to achieve her ambitions and break free from negative thought patterns.

Maggie is still homeless and lost in her second dream cycle. She continues to drive in the dark, again, reflecting her unrecognized motivation. While she looks for a dorm, this time she is drawn to the downtown area because of its close proximity to bars. We now see drinking or the importance of alcohol coming into focus. The fact that it is *dark* suggests how she does not acknowledge how drinking may be keeping her from experiencing *real* intimacy. This second cycle reveals how the crisis was created.

John continues to question his approach in the second dream cycle in a setting where he is getting on a school bus with people dressed in black suits. He wears the same suit (an image of what is expected of him), or how his motivation was adopted in the same way one is taught in school. Not only is he *not* driving, he rides as a *passenger with a group.* The dream reveals how he is exploring whether the new identity which came with his promotion is authentic or adopted.

This imagery also suggests anonymity, being part of a force and a lack of originality. Whereas the police were checking him from the sense of conscience, (whether reprimanding an employee was morally acceptable), the people in suits on the bus portray *following others* from the standpoint of conformity. His inner turmoil reflected how he does what is expected but perhaps, is not acceptable to his psyche.

The third cycle of the dream points toward a new approach and can reveal an "aha" or a breakthrough that can lead toward resolution. Cathy then drives a car *without* her father in the third cycle (letting go of his influence and preparing to *drive* alone). She observes herself from the neck up in the rear view mirror. She does not look into her own eyes, but looks around them as she decides which stray eyebrow to pluck. This is an example of the bizarre nature of the third cycle. There is an attractive male looking over her shoulder from the backseat. She sees him in the mirror, and he helps her decide how she should pluck her eyebrows.

As a resolution, she explores her adopted image by looking in the rear view (past) mirror (self-reflection). By observing herself from the neck up, the dream concentrates on the *head*, or the ideas that shape her self-image. Looking *around* her eyes offers a message about her inability to *see* herself clearly.

The attractive male appearing in a woman's dream is a symbol of activating empowerment. He embodies the transformation or self acceptance necessary to find fulfillment in relationships. As she moves beyond the male influence of her father, she attempts to see herself through the eyes of this new male character. By plucking eyebrows (which shape her expression), she is changing her response and *grooming* her perspective. She describes how the dream makes her feel good about herself.

As she incorporates this foreign or unknown perspective, the part of her represented by this male develops in a way that can be more than critical, but accepting and guiding. *The disempowered hero feels bad because she owns someone else's "stuff." She takes another look and finds encouragement to see her real beauty.* Because hair grows and is cut over time, it signifies ideas, which need to be groomed as we mature. After this sequence Cathy moved out of her dysfunctional relationship and started a new life, which better reflected her growing self-esteem. The work I have done with clients in this type of transition is the inspiration behind the Protector's Empire and the Fear of Abandonment in Chapter Four.

For Maggie, the third dream cycle is the first to occur in daylight, suggesting ideas coming into conscious awareness. She continues to look at dorms, although this time she finds one on a river (flowing with the changes) for "upperclassmen" (seasoned and mature). She looks at a dorm that the "Greek system usually stayed in during their second year," but considers living in her sorority house. *All of a sudden,* she realizes she had already graduated from college and did not need to live in the dorms. As obvious as this dream is, Maggie failed to recognize the message: *you are living as an undergrad and you have graduated.* Her dream suggested that it was time to grow up and move off campus.

She is living a lifestyle her unconscious considers to be the immature way of a college student. In her mid thirties, she wants to find a mate and settle down, yet she sabotages each relationship.

The appearance of bars and alcohol in strange places became central in subsequent dreams. This suggested she may be sedating her *unacknowledged* fear of intimacy with alcohol. Perhaps that is why her relationships are not manifesting in a healthy way. She feels alone and drinks. On her dates, there is a lot of drinking. She wants a real home and family, although she is hiding a fear of intimacy in unhealthy relationships founded on drinking.

The dream was clearly telling her to wake up, grow up and claim her mature status. *The hero wants to settle down and doesn't understand how her lifestyle is exacerbating her isolation. She is in the dark about how she undermines the very thing she says she wants.* The work I have done with clients with intimacy issues and unrecognized substance dependence is the inspiration behind the Negotiator's Labyrinth and the Fear of Intimacy in Chapter Three.

Finally, John dreams of a sinking boat, with "only the top sticking up." He calls Sears, and discovers it will take three and a half months to fix the boat. He goes into a warehouse to look for help. A guy says he should find Ed McConnell. John looks at him questioningly and the man says, "You know… your closet."

It is always this third portion which manifests in bizarre or cryptic symbolism that often humorously, reveals the way through. The "closet" reflects his adopted approach that felt foreign and may have given life to a closet character or shadow. Boats symbolize how we move through the currents of life, while water symbolize how we feel about the changes we face. When his boat sinks, it suggests the end of an old way of moving through difficulty, suggesting a needed change in approach.

Sears or the "dependable repair people" portray a systematic way of fixing something. The mechanical way the guy says: "Ed McConnell, you know…your closet…" combined with the images of men in black suits portray how John's psyche is questioning whether he is living authentically. As his identity is molded by conformity, his dream suggests he is being a front man to a hidden character he is having difficulty integrating.

The time-period indicated for repair became prophetic in resolving the conflict. Three and a half months from the date of the dream, the crisis was resolved when the subordinate was asked to resign by John's manager. In terms of untapped potential, the guy in the closet presented interesting exploratory material, since John failed to resolve the situation on his own. *The hero questions whether he is suited for this type of work. His approach sunk him and the mechanics needed to solve the problem are not something he learned in school, nor did they come with his costume or title.*

In three and a half months, his sense of authority remained in the closet, while the dependable repair people resolved the situation for him. The closet character is a portrayal of the Shadow, which must be recognized and integrated. *That person* we are afraid of becoming will actually stalk us as the Shadow until we claim its power. Dream work with clients who are integrating the Shadow provided the inspiration for the Shadow Snare of Chapter Seven.

In each of these examples, the dream revealed the opposite of what the dreamer believed. Inspecting eyebrows in a mirror may be shrugged off as *vanity,* but actually suggested just the opposite: *low self esteem* and searching for male acceptance. Driving in the dark and looking for a dorm is dismissed because we already have a place to live. However, the dream reveals how we can operate *in the dark,* which leads to an unacknowledged sense of homelessness. A fear of intimacy can sabotage our relationships because we *believe* we are facing *rejection,* yet we begin undermining the relationship from the start. The men in black suits on a school bus demonstrate the dreamer's unrecognized march toward *conformity* even while the dreamer believes he has grown in stature and power.

The boat sticking up that the Sears repair people can't fix for three and a half months displaces a complex work issue with a bit of humor. Our boat has sunk, although the situation will be resolved in three and a half months. On a deeper level, the dreamer already knows the situation will require the help of the *dependable repair people.* Going to the airport became prophetic too, when Cathy moved to a new city.

The third cycle of the dream often presents a view of the future. Hidden within this cycle of the dream, I often see prophetic vision at work, the nature of which is explored in the Crusader's Grail of Chapter Five.

In the following chapters, we explore myths from different regions to discover the healing pathway of the hero. Each offers a landscape which mirrors a lifestyle or myth we live by that becomes fodder for our dream life. The dreams of numerous clients reveal how issues can usually be classified within these eight transformative landscapes.

Chapter One
Odin and the Warrior's Wolves

Tales of the Norseman
Motivation and the Boundaries of Power

> "Great Surtur, with his burning sword,
> Southward at Muspel's gate kept ward,
> And flashes of celestial flame,
> Life-giving from the fire-world came."
>
> *Valhalla* (J.C. Jones)

There is a land where the sound of thunder is given the name Thor, and the one-eyed chief among the gods is Odin. It is a place where lightning dances from the celestial rays of the aurora borealis in a world created by nothing more than the mixing of fire and ice. The rich characters of Norse mythology fueled the imagination of Tolkien in his creation of *The Lord of the Rings*. These Scandinavian and Germanic myths have left us with the legacy of our most precious fairy tales.

The ways of the Vikings, traveling swiftly in their Dragon Ships over great distances, brought their customs and culture to just about every growing civilization in the developing world. Between 750 and 1050AD, during one of the largest migrations in European history, the Vikings started plunder-raids, conquering and eventually developing settlements in other lands. The Swedes established kingdoms in Russia. Explorers from Norway colonized part of the British Isles. The Danes conquered northern France or Normandy. They were a powerful people who drew their destiny upon a distant horizon.

More than 900 words in the English language are Scandinavian/Germanic in origin. Christianity adopted some of the attributes of the Yule season and the pagan name of the goddess Eastre into religious ceremonies. This fertility goddess had a hare living on the moon, which laid eggs and symbolized renewed life. During springtime, people celebrated the goddess Eastre as a time when eggs were delivered by rabbits.

Most of the English names for the days of the week were derived from the Norse gods: Tyr or Tiw (Tuesday), Odin or Wotan (Wednesday), Thor (Thursday) and Frigga (Friday).

The Viking contribution to civilization is obscured because of their later reputation in Europe as marauders and pirates. They left a lasting influence on England and Northern Europe, and in other places, like France and Russia, the Vikings settled and gradually merged their ways into the existing tribes. In the three hundred years of Viking dominance, they instilled a lasting heritage within the developing civilizations of those they conquered. Although they were ultimately overthrown, it was accomplished by the offspring of their own ancestors.

The mythology or *inner architecture* of the Warrior is mirrored in these Nordic stories. From a landscape created by fire (passion) and ice (detachment), we explore the conflict the Warrior faces in the character of Odin, who disengages from real human interaction. The second cycle of the story portrays how the conflict is created when he trades his disinterest in the present for increased power to overcome a sense of impending doom. Like the third cycle of dreams, the story of Odin helps us to understand the healing pathway for those too strong to show weakness. We also explore motivation as it appears in the dream setting to see how it can operate consciously or unconsciously.

Unlike the omnipotent characters of the Greek pantheon, the Norse gods appear fallible in their shortcomings, and provide clues to the *Achilles' heal* or weakness of the Warrior. Although we are often endowed with the power to achieve great things, we can get so caught up in a vision of the future that we may find ourselves battling depression and isolation in the present.

The Creation Story and the Norse Pantheon

In the Arctic Circle of perpetual light, the summer is brief and the winter is fierce. The seasons change in these Northern lands with the sound of clashing thunder. The rumbling sky is a gigantic palace, where powerful gods embark on great hunts. The voices of those who fell into the dark abyss below, will tell you how the world was once created by blocks of ice falling into the immeasurable depths of the Ginnunga-gap. These blocks banged and crashed against magnificent walls of ice before tumbling into the darkness below.

The flame giant, Surtr, lived in the South and brandished his flashing sword, sending showering sparks into the great abyss. The sparks hissed and sizzled, falling upon blocks of ice, melting the frozen sheets with the intensity of their heat. As the steam rose against the prevailing

16

cold, it changed into rime or frost. Layer by layer the frost began to fill up that great central space.

By the continual action of ice and heat, Ymir the ice giant took form as the personification of the frozen ocean. He groped about in the gloom for something to eat and soon found the udder of a giant cow. Her name was Audhumla and from her udder, great streams of milk flowed. Hungrily, Ymir drank until he was satisfied.

The cow too was hungry, and she began to lick the salt from a block of ice. She licked until the first hair of a god appeared. Slowly, a face emerged and she licked until Buri, the first god stepped forward from his frozen and inanimate world. Buri begat Borr who had three powerful sons: Odin, Vili and Ve.

As the cow returned life to the gods, Ymir, the ice giant fell asleep, and soon a son and daughter were born from the perspiration that gathered beneath his armpits. Their birth began the line of giants who would dwell in a land called Jotunheim. Thereafter, a war raged between Ymir, his offspring, and the newly created gods. The ice giant, Ymir, was ultimately overthrown, and from his corpse, the earth was created. It was upon the giant's eyebrows that Midgard or Middle Earth rested. Within his upper skull, the gods skillfully positioned the realm of the vaulted heavens of Asgard.

A mighty ash tree or tree of the universe called Yggdrasil sprang from the body of Ymir. Its roots extended from the dark, cold regions of Niffleheim below, through Midgard or Middle Earth, and up into Asgard or Heaven. This great root passed through Midgard, next to Mimir's well and three Norns or Fates carefully guarded where it rose into the heavenly realm of Asgard. First was Urdur who was old and feeble and focused her one-eyed gaze backward upon the past and so, her name signified Fate. Next was Verdani who was fearless and young, and concentrated her fixed gaze upon the present and her name was synonymous with Being. The last one, called Skuld, wore an impenetrable veil, and pointed her unopened scroll toward the future. Her name would come to represent Necessity.

From the rotting flesh of Ymir's body, a host of maggot-like creatures festered and grew. Upon discovering them, they were summoned to Asgard by the gods. They were given superhuman intelligence and were divided into two groups. Those, who were cunning by nature, and dark and swarthy in complexion, were banished underground into a place called Svartalfaheim. They were not allowed to come forth during the light of day under the penalty of being turned to stone. These Dwarfs, Trolls, Gnomes or Kobolds lived within the earth and set about learning its great mysteries. They collected bits of gold, silver and precious stones. Hiding these treasures in secret crevices, they used

17

them as tools of magic to create wondrous gifts, given to both men and gods.

The dwarves carved the Runes and guarded its mysteries, which offered the secret knowledge of life. Among their most prized creations were Odin's spear, Thor's hammer, Tyr's sword and the rope that would come to bind the monstrous wolf, Fenris. Although they were not as powerful as the gods, they were far more intelligent than men. Their knowledge was vast and extended even into the future where both gods and men sought their advice. Hiding behind rocks, they repeated the last parts of people's conversations, and mimicked words with their mischievous echo. By donning a red cap called a Tarnkappe, they remained invisible, moving about unseen, playing tricks upon the unsuspecting.

The other group was the Fairies and Elves who were more brilliant than the rays of the sun and wore delicate garments spun of a transparent texture, like dew. These fair and gentle creatures were situated in the airy realm between heaven and earth, called Alfheim. Being drawn to light, they descended at sunrise to attend the growing plants and flowers of Midgard or Middle Earth.

Mixing with the birds and butterflies, they danced in the grasses and fluttered beneath the rays of sunlight. At times, they could be seen gliding along the silvery light of a moonbeam, their laughter mixing with the sound of the crickets that chirped melodiously beneath the trees. Along with tending to the earth's growing bounty, Fairies and Elves sometimes visited dwellings to help with the chores. They would find mischievous pleasure in tangling up the horse's tails.

Chief among all of the gods was Odin who held the highest seat in Asgard along with his wife Frigga. He was tall with dark, curly hair and sported a trailing, gray beard that cascaded from his chin. He was usually dressed in a gray suit, with a blue hood and mantle representing the sky. Sometimes he would wear this gray coat and hat when he walked about the earth to observe mankind. At such times, his wide-brimmed hat was drawn low over his forehead to conceal the fact that he possessed but one eye. Odin was not born omniscient or all knowing; in order to obtain the great power, wisdom and vision he sought, he was forced to make great sacrifices.

Mimir, the great sea giant, guarded a spring that bubbled near the root of the tree, Yggdrasil where it passed through Middle Earth. In its liquid depths, lay the secrets of the future. Odin approached Mimir and asked him for a drink. Clever Mimir knew the value of what was hidden below the water, and refused Odin this gift unless he consented to sacrifice one of his eyes in exchange.

So highly prized was this vision of the future that Odin plucked out one eye and handed it over to Mimir. He sunk it down deep into the fountain where it still shines today. Upon drinking the mysterious water, Odin gained the awareness of the future, and discovered the transitory nature of everything taking place on Middle Earth and in Heaven. In this vision, he witnessed a future known as the Twilight of the Gods where even the gods were doomed to pass away. Odin saw a day would come when the hideous wolf, Fenris would devour him.

He never regretted the sacrifice. Later, he would hang himself upside down for nine days and nine nights upon the tree Yggdrasil in order to obtain the power and wisdom of the Runes. Suspended from the tree, he gazed down into the immeasurable depths of Niffleheim and was soon lost in deep thought. He wounded himself with his spear in a sacrifice of pain to gain the knowledge that he coveted. He cut the symbols of the Runes upon his spear, Gungnir, and thereafter, held power over all things. Even as he had witnessed the future, he still believed he possessed the power to change it.

As he wandered the earth all-knowing, with his wide brimmed hat hiding his missing eye, it is said that the knowledge only made him melancholy. Thereafter, he was observed with a much more contemplative expression. In time, he would send only his two ravens out to witness the activity, which took place upon the earth.

From his seat in Asgard, two ravens perched upon his broad shoulders. One was called Hugin (thought) and the other was called Munin (memory). Each morning they flew over the earth and returned at night to whisper into Odin's ear, all that they had witnessed in the world below.

Crouched at his feet were two wolves named Geri (hungry) and Freki (greedy). Combined their names came to mean the greed or hunger and insatiable appetite of wild dogs. Geri and Freki were fed the scraps of food of which Odin no longer needed. Instead, he partook only in the sacred mead or wine, subsisting on only wisdom.

In time, only the Great Hunt would come to cheer his spirits.

The Great Hunt and the Yule Season

After the time of harvest and before the onset of winter, the roaring winds whipped fiercely against the leaves of the trees, and the thunder rumbled from the billowing clouds above. Townsfolk recognized these sounds as the onset of the Great Hunt.

Odin, as the Wild Huntsman led his son Thor, god of thunder, along with a train of snorting horses and baying hounds on a hunt for

19

disembodied spirits and the souls of the dead. It was an invigorating ride across the skies where the thundering wind spun the rolling clouds in its wake. The Great Hunt had the effect of tugging the last remaining greenery from the earth. Since the winds blew more ferociously during winter, peasants would leave gifts of grain out in the snowy field for the flying host and his horses as they passed overhead. Also called Thor's month, the festivities peaked during the winter solstice or the longest night of the year. The feasting heralded the return and resurrection of the sun.

Peasants celebrated in knowing the days would commence to grow longer. They made a Yule wheel that symbolized the sun, wrapped it in straw and place it at the top of a mountain. It was set on fire in a huge blaze that was sent rolling down the hill. This twirling, tumbling wheel of fire represented the new sun and the birth of the year to come. In later times, they burned Yule logs, which would be kept burning all night lest it portend a bad omen for the year to come. The next morning, the ashes were carefully gathered to ignite the burning log used in the celebration the following year.

Many ancient cultures used a world tree as a symbol representing the sun's rebirth. Decorated with stars, orbs and crescents it symbolized a time when peasants celebrated the changes taking place in the natural world. The ancient Roman autumn festival of Saturnalia also celebrated the death of the old year with a similar world tree.

The gods and goddesses of Norse mythology were equally adventurous and brave and women enjoyed as great an honor in these myths as the men. The warrior maidens were called Valkyrs. They wore helmets of silver or gold and red corselets. Brandishing spears and shields they rode white steeds into battle led by Freya, the goddess of love. The bodies of these goddesses were often carved onto the front of Viking ships.

Tyr and the Wolf, Fenris

Along with Thor, Odin had another son named Tyr. He was the one-handed god of war and justice. Considerate and kind, the legend of his bravery is told in how he lost his hand in the jaws of the Wolf, Fenris.

The fire giant Loki is one of many Trickster characters like Hermes/ Mercury of Greek/Roman mythology, and Coyote/Hare of the myths of the Americas. Like Hermes, Loki tricked his way into the Pantheon through wit and charm and by becoming Odin's blood brother. Yet, he was a giant and therefore an enemy of the gods.

Loki married the giant, Angur-boda from Jotunheim who bore him three monstrous children: Fenris the wolf, Hel the goddess of death and Iormungandr the serpent. They were hidden in a cave until they grew so large the gods soon discovered them. Odin knew the birth of these monsters would ultimately lead to the destruction of the gods.

Using protective measures, he cast Hel into Niffleheim. She would continue to grow and reigned over the dead, although she would be unable to leave. He flung Iormungandr into the sea where he grew larger and encircled the earth in such a way that he could bite his own tail.

Although Fenris was a tiny wolf pup, he was already ferocious. Odin knew the truth of what he would one day become and believed if he brought Fenris to Asgard to be cared for and loved by the gods, perhaps he might be tamed. All of the gods and goddesses, with the exception of brave Tyr, trembled at the site of Fenris. Tyr, who was afraid of nothing, approached the wolf and thereafter fed and cared for him. Daily, Fenris increased in size and power until the gods came to realize he would need to be restrained. Only by binding him, could they hope to control him.

Fenris allowed them to bind him because he knew he could break free from any fetter they used. Time after time, they tied him only to find that with a mere shake of his head or the wag of his tail, the fetter would be broken. To Fenris, it was a game, and he grinned and leaped with delight. After several attempts, the gods soon realized restraining Fenris was futile. It was decided that the Dwarves of Svartalfaheim should be summoned to fashion a binding to contain him. The Dwarfs were proud to think that it was left to them to make a fetter which would restrain the monstrous wolf.

"We can make it," they had said. "Out of six things, we will make it." Skillfully, they spun a silken rope of six unfathomable essences: the sound of a cat's footsteps, hairs from a woman's beard, the roots of stones, the longings of a bear, the voice of fishes and the spittle of birds. As a magical binding, not only was the rope unbreakable, but the harder one pulled the stronger it became.

Fenris grew suspicious when they approached him with such a flimsy cord. He knew such a tether had to have come by way of magic. He demanded that one of the gods should put their hand into his mouth as a token of good faith, and to guarantee that no magic was used in its making. If not, Fenris refused to allow them to fasten it around him.

It was futile. Dejected and forlorn, the gods exchanged worried glances because they realized they would never be free of Fenris. Suddenly, Tyr stepped forward and bravely thrust his arm into Fenris' great jaws. The gods could only stare in disbelief. They quickly fastened the rope around Fenris' neck. The monstrous wolf shook his head and he leaped. He pulled in every direction and could not break free. The more he struggled, the stronger the tether became. When the gods saw how indeed,

Fenris could not break loose, they were jubilant. Angrily, Fenris bit off Tyr's hand.

Just as Odin had sacrificed his eye to obtain his omniscience and vision of the future so too, did Tyr prove his courage and dignity by sacrificing his hand so the gods might endure.

Motivation in Dreams

All good stories are founded upon a character's *motivation*, or what drives the hero on an adventure. Odin is driven by a sense of impending doom that *threatens* his power. Motivation drives us forward in life and is portrayed as *transportation vehicles* in dreams. The details surrounding the vehicle /vessel, whether or not we are driving, crashing or moving across a choppy sea will portray our current state of autonomy as we embark on the adventure of our life.

In some cases we are aware of our motivation and other times, we are not. Driving at night is a clue that we are exploring motivation unknown to us. Whether or not we are driving portrays how we are currently taking the reigns of self-responsibility.

Water signifies the unknown. It represents how we can be fearful of not being able to control the current, or where life is currently leading us. These types of dreams reflect whether we are learning to take control of our vehicle (motivation) or how we might trust the current (life experience) is taking us where we need to be.

When the Vikings mastered the art of transportation and the use of the sail, they burst upon history as uncivilized barbarians and pirates. Although they plundered and raided what remained of the Roman and Byzantine Empires, they also colonized much of early Europe through their power.

No other folk tales have left more of an indelible mark upon the nursery, or brought such a richness of fantasy to the world of children. This is especially true in the education of the 3-6 year old, when the growing ego and the will are believed to manifest. It is therefore appropriate to turn to this culture to explore the *kindergarten* of how our power manifests. In the first stages of empowerment in the individual we can come to appreciate the motivation behind the Warrior's tale.

Sigmund Freud was the first explorer to chart the unknown regions of the psyche, utilizing dreams to explore its hidden territories. He believed the *ego* was the center of consciousness and was birthed slowly from an oceanic sense of connectivity to everything. He labeled this ocean the *unconscious* and its smaller continents the *id* and the *ego*. Nietzsche, inspired by the ideas of Darwin, first used the word *id* to describe the part of our nature that was impersonal, unrefined and subject to natural law. Recognizing that some segment of the ego remained *uncivilized*, Freud labeled it the *id*.

He believed the compliant part of the id donned the mask of conformity to evolve into the ego. Dreaming allows us to dissolve back into the id's oceanic realm, specifically because the mask and the controls of the ego are inactive during sleep. In this way, the realm of the id inspires our dreams to keep us expressing our uncivilized *naturalness*.

As children, we set sail from the *id's* instinctual realm, and begin to recognize or remember something or someone. When we know in this way, consciousness and the ego are developing. Something catches our eye, and we want to reach out and touch it. Accomplishment comes from the monumental journey of crossing the endless expanse of the living room to explore. On this early journey, we were sometimes watched and rewarded with a tussle on the head. A conditioning process begins where this type of accomplishment can become a method for receiving more attention and love.

Like Fenris, we approach the challenge and grin with delight. Perhaps nobody was watching when we crossed the room with our willful determination, and ran headlong into the coffee table. We may have experienced nothing but pain in return for our heroic efforts, or were punished for touching things. We become skeptical about venturing beyond these *unidentifiable* or ambiguous boundaries. These boundaries will become rich fodder for our dream life. Contradictions and illogical idea sequences are constantly explored to uncover the ways they disempower us when we are older.

The Norse gods make heroic sacrifices to increase their power over monsters and giants. We too, explored a world inhabited by giants and enjoyed a type of boundless awareness. We may recall drifting between this realm of fantasy and being prompted toward conscious awareness during a time when grown ups were focusing us outward, and teaching us about the world we were growing into.

As we grow, we organize the world into a myriad of concepts and words. Life becomes more complicated and the ego becomes, in Freud's words: "a shrunken residue of the much more inclusive, more intimate bond between the ego and the world about it." Thereafter, this boundless perspective will only resurface during dreaming where we dissolve back into the instinctual and fantastic realm of the id.

The Psyche's Cast of Characters

The developing psyche can be viewed as characters emerging upon a stage. First on the scene is the instinctual and primitive *id*, which will be reigned in by the developing *ego*. Like a charioteer who controls a group of horses, the ego must reign in and gain control of the id's desires. Each horse represents various desires for satisfaction, to overcome hunger, fear and to receive affection and encouragement on our road to empowerment. In time, we must also gain mastery over the environment.

The charioteer *(ego)* must balance the instinctual nature of the horses *(id)* against the demands and terrain or what is perceived in the outer world. If that weren't difficult enough, the charioteer *(ego)* falls under the influence and demands of a back seat driver *(superego)*, which can criticize and direct it's every move. Freud believed the superego manifested along side of the growing ego as an *alter-ego* that enforces the disciplinarian tapes adopted when we were young. It is created from the times in our life that we heard and assimilated *what we should and shouldn't do*. Joseph Campbell, a pioneer in the study of the mythical symbols of transformation, labeled this self-critical aspect *"thou shalt."* This sense of conscience will continue to shadow us on our journey.

Natural urges of the id can be controlled by either the ego or superego before being expressed. The *will* can be viewed as the reins, or negotiation process between the characters. The charioteer (ego) uses controls to manage the horses when we apply the will consciously. At the same time, obscure boundaries or illogical ideas allow the superego to "manage the horses" and operate less consciously. *Psychic health requires balance where no one character is suppressed or overwhelmed by another.*

An initiative, which begins as an act of will can, through repetition, become habitual. In Chapter Two we will explore how an instinct like fear, when unchecked, can grow out of proportion to develop into an uncontrolled state of anxiety. During depression, we can fall prey to a type of *conversion* where the reins of the will are usurped from conscious awareness by the *unfathomable essences* of the unconscious. We dream of doing something in the dark or riding as a passenger when our will to go forward or self-motivation is no longer operating under conscious control. In this way, dreams often reveal how we become lost. Dreams of reading red writing can also be a wake up call to explore this.

Undoubtedly some aspect of the psyche leads us toward wellness when we dream. At the same time, we must acknowledge that another aspect acts a gatekeeper in upholding the status quo.

The unconscious shifting of the reins is often portrayed in dreams of vehicles or buildings with doors or windows that cannot open. Sleep's mythology rarely presents the actual body part that is undergoing conversion or *dis-ease*. The ideation behind dreams will portray the part of the body that is holding unprocessed energy as symbolism associated with movement (vehicles) or beliefs (the upper and lower floors of houses). The dreams of clients facing illness present this type of setting as the first cycle, while the second cycle shows them searching for *or protecting* a precious treasure. The treasure of course, is the *unacknowledged conflict* which is carefully guarded by the gatekeeper. I have often observed the clue to their disempowerment represented by the landscape of the third cycle, in which they are searching for a key or something lost.

The search for a lost item usually presents the clue to our disempowerment. We may search for a purse or wallet when we are changing occupations, or during a period when we are questioning how we will provide for ourselves. Searching for an unknown child can represent our attempt to discover an emerging and unknown part of our potential. Looking in religious buildings can represent exploring critical conscience or the realm of "thou shalt" when we are trapped in a transformational process. Searching in a school setting is often associated with exploring conformity or what we have learned and adopted. When our sexuality is repressed, we can dream of reading newspapers on a bed, portraying the idea of discovery (reading), the pressure of conformity (newspaper) and how we can express ourselves more naturally (bed). Sexuality is also associated with the bathroom where we come clean and get naked at the same time.

As we attempt to give expression to our natural urges, we succumb to the demands of conformity to fit in. The psyche is always negotiating its more *natural* desires against the disciplinarian tapes of what we should and shouldn't do.

When we are depressed, we can succumb to highly critical childhood tapes. *"Stop crying...don't be a baby...come on, get up...what is the matter with you?"* If we believe we are not allowed to show weakness, a physical symptom without a biological basis can sometimes manifest. It becomes the unconscious shifting of the reins to something other than conscious awareness.

The Drive for Power

The need to exert power is sometimes viewed as a need to dominate or control others. However, if we look deeper, we find the need to control manifests in proportion to our insecurities. In dreams, insecurity is often revealed by sliding foundations, choppy waters and terrestrial events which are beyond our control. Natural disasters and their meaning in dreams will be explored more in depth in Chapter Seven.

Like the Norse gods, the crisis faced by the Warrior or over-achiever is sometimes funded by an early environment that may have been perceived as threatening. Perhaps it was highly competitive and demanded an extra dose of willfulness. During the first few years of life, we either trusted that our needs would be met, or we behaved more aggressively to take care of ourselves.

What may have started as a need for love and competence transforms into a need to gain mastery over an environment, in which we felt threatened. Later, this may develop into an extremely willful approach or controlling tendencies. The less than perfect gods of Norse mythology develop power against the backdrop of monsters and evil giants who emerge from the landscape. In dreams, the monsters of the psyche are always challenging us to unleash our powerful faculties as a mechanism that ensures our wellness.

What begins as the motivation to seek positive reinforcement and accomplishment can turn into the endless process of building self-esteem to offset a fear of inadequacy. When achievement does not bring a sense of satisfaction for the long term, we know we are an over-achiever.

Our drive for self-esteem can lead us to set unrealistic goals that can also lead to defeat. Although we may achieve our goals, this drive is not necessarily based on an equal balancing of all basic needs and *something* always remains missing. Using accomplishment to overcome a sense of inadequacy, we are actually motivated by a need to gain acceptance. Eventually, the lack of a balanced reward system leaves us feeling empty. To compensate, we substitute *admiration* for love and real intimacy.

The Warrior/over-achiever will work long hours, neglecting the family and experience work as the only means for achieving a sense of reward. Success and power can only be achieved by developing even greater goals. The self-sufficiency and achievement cycle developed in early childhood serves the single executive, although it can lead to crisis for anyone trying to build a family or experience a normal relationship. We see this lack of balance in the growing group of forty-something female executives. They realize all too late, how they have perhaps missed out on the joy of having children. We find a similar crisis experienced by the successful businessman who comes home to find his family has left him.

Over-achievement is not just the mythology of the business executive; it simply coincides with a lack of balance. We can be overly focused on our role as a caregiver, which can also leave our authenticity

26

arrested. "Barb" is a doting mother of four and a faithful wife. She described a dream where her husband, children, younger sister and her children were all going on a trip. Barb was packing and couldn't find something *very important*. She couldn't recall what it was she was searching for, although she knew it was the reason she had been left behind. This left her feeling quite unsettled.

For a woman who has not had children, this type of dream might manifest as being late, portraying a sense of being tardy in terms of life stages, or the appropriate time to have children. In this case, what stood out was that Barb *did not know* what she was searching for. She was exploring her identity by packing clothing that represented the costume she wears in the role of mother and older sibling. In every way, she believed she should have been leading this adventure. She is the one who is always in control.

She was about to take a girl's trip with women who did not have children and her motivation to go away alone underwent a type of self-scrutiny. She probably felt the subtle fear that comes when the only role which validates her identity and sense of achievement is suddenly not important. While the sense that everything would be okay without her may have been unsettling, *the mystery* behind her searching was the key.

Since she was searching for clothing, she was exploring an identity that is unknown, aside from her role as wife and mother. Perhaps her desire to be away from her family unleashed the finger wagging tapes of "thou shalt." It may have seemed she was looking for *something else* which may have felt morally wrong. In reality, finding time to reconnect with others as an individual is an important aspect of balance and wellness. After all, the theme of the dream was how everything would be okay with out her.

If balance is not achieved, regardless of how well we do in one aspect of our lives, we may fall into a type of depression. Odin is the first character who will demonstrate our pathway to wellness and balance. In this story, he seeks greater and greater power, testing his strength and will in an attempt to overturn a sense of impending doom. This knowledge makes him melancholy. As he begins to distance himself from human interaction, his behavior resembles an over-achiever moving into depression. He allows the ravens and wolves to take over his everyday interaction.

Wild animals in dreams can portray instinctual feelings that seek to break free, so we can reclaim our more wild and natural self. The various animals appearing in dreams represent natural aspects and how they are expressed. Animals can attack us in dreams when we have an emotional outburst during the day that appeared to come out of nowhere.

Chances are, we were carrying an issue which was left unprocessed and the slightest difficulty could have upset our house of cards. While we do not own our emotions, in dreams they will be personified as something wild and threatening that comes *out of the woods*.

Animals, however, represent different things. For example being attacked by a bear is different from being attacked by a wolf. Most bears are associated with ideas like the teddy bear or maternal protectiveness and can represent feelings associated with the mother that we carry forward. Tigers can be sexual, while elephants are associated with the power of an enormous emotional response that when repressed, can trample over us. Wolves are associated with stories like Little Red Riding Hood or Peter and the Wolf. They stalk the hero and are aggressive. Their teeth can pierce the skin, bringing forward the idea of drawing blood or representing feelings. Being attacked by a wolf portrays how feelings (blood) or unprocessed aggression (teeth) attempt to break through the surface (skin/feelings).

If aggression is not actualized, it finds life in *The Mythology of Sleep*. The wolf pup, Fenris, can be viewed as a symbol of this psychic conflict, embodying aggressiveness that was continuously nurtured, yet is temporarily restrained (through depression). In this story, restraining or *repressing* energy portrays how it can take on *monstrous proportions*.

Odin's behavior foreshadows what can happen when we disengage from life after continuously funding power and aggression. We know Fenris will someday lead to the hero's undoing.

The Mythical Setting of the Warrior

Odin's inability to be in the present is central to the plight of the Warrior/over-achiever. He does not begin to disengage from the world until he sacrifices his ability to use both eyes to view the present. In dreams, the eye is an objective representation of our perspective. Since it is sacrificed, it portrays how we can lose sight of the present by focusing on something else. He becomes focused on an impending crisis and when we have a sense there is no longer light at the end of the tunnel, we fall into depression. Sending only the ravens, *thought* and *memory*, out into the world of experience as scavenger birds, he observes human interaction from an emotional distance. This allows him to be removed from real experience. He is caught up in a vision of the future, the domain of all achievers who can never really participate fully in the present.

This mythological landscape embodies a world created by the *fiery flame* giant Surtr (passion) who flashes his sword (aggression) and sends showering sparks into the great abyss (*of emptiness*). The continual action of more heat (*passion*) against ice (*no feeling*) then creates Ymir, the ice giant who is described as the *embodiment of a frozen ocean*. We can grow in stature to become, in a sense, *a frozen giant*, and this is all that will remain of our oceanic feeling of connectedness to the world around us.

This *frozen ocean of a giant person* becomes our unacknowledged shadow. It what created by the *unfathomable essences* growing beneath the surface, and must be conquered if we are to build Middle Earth or a *real life* upon its carcass.

"Michael" is a Warrior/over-achiever who has been HIV positive for 15 years. He has remained *physically* healthy due to medications, although he dreams of skinny man chasing him. This imagery is self explanatory and yet, he describes this recurring dream as a nightmare where he awakens in a state of panic. As a representation of his shadow, its significance remains a mystery to him. He is too busy building his empire to process his unacknowledged fears in a way which might lead to a type of integration that is acceptable to his psyche. He is an achiever in every sense of the word and nothing can get him down. He describes a life of emotional outbursts and isolation before he quickly moves to the next conquest. Unacknowledged fears can make us profoundly unhappy, even while the cause remains a mystery to us.

The shadow recurs in dreams so the crisis can be uncovered and processed. It appears threatening in dreams because it captures the *sole imagery* that can topple our house of cards so we might heal. Its message is simple: *not acknowledging and integrating our fears can overwhelm us in an unhealthy way*. The dream is ever attempting to offer a healing pathway for the dreamer. It is not the HIV that Michael is battling; he is extremely successful and healthy. His battle is with unacknowledged depression and he has yet to build Middle Earth (a place where the living can thrive) into his mythology.

Anyone who has lived the life of emptiness found at the top of the corporate ladder can attest to the rude awakening which comes from recognizing how professional success does not equate to real fulfillment. Transformation occurs when we awaken to the meaning of our *real* journey to discover life in more fulfilling ways. Focused only on the future because of a present we are unwilling to acknowledge, we do not incorporate what unfolds as a message that might awaken us to our destiny. When a client overcomes a sense of denial to become present, I often find they access greater energy that can become regenerative power. We are endowed with healing mechanisms that have ensured our survival since our beginnings. Denial creates a frozen *inner* landscape that reinforces the mythology of isolation. The weakness we run from *in here* becomes the motivation of endlessly having to prove our power *out there*.

29

Like Michael, Odin develops his power to demonstrate how will alone can prevail against whatever fate may throw at him. At the same time he is certain the future holds only doom. This is not a healthy way to approach life.

In the description of the Norns, we find another one eyed character, gazing back upon the past as Fate. While Odin has one eye focused on the future, the other looks back upon the past and real participation in the moment is non existent. Unable to let go of past experiences, and expecting only crisis up ahead, we actually stalk adversity and enact a lifestyle of preparing for constant battle.

The second Norn is *fearlessly* fixing a concentrated gaze upon the present as Being. If we believe we may be found deficient in the moment, all of our attention will be directed toward a future where we will have the opportunity to one day prove that we are powerful. The past may have appeared threatening, although we have the power to stand in the present and change our experiences. To stand in the present however, requires fearlessness, and courage should be second nature to the Warrior.

To most people, being in the present does not involve fear. There is something about revealing fallibility that is frightening to a Warrior who is too strong to show weakness. Living in the future of Necessity creates a lifestyle where we do not develop the sense of ease which allows us to remain rooted in the present. At such times, we may actually feel claustrophobic.

We can't help ourselves; our innate magnetism and energy quickly propel us to take control and assume the role of leader. Interacting as leader to the group is the closest thing resembling human intimacy to an over-achiever.

In childhood, we may have developed a sense of inadequacy because we were faced with issues that humiliated or shamed us. It could have been as harmless as experiencing neglect, although a sense of inadequacy can arise from recognizing that our fire burns brighter than those around us. For whatever reason, we may not have blended easily into the group and began exercising traits which overcompensated for our feelings of *not fitting in*. Most over-achievers are said to be born leaders as children. This is because leading the group allows us to remain in control. Being in control ensures nobody can break through our barrier.

Likewise, when we experience something painful in the present, we may not recognize the part it plays in revealing a more fulfilling sense of destiny, until the time has passed. The third Norn wears an impenetrable veil, perhaps knowing the future must remain a place of endless possibilities. She is called Necessity and holds an unopened scroll, pointed toward the future.

Someone who is depressed may believe *thought* and *memory* alone can take the place of human interaction. Should the Warrior experience depression brought on by isolation, the situation can become a trap. An aggressive character, fundamentally too strong to show weakness might experience depression in the only way a powerful psyche will allow. Like the impaired characters in this story, an unresolved conflict may be forced to develop as a physical symptom until the *real* crisis can be resolved.

The Conversion of Energy

During the late nineteenth century, Josef Breuer was using suggestibility and hypnosis to treat patients with physical symptoms which did not have a biological basis. Breuer used hypnosis to induce or remove a *physical* response in his patients. After observing Breuer's work, Freud decided there must be a powerful psychological factor in the creation of some symptoms. He formulated the idea that *psychosomatic* symptoms could manifest when mental processes were withheld from conscious awareness. He observed how conflict that is repressed or left unresolved allowed energy to be diverted into bodily symptoms. Psychosomatic does not mean imaginary; it develops as a sympathetic or autonomous response to a psychological conflict.

The work of Breuer inspired Freud's idea of the unconscious, leading to his pioneering work in psychoanalysis. By studying dreams as the messenger of unconscious information, he began to explore the repressed inner life of his patients.

As Odin withdraws from everyday interaction, he embodies what happens during depression. He is melancholy when he believes there is an impending crisis that is beyond his power to resolve. The two ravens *(thought and memory)* at his shoulders, and the two wolves *(hungry and greedy)* at his feet, begin to take over his everyday functions.

In dreams, birds are symbolic of conscience and our pursuit of a higher awareness. They often portray morality and a spiritual perspective, symbolic of how we view Freud's idea of the *superego* or Campbell's *thou shalt*, which can stand in judgment of us. Re-playing childhood tapes at our shoulders of what we should and shouldn't do, these messages can come to represent an idealized replacement of *the world below*.

Geri and Freki are wolves with names that suggest the insatiable appetite of wild dogs. They actually feed on Odin's condition and disinterest in experience. As wolves, they too, represent the instinctual power of aggressive energy, usurped from our conscious control when *the reins of the will* are no longer under our control. As the will is handed over to the unconscious characters of the story, energy is *converted* or turned back upon us until the real crisis can be acknowledged.

In the northern regions, ravens and wolves maintain a symbiotic relationship. The raven will scout over distances for potential prey and when it spots an injured or defenseless creature, it cries out to alert the wolves. This behavior captures how conscience (ravens) can manipulate instinctual energy (wolves) to do its bidding, something explored in depth in Chapter Six. Being scavenger birds, the ravens await their turn to descend upon the leftovers. Should the charioteer lose interest through depression, the unconscious characters can gain access to the reins of a powerful will.

Since the superego developed as the voice of the parents to control the child's desire to act on every impulse, Freud believed it had a close relationship to the id. We often fail to realize how much power remains behind the disciplinary tapes of our childhood, and conscience may evolve into a type of self-condemnation. As the ego matures, it still remains subject to the superego's domination and criticism. Just as the child was trained to obey the commands of the parents, so too, does the powerful energy of the id fall prey to the dictates of the superego. Its historical mastery over the id, gives the superego easy access to this unconscious and instinctual realm.

In this story, both are given *an inordinate amount of freedom and power*. Dreams provide clues to the *unfathomable essences* which trap us. These unfathomable essences are used to make the rope that will come to restrain Fenris, and we see how unconscious conflict can take on monstrous proportions. Ultimately a physical symptom becomes the unconscious expression of internal crisis.

Fenris personifies how natural energy can grow out of proportion to a point that will soon threaten the hero. This is why those who are too strong to show weakness must convert depression in the only way a strong ego will allow. The physical symptoms allow us to have a reason other than failing, for taking a time out. The symptom becomes disempowering only while the underlying crisis remains unresolved.

Psychosomatic illness is the unconscious production of physical symptoms due to psychological factors which do not fall under voluntary control. We have yet to understand the extent of how all illness may be induced by psychogenic factors, although this type of condition is well documented. While it is a condition altering or impairing a physical function suggesting a physical disorder, physical mapping cannot account for this loss or distortion of neurological function. It is the expression of an underlying psychological conflict or need and manifests as symptoms of weakness, paralysis, sensory disturbances, pseudo-seizures, and involuntary tremors. Like the characters in this story, debilitation oftentimes affects only *one* side of the body.

Just as Odin sacrifices bilateral sight, deafness or blindness can manifest bilaterally. The symptom often enables a person to avoid some type of irresolvable conflict at home or work. While the conflict may not be apparent to the individual, it can usually be observed in dreams symbols of windows or car doors on one side that will not open.

Conversion symptoms are more prevalent in people who are *too strong to show weakness,* or those in an environment that does not allow for failure. Symptoms can be brought on by the long- term stress of conquering, which is why this condition appears more frequently in military personnel or childhood sport prodigies. We see the manifestation of illness or the conversion of will playing out in the story of Tyr. The Odin cycle of this story captures the conflict and its creation in the symbolism of depression, while Tyr portrays how we can fall prey to unconscious disempowerment.

The Unintentional Sacrifice

Tyr, the one handed god of war and justice, offers a picture of the conversion which can take place when we remain in denial of our depression. Deities of war appear in many mythologies although these heroes are not always expressions of aggression and a desire for war. Tyr is also the god of justice, representing the need for balance, nurturing and protection. Tyr reared and tended to the basic needs of Fenris as a representation of continuously nurturing aggression. Both Tyr and the wolf will fall prey to a strange type of restraint; Tyr will be forced to sacrifice the use of one hand to subdue the wolf.

Aggressiveness is how we need to defend and assert our power to compete and win when interacting with others. Some Warriors are simply unable to process and assimilate defeat. Should we be faced with circumstances that we are powerless to solve, we may become melancholy and withdrawn. Among other types of crisis, such as the dissolution of family due to our ambition, the loss of esteem cultivated from our interactions with others may lead to isolation and depression. Avoiding human relationships and close interaction with others, we may be fearful of having our shortcomings or weakness exposed. This may be taking place, whether or not we realize it. Warriors who thrive on receiving the approval of a challenging caregiver may become disoriented and depressed when this caregiver passes away.

While a conversion disorder demonstrates one type of psychosomatic manifestation of illness, it provides a model for

33

understanding the enormous power of unconscious processes. Studies show that anywhere from 8-10% of patients admitted to hospitals, have a somatization disorder. Many doctors identify stress or anxiety as being *the silent killer* and believe this percentage to be much higher.

When there is a psychic conflict requiring resolution, a type of innate check and balance system kicks in, urging us toward wellness. As an imbalance occurs, the psyche moves to divert energy into a type of self-restraint until the crisis can be resolved. *"Without your hand, you are effectively disempowered."* A Warrior can no longer fight without the hand that holds the sword.

The characters of Odin, Tyr and Fenris become our first example of how natural mechanisms move to make us well. We understand the mechanisms of psychosomatic illness, and dreams can shed light upon the pathway to psychosomatic healing.

When a comprehensive and expensive medical diagnosis can find no basis for the condition, we have the opportunity to explore the real root of our *dis-ease*. We are, in a sense, *victimized* because it is *unconscious*. The symptoms do not follow the normal patterns of physiology and yet, we cannot admit how some part of our lifestyle has fallen out of balance.

Tyr embodies how we can remain oblivious to the ramifications. *"I will put my hand in your mouth to prove that we are not going to restrain you."* This demonstrates how we can remain unconscious of the processes which come to paralyze us. The normal economy between the ego and its instinctual energy manifests as a type of embargo. By tying up one (Fenris/id) and removing the hand of the other (Tyr/ego), the internal conflict remains symptomatic, only while it is unacknowledged.

This is not to say the symptoms are imaginary. On the contrary, while the cause remains unconscious, the condition is debilitating. The rope that restrains Fenris was created by *unfathomable essences* and as a magical binding it personifies the immense power of unconscious processes. Freud described conversion as how energy it turned backward and the harder one pulls, the stronger we are restrained by a binding created in this way.

Physical manifestations of psychological conflict can manifest in other ways, as we shall see in later chapters. In this case, it is the Warriors inability to demonstrate weakness combined with the development of an aggressive inner life which provides the mechanisms employed by the psyche. Dreams of being chased, landscapes of fire, ice, aggressive animals and larger than life monsters that threaten us manifest as our shadow life in the symbolism of how dreams seek to return us to wellness.

The Healing Journey

Aggression applied by the individual, reflects a courageous spirit in pursuit of the boundaries of power. This fearlessness and courage is demonstrated in the image of the Vikings, sailing across a vast and unknown sea. Most of our greatest explorers came from this region and were subjected to miserable conditions yet, stand as a monument to human endurance. They are the heroes who paved the way for our future.

Alfred Adler was the first psychiatrist to recognize the importance of the drive for power and success along with the sexual and hunger instincts. He coined the word *"inferiority complex,"* as an unconscious sense of worthlessness. He described *compensation* as the process of being driven into challenging situations to prove these deeper misgivings of inadequacy to be false. Understanding the fire behind needs, drives, and impulses can reveal compensation as the reaction to real or imagined weaknesses. He taught patients to identify practical circumstances, real opportunities and real limitations.

Conflict and frustration are implicit in the gulf which exists between aspiration and achievement. By discriminating between feasible and necessary goals and impractical, non-rewarding goals, we begin to pursue the one and learn to discard the other.

The Sagas end with a great battle fought between the gods and monsters as a final war without victors. Similarly, dreams reveal how the psyche battles against the ambiguous boundaries and beliefs that keep us from living authentic and well in the present. The promise of rebirth is symbolized as all of life perishes, although a new earth is created in its aftermath. When the monster is overthrown *Middle Earth* is built upon its carcass. This is the inspiration to recognize how constant battle comes at great sacrifice. Dreams always provide the clues to understand how our past way of approaching experience can be transformed so life can become more fulfilling. If we ride as a passenger in a vehicle, we know we are not in control of where we are going.

Renewal offers a type of human interaction where we can strive for win/win situations. Riding off to battle, conquering the weak and defenseless in a demonstration of power, will only lead us into more battles. If our journey calls us to conquer and to live in a vision of the future, then like Odin, we too, may discover a melancholy existence we are powerless to change. Our actions in the present become the seeds of a future which can only be changed by what we do *here and now*.

One day the Warrior/over-achiever must recognize outer accomplishment as only one aspect of a balanced life. As we learn to become present in daily interaction, we discover it is *our weaknesses which make us human.* We are a very social species and were never meant to exist alone. Like any good fairy tale ending, all Warriors must come home one day and make peace with the present to experience a life of living happily ever after.

Chapter Two
Isis and the Survivor's Famine

Stories of Ancient Egypt
Instinct, Anxiety and Developing Self-Worth

"Even though the rebels have been defeated,
the world can never be the same again."
The Book of the Heavenly Cow

Like the oceanic, instinctual realm of our early beginnings, the myths of ancient Egypt reveal an all-inclusive and nurturing type of sensitivity. Family life was guided by steadfast Isis as goddess of love, mother of Horus and wife of Osiris. Family dysfunction also plays a part in their myths, although ultimately the heroes prevail.

The myth of the Survivor's Famine is personified in these stories. On a journey to develop self-worth, we must overcome crisis and famine *within* to establish sustenance from internal reserves. Isis the grieving wife, Horus, the survivor child, Osiris, the wounded father and dysfunctional Uncle Seth all lead us into a landscape of rebirth. In the mythical world of ancient Egypt, we explore a desert setting and the barren imagery that reflects the inner mythology of one living in a survival mode.

The Setting in Dreams

The setting in which a dream takes place can be viewed as a metaphorical representation of our *current frame of mind*. As we saw in the Warrior's Tale, a dream set in an icy landscape can suggest how we grow cold and distant from life. Rickety or half built structures appear commonly in dreams because houses and buildings portray our inner architecture, which can only be partly constructed and undergoes renovation as we grow. A more commercial setting becomes a snapshot of how we are approaching work or what will lead to a sense of self-worth. Just as different settings make us *feel* differently, the setting becomes the landscape that allows us to understand what is going on inside of us.

In Egypt, civilization took root in the Nile valley where the marshes to the north and the deserts to the south, east and west offered protection from outside invaders. The yearly inundation of the Nile became the life-giving source of a growing agricultural community.

Their gods were half human and half beasts and the Egyptians learned to defy gravity and the human limitations of strength by building their massive structures. Even death could not conquer them and they developed methods to ward off life's natural process of decay. They were the first culture to establish the calendar based on the solar year of 365¼ days, dividing the days into 12 months. This provided a year of three seasons of four month cycles, enabling the farmer to predict with accuracy, the times of planting, flooding and harvesting.

Since the overflowing Nile was central to their agricultural existence, their pyramids, in addition to being resurrection vehicles for kings were also ancient observatories. These structures allowed for the observation of the specific placement of the Dog Star, Sirius which coincided with the annual inundation of the Nile. From a cloudless sky, Egyptians tracked the movement of the planets easily against the constellations. They studied the sky to understand the strange behavior of this life-giving river.

The Nile bestowed life as a benevolent deity whose gifts were received gratefully. When the monsoon rains and melting snows brought an increase to its waters, it flooded the low-lying valley and Delta, leaving behind a thick layer of silt. As the water receded, the fields were planted. Some years, they grew more than was required to feed the population and at other times, the river failed to be high enough to reach their fields. By managing a surplus of reserves, they balanced themselves against the unpredictable behavior of the great river.

Magic was central to their existence, giving them the power to control every aspect of the environment. Reality was symbolic, in the sense that *their idea of it* allowed them to transcend the hardships of daily life. They believed magical symbols allowed one to penetrate the deeper aspects of existence. This magic was inspired by what could be understood and predicted. After all, they had witnessed the returning cycle of the cosmos, the annual inundation of the Nile, and the predictability of the seasons. Through investigation and the establishment of *maat* or order, they believed they came to orchestrate and control all phenomena.

Only death would come to threaten the living, with its unpredictable power. Yet, through ritual and technique, death was interwoven into daily life. They built a culture where they interpreted life in a way that death gave it added meaning.

It took seventy days to mummify the king and carry out his funerary rites, yet when we open his tomb, we find him preserved in a heroic and death-defying feat. He is the true Survivor, grinning at us from a world where even the ravages of time cannot destroy him.

The shadow of the Survivor casts an image of a glass half empty. Life is never far from the idea of death, stemming from the early belief that the world is full of peril. An early sense of crisis perpetuates the myth that *"the world can never be the same again."*

The Pharaoh orchestrated the great agricultural machinery which fed the growing population. Even during times of drought and famine experienced in other areas of the Middle East, the Egyptians accessed food from the surpluses in their granaries. In Hebrew stories, Joseph and his brothers were said to have migrated to Egypt during such conditions.

The divine order placed Egypt in the center of a world, surrounded by the primeval waters of *nun*. From these waters, the Nile received its life-sustaining power and gave birth to the original creator. Although the Pharaoh was the incarnation of Horus on the earth, Isis shines as the goddess of the people. There is a marked femininity in their Pantheon and in the watery and womb-like processes of creation. In ancient Egypt, women were equal to men and could become landowners and scribes.

Isis is one of the oldest deities and represents the ubiquitous mother goddess. Her image, with infant Horus in her arms is one of many mother/son representations which survived to inspire later images of a divine mother and child motif. Her prominence may be due to the fact that the creator, Atum-Ra was unapproachable and remote. Perhaps the focus on agriculture was distinctly feminine as seeds were birthed from the womb of the earth. Where the Warrior's assertiveness might be classified as *masculine,* we look to the introspective world within and what may be called *feminine,* although applicable to either gender to understand the dynamics of the instinctual realm.

In the Eighteenth Dynasty and start of the New Kingdom, there was a renaissance of the arts and the Egyptians adopted the use of the chariot, expanding their commerce into new realms. Although the female pharaoh, Hatshepsut, ruled during this period, it wasn't the strength of Isis which gave her power. Before the Assyrian and patriarchal dominance of the Middle East, we find many matriarch rulers of these regions as priestess-queens.

As we move away from how motivation is portrayed by transportation vehicles in dreams, we explore instinct and anxiety and its symbolic representations as murky waters and reptiles. Our unique nature requires expression and when we can find ways of tapping it productively, we develop self-worth. Dreams that revolve around food and kitchens often coincide with work imagery. They capture our sense of self-worth and the ways in which we are trying to find fulfillment in what we do.

We tend to view feminine qualities as more introspective, yet introspection is required of both sexes, if we are to understand how the inner landscape reflects itself upon experience. Females appearing in the dreams a male indicate how he is exploring his sensitivity. The male appearing in a woman's dream portrays how she is exploring her more assertive qualities. Both aspects represent functioning parts of a healthy psyche, when fully integrated and effectively empowered in life.

With a cessation of action, the mind is able to reflect on its experiences and yet, sometimes we can become lost in the inner terrain. In the Survivor, we see the necessity of bringing healing to the inner world and the need to channel our instinctual energy more productively. In this way, we can tap our refined sensuality on the road to developing authentic self-expression in the outer world.

The death of Osiris and his transformative journey becomes our backdrop to explore the many stages of the Survivor who must traverse the underworld (unconscious) to resurrect a sense of power in the outer world. It is a necessary journey through a wasteland where we initially lament our sad fate in a dialogue of loneliness and despair. His grieving wife, Isis, searches the land for her disempowered husband. Rising as the most powerful deity of antiquity, she embodies the need to explore the inner terrain (feminine) to resurrect our power and apply it as assertiveness (masculine) in the outer world.

As Survivors, we are almost reptilian, with a personality perched on all fours, operating on vigilance and apprehension. Earthy and sensual, we are on a journey to discover how the sustenance sought in the outer world must be cultivated within. We emerge from a symbolic desert landscape, divided by the unconscious waters of instinct, which flow as if by magic, from a mysterious realm to sustain us. Our sense of reality is arrested and our mythology revolves around believing great sacrifices or magic is required for our survival.

Yet, through these myths we can see the representation of how instinct comes forward, and discover the pathway to achieve *maat*, or order within. When we compose the inner terrain, we find this order *magically* reflected around us.

The Creation Story and the Egyptian Pantheon

In the fertile valley at the rivers edge, time moves in a circle, just as the cosmos can be seen to revolve and return in a perpetual cycle. Life

40

endures because the river Nile swells and brings forth nourishment, demonstrating a constant rhythm of renewal. Time is not linear, for transformation is a place without boundaries. Death and rebirth are interwoven aspects of life, which takes on more meaning within the confines of death. Time, however, is experienced differently for both, because a moment in the land of the dead can become a lifetime for the living.

First was a dark, watery realm of unlimited depths and chaos. These primal waters, called *nun*, surrounded the world and became the source of the Nile. In *nun*, the creator was in an inert state without gender. Yet, this state contained the potential for all of life where *nun* became the father and mother of all things.

The creator was alone until the heart started to beat and the feelings were felt. Sensations began to arise from within, and in this awakening, the creator began to feel. The first thoughts manifested as insight, allowing for the visualization of other forms. Through the power of speech, the creator began naming these thoughts. Differentiating the elements of chaos, the creator brought forward the Ogdoad, or eight amphibious deities who fertilized the primal waters. The creator established *maat* or order out of the chaos, and the power to bring thought into reality was called Heka or magic.

Obeying a primal instinct, the amphibious Ogdoad manifested the invisible power of the breath of life. This breath created the atmosphere that allowed the creator to come into being. By giving birth to his twin children Shu and Tefnut, he evolved as the creator Atum (primordial) and Ra (sun). The creator was called many things but was known as Atum-Ra or simply Ra.

From the breath of his nose, Atum-Ra created the air god, Shu. Through the breath of his mouth or the word, he brought forward Tefnut, goddess of moisture. The primeval waters were dark, and soon Atum-Ra was separated from his children. He removed an eye as "The Sole Eye" or disc of the sun and sent it out in search of his children.

This eye was a goddess, called the Daughter of Ra, who became the light emanating within the darkness. Although the twin children, Shu and Tefnut were lost within the dark primordial depths, Shu cleverly created a void, so the eye could shine forth for the first time. Through this illumination, the children were no longer hidden. When it shone upon the twins, the Sole eye returned the children to Atum-Ra. She returned to find that in her absence, the creator had replaced her and she grew angry. To appease his daughter, Atum-Ra transformed her into a snake and put her at the place of honor upon the forehead.

In a mixture of joy and sorrow, Atum-Ra wept at the sight of his children and from his tears, all of humanity was created. He animated the newly created bodies by bestowing them with the breath of life. Atum-Ra had effectively transferred his divine essence and emotions to humanity and his tears reflected the vicissitudes of feeling.

Shu and Tefnut gave birth to a son called Geb (earth) and a daughter called Nut (sky). These offspring embraced so ardently that immediately the gods feared they were trying to become one. Although Nut conceived children, she refused to give birth to them. Knowing this would reverse the process of creation, Shu created another void to separate the earth and sky. This separation allowed Nut to give birth to Osiris, Seth, Isis and Nephthys. Together, they became the great Ennead or nine gods of the Egyptian pantheon.

The divine realm was in the sky, and Egypt was placed at its center. The underworld of *Duat* was the realm of the dead. The creator set about making creatures by naming them. He made the birds, reptiles, cattle, fish and all living things on the earth. In the space created by separating the earth and the sky, these creatures were able to continue breathing the air as the divine breath of life. When the sun rose, it drove away the darkness and the miracle of this first sunrise or perfect moment repeated itself everyday. Sunrise is always a daily representation of eternity.

Just as the heart had stirred and the tongue had spoken to establish *maat* in the chaos, so too, would the heart and tongue of the individual have control over all other parts of the body. Thus, the creator was in each body, thinking and commanding everything he wished as the divine order comes into being through the heart.

Shu represented Eternal Recurrence and Tefnut was Eternal Sameness. This principle was the great cycle, in which everything would need to change to survive and yet everything remained fundamentally the same. The presence of maat in everything ensured this continuity.

Nut ruled the heavenly bodies and arched across the sky as a giant cow observed in the starry markings of the Milky Way. The heavens were a liquid place where stars floated in boats. It was Nut who pulled the dead king up into the heavens to live as a star.

The True Name of Ra

Through the power of naming the creatures, Atum-Ra had created the world. He kept his own name concealed in his stomach to protect it from any enemies who would use it against him. He was known as Atum-Ra during creation and had come to be called Ra, which represented the sun. The only deity to challenge Ra's authority was Isis who was said to be "cleverer than millions of gods." As a powerful goddess, Isis knew everything except the real name of Ra.

Her husband Osiris was the ruler of Egypt but she knew one day, her brother, Seth would try to destroy Osiris. She also knew she would give birth to a son named Horus who would rule Egypt. In order to ensure this throne for her child, she would need to know the true name of Ra. She began plotting a way to discover the true name of this powerful deity.

As Ra grew old, his mouth drooped and he began to drool. Isis gathered some of the saliva when he wasn't looking and mixed it with the earth to create a snake. She breathed life into the snake and when it awoke, she left it at a crossroad where Ra was sure to pass by. When he crossed the road to view his creation, the creature bit him.

The poison burned and Ra screamed until he was barely able to speak. His lips were trembling and his limbs were shaking. He knew he had not created such a snake and summoned his children for help. They were very distraught and Isis too, pretended to be upset. She swore that if any of his creatures had done this thing to their father, she would destroy them with her powerful magic.

Ra recounted what had happened, and soon grew cold like water and hot like fire. He was drenched with sweat and began to lose his sight. Isis pleaded with Ra to tell her his true name. She told him how she could cure him, but only by invoking his true name in her incantation. Ra was barely able to speak, although he told her he was the creator of life and all creatures. Isis knew this was not his true name, and she continued to press him. He said he is Khepri in the morning, Ra at noon and Atum in the evening. Isis grew impatient and told him she could only cure him with the use of his real name. Ra was weak, although he finally leaned forward and whispered this name into her ear. He assured her that while her husband Osiris would someday become ruler of the dead, her son Horus would ascend as ruler of Egypt and the ruler of the living.

Osiris and Seth

Osiris ruled Egypt, while his brother, Seth was the ruler of the lifeless desert. Osiris was loved for bringing agriculture and sustenance to the people, but Seth could only bring forth barren lands and famine. Seth was jealous of Osiris and his loving relationship with Isis. He was determined to destroy Osiris and usurp his birthright.

As Osiris passed by one day, Seth measured his shadow against the sun. Later, he built a beautiful casket of fragrant wood, designed to fit his brother. He intended to use it to be rid of Osiris once and for all.

43

During the night of a great storm, he called the gods together for a feast, and each admired the casket that Seth had placed in the entrance hall. They were amazed at the fragrant smell of the wood and enchanted by its beautiful carvings. All took turns lying in it, until they eventually retreated into the dining hall.

It was late when Osiris arrived, and when Seth greeted him, they were alone. He convinced Osiris to try out the casket and when he did, Seth and his attendants nailed it shut, sealing it with hot lead. The gods heard the hammering and came out to investigate, but they were too late. The evil ones, led by Seth carried the casket out into the desert night. They flung it into the Nile where Osiris died of suffocation.

Although Isis was in Coptos, she heard the lamenting gods and knew something had happened to Osiris. When she learned of what Seth had done, she went out to find her husband, searching all of Egypt by traveling along the Nile. The casket had drifted into the Mediterranean Sea and the current brought it to the banks of Byblos or modern Lebanon. A small tree grew near the casket and eventually, it grew so large that it enveloped the casket inside of its trunk. The sweet smell of the wood permeated the tree and made it famous throughout the world. When Isis heard of this tree, she immediately set off for Byblos.

In the meantime, the King and Queen of Byblos had heard of the tree too, and ordered it to be cut down and carved into a pillar to adorn their palace. When Isis arrived at the shoreline where the tree was said to have grown, she found only a stump. She sat on the stump and said nothing for many months, cutting a lock of her hair as a sign of mourning.

The royal couple heard of the beautiful and sorrowful woman who remained near the tree stump. They summoned her to their palace, and Isis captivated them by nursing their child with only her finger. They asked her to stay and become the child's nurse. Each night, while they slept, Isis chipped away at the pillar and threw the wood chips into the fire. In this way, she tried to separate the body of her husband from the wood. As she worked, she placed the royal child into the flames to keep it safe and warm.

When the Queen came into the room, she was horrified to find her child in the flames. Angrily, she grabbed the child and held it to her breast. Isis temporarily became a swallow, flying around the pillar and spoke to the Queen's heart. She explained how the fire would have made the child immortal. Now, all the child could hope for was a long life.

Isis changed back and recounted the story of what had happened to her husband. The royal couple took pity on her and ordered the pillar to be split, so the casket could be removed. Isis returned to Egypt with the casket and when she opened it, she drew her dead husband to her breast and kissed him. This bestowed the breath of life needed to revive him.

Isis and Osiris did their best to hide from Seth. Of course, Seth knew Osiris was alive again, because the fields grew lush and green, while the desert receded. This time he attacked Osiris as he slept. He cut him into fourteen pieces, scattering his body throughout the land. Isis was overcome by grief when she learned how her husband had been dismembered. The grieving sisters became birds and were able to travel great distances to gather the parts of his body. Once assembled, Isis believed she could revive him again.

Osiris had found himself cut off from the land of the living. Left to wander through the underworld, he lamented his fate to Atum Ra. The powerful god consoled Osiris, by telling him he was now Ruler of the Dead and that a day would come when he would be resurrected.

As Isis wept over her dead husband's body, she was told how Seth had poisoned the hearts of men. The soul of Osiris was now in the land of the dead where he had been made its ruler. He was judge of the underworld where all souls would gain immortality at death, and be reunited with their bodies upon the resurrection. This resurrection would take place on the day Ra penetrated the dark underworld with his light, allowing Osiris and the souls under his care to rise again in life.

Knowing she was to give birth to a divine child, she held the lifeless body of Osiris and fanned the divine spark, allowing his seed to be planted within her. Soon she was pregnant. Known as the child who is "king even in the egg, the gods bowed down to the unborn king, Horus."

Horus and Seth

After the death of Osiris, Seth once again usurped the throne to rule Egypt. His parched deserts began to overwhelm the fertile fields, causing famine throughout the land. Mothers were unable to sleep at night because of the cries of their hungry children. People began fighting and stealing from each other over what little food remained. Isis had to help Horus to become Egypt's rightful king. She knew he would avenge his father's death and overthrow his usurper uncle Seth. Horus would be the one to bring peace and prosperity back to Egypt.

Once Horus was born, she hid him in the marshes of Chemmis. During this time of famine, Isis had to leave the child alone while she went out to beg for food. At such times, seven scorpions attended her. During one of these excursions, Isis came upon a rich woman and asked her for food and shelter but the woman refused. A poor fisherwoman overheard her plight, and offered Isis the larger portion of what little she had caught that day.

When the scorpions learned how the rich woman had treated Isis, they punished her by killing her child with their poisonous sting. Isis heard the woman lamenting in the night and took pity on her, immediately restoring life back to her child. The rich woman was eternally grateful and wanted to reward Isis. Instead, Isis asked her to give her gifts to the poor fisherwoman.

Horus the Survivor Child

Isis had asked the marsh creatures to protect Horus while she was away to keep him safe from his enemies. He was secretly hidden on a floating island inside of a papyrus thicket. Even as a child, Horus was said to hold power over the crocodiles, hippopotami, scorpions and snakes. Yet, one day, a very strange snake, believed to be under the spell of Seth, came upon the unsuspecting child and bit him. Isis held the sick child and watched as his life drained away. In great distress and sorrow, Isis brought the plight of suffering not only for herself, but all of humanity to the attention of the gods. She begged them to set right the earth, overthrow Seth and restore her child's health. Although they felt sympathy for the goddess, Seth was equal in power to them and they could do nothing.

The cunning goddess commandeered the solar barque and stopped the movement of the sun across the sky. Its progression was halted until such a time that Horus could be cured. The gods were shocked and outraged at the way in which she had defiantly interrupted *maat*. Ra had no choice but to descend to the earth and drive the poison from the divine child.

On another occasion, Isis would have to save Horus when he developed a severe stomachache from eating a sacred fish. Horus came to be called the Survivor Child and was pictured as a naked young boy, often with a shaven head and plaited side lock. He was sometimes depicted as "the infant with his finger in his mouth," as the deity who could vanquish dangerous snakes and reptiles. He was known as the protector of women and children. Oftentimes he was shown sitting in the lap of his mother and would come to represent the divine promise to relieve the suffering of humanity.

As Horus grew, he and Seth fought many battles which disturbed the entire cosmos. At one point, Horus challenged Seth to a race in stone boats. While Seth used real stone, Horus painted a wooden boat to look like stone, and when the race began, Seth sunk. Horus finally triumphed after a Divine Tribunal convened. Seth pleaded his case to justify his violence toward his brother and nephew, but failed. He claimed he was the strongest of the gods and this should give him the right to rule. Horus stressed how legitimately, he was ordained as Egypt's ruler. The gods ruled in Horus' favor.

Upon first arriving in the underworld, Osiris was too weak to achieve the transformation necessary to become its ruler. Because his child had overthrown Seth, both Horus and Osiris gained their power to rule effectively in their respective realms. Horus, the son ascended as ruler of Egypt and ruler of the living, while Osiris, the father became ruler of the underworld.

Biological Processes

In 500BC, the Greeks were describing a world composed of *atoms*. We can't help but wonder if they borrowed the word Atum as a primordial state from the Egyptian myths. In this story, the creator was alone in *nun*, until the heart started to beat. From the creation of the Ogdoad or eight amphibious deities, the power of breath was created.

The human brain contains remnants of our ancient past and has developed three progressive areas. Labeled as the *reptilian, mammalian* and *rational brain* they function in an interrelated manner and have retained, in the words of Dr. Paul MacLean: "their peculiar types of intelligence." At the base is the most primitive *reptilian* area, responsible for self-preservation and the regulation of cardiac, pulmonary, digestion and instinctive reactions which make us fight or flee. The reptilian motor center reacts to vision, sound, touch and chemistry. Like the amphibious Ogdoad in this myth, the reptilian center of the brain controls our vital processes such as heartbeat and breathing.

When mammals thrived in a nocturnal existence, *smell* rather than *sight* was the dominant sense. These aroma circuits or odor pathways are believed to have become the outline of the *limbic system* or the emotional area within the *mammalian* brain. This is the area that generates the parental care of mammals: playfulness, vocal calling and emotion. Emotion and mood originally evolved from neural structures allocated only to the sense of smell, which either attracted or repelled. Over time, these two simple responses have become the complicated emotions we experience today. The final area is the *rational brain*, a highly complex portion which produces language and intellectual ability.

All vertebrates, including mammals, birds, reptiles and fish have a *hindbrain, midbrain* and *forebrain*. The forebrain in man differs from mammals and reptiles the most in its ability for complex problem solving. The hindbrain has almost no differences. Reflexive or autonomic behavior is controlled by the older portions of the brain, which hold tremendous power over our functioning.

Like the Warrior's Tale, the Survivor's Famine is a reflection of how the charioteer does not have mastery of the psyche. Instinctual impulses that are unchecked can have unusual freedoms. In the case of the Warrior, there is a need to develop power and mastery over an environment which appears threatening. With the Survivor, there is always a sense of threat with little or no attempt to reign in irrational fears.

The beliefs of the ancient Egyptians reflect the Survivor's belief that the power remains *outside*. Through a process of magic or alchemy: *merging with another, large amounts of nourishment, the alchemy of converting responsibility into victimization*, we believe we can transcend our internal hunger. Unfortunately, disowning power and lacking the discipline to control our fears can lead to uncontrolled anxiety states. Unlike the Warrior who seeks achievement to increase a sense power, the Survivor does just the opposite and *reinforces* an innate sense of powerlessness.

The reptilian center, regulating the flight or fight response may be what creates a *free-floating anxiety state* when not under the control of the charioteer's reigns. The condition of Ra after being bitten by the snake resembles a panic attack. He grows cold like water and hot like fire. In addition, he is drenched with sweat, grows dizzy, and is unable to walk or see.

Whatever process began the reinforcement that our basic needs could not be met can develop into an anxious personality. In a sense, we are driven freely by the lower centers of the brain.

With the Survivor, we find anxiety awakened and integrated as part of the personality. In the early environment, we may have experienced a sense of danger that was left unresolved. Unlike the Warrior who develops mastery over the environment, this may have appeared impossible to the Survivor. Instead, we distanced ourselves from this excited energy and allowed it to co-exist as a part of our personality. Our inner mythology is personified by the characters of Horus the Survivor Child and Grieving Isis. They embody how we may have been forced to become the parent or nurturer to a grieving caregiver.

The way of the Survivor is not an image of the charioteer driving the horses, but the horses driving the charioteer in a state of panic. As we have seen, our *unfathomable essences* can be sent underground to manifest in a type of *dis-ease*. Whereas the Warrior's aggressive energy is checked and arrested, the Survivor's unchecked energy dissipates as anxiety. Ultimately, this energy could be more productively channeled toward authentic empowerment.

The Mythical Setting of the Survivor

Nancy dreams of going back to school (learning) where she is forced to live in a communal setting (integrating new aspects). She has to take showers and get naked with other women, portraying how she is beginning to reveal herself through dream work. She feels extremely uncomfortable and decides to run away (flight). She is sad because she is leaving and begins packing, where she notices how everything in her suitcase is inside out and dirty (negative self assessment). She gets angry because she doesn't have time to wash her clothes or get organized before going. This portion shows the conflict of her inner setting.

In the second cycle, she dreams of a gun battle (fight) where she has to get the women and children out of the building. Her dreams are a clear portrayal of her continual fight or flight response. Since everything in the dream was a reflection of her inner turmoil, all that she protects (getting characters to safety) cannot be separated from what she runs from (negative self-assessment).

When she first began dream work she was in a constant state of anxiety and hid the fact she was bulimic. Since her inner world was in a constant state of turmoil, bulimia allowed her to live in the illusion that she had some type of control over her body. Amazed at the guidance which came forward from her dreams, she discovered a newfound respect for the direction that came from within. Her dreams became the foundation upon which she could build her self-esteem.

She became more relaxed and had incorporated a healthy diet and exercise as the healthy type of control necessary to give her a sense of *real* accomplishment. Once she had learned to recognize the irrational nature of her fears, she was no longer riding sidesaddle to her anxiety states. Her last dream was of receiving a gift (wisdom) on a boat (motivation) going over a calm sea (ability to understand and compose her inner setting).

When energy is created, it cannot simply vanish and it has to be discharged. When it is repressed and irrational, it may be released quickly in a full-blown panic attack or slowly, through a free-floating anxiety condition. This arises when we are forced to live a life of fear where we *believe*, either consciously or unconsciously that our survival is always at stake.

Unlike Odin who sacrificed an eye to see the future, the sacrificed eye of Ra becomes a daughter who grows angry to find that in her absence, she was replaced. She is the one who must go out in search of the children in peril. In the early environment, the Survivor often cared for other siblings and was denied a normal sense of childhood. In this story, she goes on a tirade and is eventually appeased. This demonstration of anger and appeasement will ultimately bring its own reward system.

Like the ego, the eye of Ra or the disc of the sun was created to go forward and illuminate or make sense out of the darkness. The ego must shine its light over the waters of the unconscious to compose it. Instead, the Daughter of Ra wants to reverse creation and return to her primordial condition. She is turned into a snake and placed at the center of the forehead as a symbolic representation of how reptilian urges can take precedence over logical processes. Labeled as one, whose anger must be appeased, the family tiptoes around us to avoid our tirade. This is the shadow a Survivor carries forward from childhood.

Anxiety is a normal, adaptive response to a stressful situation. However, when it is too frequent or becomes irrational and symptomatic, it can develop into a *generalized anxiety condition, phobia or obsessive-compulsive disorder*. In a chronic anxiety disorder, the symptoms are long lasting and are expressed in motor tension, autonomic hyperactivity, apprehension, and vigilance patterns. This energy can make us appear almost reptilian, in the over-development of an instinctual fight or flight posture.

Survivors often were caregivers as children, who were never cared for themselves. Condemnation for the grieving caregiver makes all relationships difficult for us because at some level, we have to make peace with the *role modeling* we adopted either consciously or unconsciously. We were bequeathed with an inherent sense of ugliness which leaves us feeling unworthy. The cycle of anxiety and unresolved anger can become a lifestyle where we are always feeling empty. Like Nancy's dream, we are running away from something that is within.

When we feel empty, we may create a reward system which revolves around self-gratifying behavior. Sometimes we may feel powerless to deny our hunger. Overeating may initially reduce anxiety, but oftentimes becomes habitual or compulsive to create an even more diminished self-image. While our care-giving skills are pronounced, we tend to give in to all of our urges. This diminished self-image may also lead to self-abuse as in the case of bulimia or anorexia.

We compulsively seek order in proportion to the disorder we feel within. In this case, *nun* (nothing inside) truly becomes the father and mother of all things. We live a life of seeking instant, yet unfulfilling gratification. How would our lives be transformed if we channeled this enormous energy away from reinforcing self-destructive behavior and toward the pursuit of real fulfillment?

Projection and Diminishing Self-Worth

The Egyptians projected reality into incantations meant to keep them safe. *Projection* is the process of attributing to others, what we deny in ourselves. In relationships, we are often attracted to individuals of opposite character traits. While we project our power onto others, our own sense of self worth remains arrested.

Nut and Geb embrace and like the Eye of Ra. They too, want to return to a more primordial condition. Their desire to become one reflects the Survivor's pronounced neediness toward others. We may recognize how we can care for others, while remaining unaware of how needy we have become.

The Egyptians learned to balance their resources against the unpredictability of the river of life by using granaries to store food. From these established internal reserves, they were no longer forced to succumb to fear, brought upon by the threat of drought and famine. Building granaries gave them self-sustaining power and allowed them to thrive, regardless of the river's unpredictability. The Survivor's Famine can be transformed when we build inner reserves or a foundation that allows us to gain mastery over our irrational fears. By turning inward, we begin to take inventory of our sensations.

When we take control of the reigns, we no longer let fear drive us, but we channel its primordial energy toward accomplishment. We begin to recognize the unsubstantiated nature of our anxiety. Feeding anxiety without taking note of its unrealistic nature will only increase the power it holds over us. This is not unlike a wild horse, hijacking the charioteer on a chaotic ride of life and death proportions.

The Survivor usually demonstrates enormous earthy sensuality and evolves as a pronounced nurturer. We are the connoisseur of life's pleasures and sensory experiences, as if we have crawled through life, experiencing it up close and personal. There is an incredible texture to our sensitivity, which is usurped in the ritual of self-defeating behavior.

Instead of magic or quick fixes, we observe our sensations and take control. Like Nancy, discovering the wealth of guidance that arises within can lead to a sense of fulfillment and self-worth. In a sense, we re-parent ourselves for what was lacking in our childhood. Later, we can redirect this energy toward building internal reserves to sustain our sense of self-worth. Balance requires we implement other reward systems into our lives. *We soon discover how our hunger diminishes when our life becomes rewarding and our sense of accomplishment begins to grow.*

We are not lazy; we are fearful and undernourished. If we feel anxious, we *stop, listen* and *investigate* the immediate surroundings. *Being still and observing these feelings is paramount in this process*. If there is no real threat outside, then we can begin to see the real root of this internal tension. This energy can then be applied more productively toward growth and empowerment.

By setting goals that are accomplished, we acknowledge how our self-esteem increases. If we do not set goals and accomplish them, the cycle goes in reverse. Just as unhappiness is the hunger pain for change, anxiety reflects rising energy that can teach us something about the world *in here*, with little relevance to the world *out there*.

If we choose to treat ourselves in a dysfunctional way, much energy will be turned inward as we literally torture and degrade ourselves for failing. The Survivor's mythology then becomes a reflection of Seth's wasteland.

"Linda" is a Survivor and lived with a mate who validated her unworthiness by constantly telling her she was overweight. She supported him financially and believed she was the *ultimate* caregiver. She projected her inner mythology and the life of an unacknowledged Seth character onto her partner. He took control of her life, usurping her wellness without giving anything in return. Since she could not own her condition, she was like Osiris, wandering through an underworld of self-pity.

She dreamed of having a photograph taken with an unknown Chinese child. The Chinese infant represented two things: a way of being which was *foreign* to her, as well as the *birth* of a new *perspective*, represented by the camera. Like the birth of Horus, accompanying an unknown child coincides with new growth and the move toward empowerment. This dream was attempting to help her awaken to a new (foreign) way of being.

Satisfaction and empowerment come when *we make the decision* to understand our inner world and why we accept a lifestyle that is degrading and unfulfilling. *We find when we are whole as individuals, our relationships provide an opportunity to share, rather than take what we feel is missing.* At the same time, giving of ourselves in an unbalanced way is always a reflection of our low self-worth

The Symbolism of Reptiles

Reptiles and snakes play a prominent role in Egyptian mythology and in dreams we find these creatures representing biological processes which remain *below the surface* of awareness. Dreams of reptiles often indicate how we are currently integrating the fight and flight response, our instinctual drives for survival, or our sexual impulses. This area of the psyche is the most primitive and therefore, if we can activate these

52

powerful energies, we can tap our most fundamental and vital regenerative power. In the same way we evolved from an oceanic and reptilian beginning, we still experience metamorphosis.

There is a profound energy driving our species to survive and adapt. This power, when channeled productively, provides us with the resources to transform difficulty into success. When this energy is turned inward, like the Daughter of Ra, it can manifest as seething anger or panic attacks.

Feathered serpents, flying dragons and the devouring snakes of world mythology embody metamorphosis. Challenging the hero to a game of survival, those courageous enough to move beyond fear programming are always rewarded with symbolic treasures (released repression), swords (enlightenment) or keys (awakened sexuality). As guardians of what remains below awareness, through flight they achieve an extraterrestrial perspective. Roosting in the hidden realms, they are the timeless messengers of how we can access our regenerative power.

The snake devouring its tail appears in virtually every ancient culture and symbolizes the journey of life where the new continuously emerges from the old. Two entwined snakes around the staff of Caduceus is the emblem of a physician, revealing the snake to be a healing image of wholeness and wellness. Shedding and adopting a new covering each year, this revered and potent reptile embodies metamorphosis and the cyclical aspect of renewal.

Snake symbolism has undergone a different type of metamorphosis. Our ancient stories reflect the ways we once celebrated terrestrial phenomena. Over time, the snake would come to lose the transformative inspiration of its ancient heritage. As new symbolism was re-packaged for mass consumption, these older, yet more powerful symbols became evil. We can see the enormous power of the snake worshipping cults, along with the fertility goddesses of antiquity in the way both were castigated by the emerging patriarchal sects.

In the early part of this millennium, words like satan and Lucifer were mistranslated from their original meaning. Satan is used in the Hebrew story of Job, when he was lamenting that he did not know what issue his *satan* had taken with him: "If only I had the indictment *my adversary* has written against me." Satan was a Hebrew word which meant *any adversary*.

Similarly, Lucifer meant Bearer of Light and in ancient times, was the name of Venus, the star that rose as the Morning or Evening Star. In these same stories, the word Lucifer is used only once in Isaiah's use of "Lucifer who has fallen." Isaiah was writing about an historical and prideful Babylonian king, Tiglath Pilesar III. He used the word Lucifer to compare this arrogant king to the planet Venus, when it boldly rose before the sun in the morning. As the Morning Star, Lucifer or Venus was always viewed as an imposter of the sun. In their newly packaged form, these symbols now give us permission to remain victims. Our dreams reveal how light always overcomes darkness and in the end, the hero is redeemed when the monsters (transformation barriers) are vanquished.

Snakes, scorpions and stinging insects in dreams represent the biting and poisonous nature of repressed feelings and anger turned inward. Dreaming of a snake signifies the repression of natural and instinctual drives or the move to allow for more natural (sexual) expression. Whether the snake represents the unleashing of repressed sexual urges, or whether it is a symbol of death and rebirth, it signifies healthy and necessary energy which must find expression.

Seth embodies the adversary of Osiris and becomes the shadow of the disempowered *hero*. When "Nancy" had to get the women and children out of the building, she was hiding from a similar "closet" character who ruled her inner wasteland. Seth is one representation of how ignoring the famine within (low self-image) leads us to project it *out there*. He wants to usurp the power Osiris has, rather than support him, and projects his famine onto everything. Ignoring the value of what lies hidden *in here* can turn all experience into crisis. When psychic famine occurs, he converts what should have been a fertile landscape into a desert. A journey to the underworld (through dream work) has to be taken by the hero before the dysfunction can be identified, and the power given back to the appropriate characters of the psyche.

First Seth creates a casket for Osiris, in the sense that self-destructive behavior always has one goal in mind. This process didn't really kill the hero and he is brought back to life, further demonstrating how self-destructive tendencies can become a lifestyle. Real crisis and the ability to transform the wasteland finally occur, when Osiris is dismembered, destroyed and sent into the underworld. Forced to walk in the land of silence, he laments his fate, complaining in a true Survivor fashion. Yet, his consolation comes in knowing he will eventually come to rule (control) this *underworld* or hidden wasteland within.

"Beverly" is in a relationship with a married man. She dreams a woman is shot and killed and she is not sure whether she should tell the woman's sister. The dream brings several symbols out into the open. The gun represents the sexual feelings which are causing her pain, while blood represents how her feelings are coming to the surface. The assassination of the (unknown) female character portrays what is actually taking place in her underworld. Her psyche has cleverly painted the idea of unacknowledged pain with a character assassination, something which goes hand in hand with an affair. The decision about whether she should tell the sister related to how she needed to own up to *what she fails to tell herself*.

After facing her issues, she too, dreams of accompanying or protecting an unknown child. This child is *wounded* and by recognizing what she was *really* feeling her dream helped her exit a dysfunctional relationship.

The hero must embark on a transformative journey in the same way Osiris takes back control of the *underworld*. Horus, like the child that appears in dreams, represents the rebirthing of our *real* self. When usurper Uncle Seth is overthrown, the empowered heroes take control of both the underworld (unconscious) and the kingdom (consciousness).

Approaching any unknown or undesirable event can be fearful. This is why we sometimes live in denial, feeling sorry for ourselves. We push an event which might transform us into a place where it remains hidden, even though it retains enormous energy within the unconscious. Repressed energy will find expression and when disowned, can appear in the form of the adversary, whether in dreams or in daily life.

Repressed childhood anger is another way of describing unresolved childhood pain. If we can be fearless enough to allow painful truths to come forward, we can come to terms with the past and allow the healing process to begin. Many people have the illusion that forgiveness is something given for the benefit of another. *In reality, forgiveness is the freedom we gain when we are unshackled from the monuments we build to remember our anger.* Like Cathy who no longer allows her father to drive her as she dreams of packing and going to the airport, we give nothing away that we need to carry with us anyway.

The Grieving Caregiver

The suffering of Isis reminds us of the early experiences of someone, forced to witness suffering or weakness in the primary caregiver. As a Survivor, we may carry resentment if we feel this caregiver's behavior drove the other caregiver away. There is a pronounced sense of helplessness that developed when we realized our needs could not be met. It is compounded when we were forced to care for the grieving caregiver and other siblings. What remains unacknowledged however is the unrecognized *identification* with the primary caregiver. It can further exacerbate a belief in our helplessness. Even while we demonstrate a profound ability to nurture others, we cannot find it within to nurture ourselves.

We tend to own aspects of our parents whether or not we realize it. The process of caring for the caregiver oftentimes forces our development into fast-forward before we are able to grow strong and set internal structures for balance and wellness. This may be how we never grew to feel safe.

Isis uses fire in this story as a form of alchemy. In dreams, fire represents passion or anger, and the burning or gnawing sensation that occurs when we experience frustration. The fire also represents the unresolved anger we may carry forward as resentment. Frustration can arise when we feel powerless to achieve our goals. When we gratify every desire and compulsively act upon every urge, fire grows by what it consumes. It models obsessive-compulsive behavior which isn't about achieving satisfaction, but controlling the inner chaos that only reinforces a sense of powerlessness.

Unlike earth, air and water, fire is the one element which has made us like gods. It can reflect our desire to destroy something but it can also become symbolic of the divine power to refine our base nature. Like the phoenix, this mythical bird transforms itself through fire and rises, renewed from the ashes of the past.

Just as Isis must find Osiris, we must resurrect our dead and dismembered ability to move *fearlessly* through the world. Sometimes we simply recognize how *something must pass on* or exists in the past, as in the case of the negative influence of a caregiver who we may have to mourn and release. Through this transmigration and the birth of Horus, (empowered child) we are reborn.

Without turning inward, we are disconnected from the part we play in stalking adversity. Only through our relationship to Isis or the feminine approach to introspection, do we discover how the inner terrain is reflected upon each experience. We can fan the divine spark to create something new and give birth to a new perspective. When we overthrow Seth, our experiences are *magically* transformed.

The Healing Journey

When life is reduced to the mechanized process of instant gratification and compulsions, life has died and our senses are dulled. By allowing our sensual nature to experience a type of rebirth, we approach the outer world renewed. We come to recognize our connectedness to life and touch again the evolving world of experience. In the last chapter we had to unleash ourselves from the future, now we must truly disconnect ourselves from the past.

The Survivor's unacknowledged mythology can manifest in dreams of reptiles moving beneath murky water or turbulent seas that threaten to engulf us. We can dream of barren landscapes, and biting and poisonous creatures that weave webs and appear as a threat, no matter how tiny. This is symbolic of our obsessions and unacknowledged self-abuse.

We can establish granaries to nurture an internal sense of self worth, which is validated by the way we have always nurtured others. Happiness does not come from making changes in the outer world, yet once we heal the inner world the outer world is experientially different.

At the end of our work together, "Liz" dreamed of a tree house with furniture made from branches and leaves. From its porch of twirling vines, she watched the world below. She saw a fox hunting a small bird, although the bird escaped and flew up to her. She looked at the bird that smiled "a bird smile," and watched the sunset, feeling good about herself.

Her dream work began in an effort to overcome her obsessive and perfectionist tendencies. She was oblivious to her anxiousness, although keeping busy kept her from enjoying life. Keeping busy is often a sign that we do not want to face a difficult issue. This was one of her last dreams after having a series of dreams of dirty bathrooms. The bathroom is a place where we come clean, although she was fearful that looking within she would find something dirty. This portrayed her disconnect from her sexuality.

In the end, the tree house became reflective of her budding natural and organic self. Her fox-like hunting and cleverness no longer succeeded in trapping her ability to fly or see the world below. Sexual issues came forward in her dreams which became necessary for her transformation. She made profound changes in her life, much to the surprise of those around her. These changes better reflected her earthy sensuality and sexual desires. In fact, she is in a new relationship and just gave birth to her first child. It became obvious her perfectionist tendencies were a way of distracting herself because she did not want to face what was lacking in her relationship at the time. The last time I saw Liz she was smiling "a bird smile," and holding her beautiful baby.

The creator used the heart to guide humanity and to establish order or *maat* in the world. Just as the heart had stirred and the tongue had spoken to establish *maat* out of chaos, so too, would the heart and tongue of the individual have control over all other parts of the body. If we can take a moment to listen, the heart will speak volumes. When we can no longer hear the heart, we can turn to our dreams for guidance.

By recognizing the unrealistic nature of our fears, we can overcome the degrading nature of compulsive behavior that keeps us from fulfillment. For the Survivor, no amount of magic or nourishment can bring order to a chaotic outer world. The call to turn inward, where we can understand and compose the inner terrain, once completed, creates what can only be called a miracle. Our beliefs shape our experiences and our experiences shape our beliefs. When we change our internal beliefs, we observe and react differently. This affects the way the world responds to us; it is always wrapped together in this way.

Jung said: "Who looks outside dreams; who looks inside awakes." We cannot control the outer drama and unfolding events around us, no matter how powerful we are. Yet, we can turn inward where we are empowered to create strength and order. By establishing *maat* within, it is reflected around us. This is the miracle that occurs when we return light and calm to the inner terrain. We find without doing anything, the outer world mysteriously changes.

Perhaps this is the magic the Egyptians lived by.

Chapter Three
Theseus and the Negotiator's Labyrinth

Myths of Ancient Greece
Depersonalization, Addiction and the Fear of Intimacy

"In the deep still woods upon the Thracian mountains
Orpheus with his singing lyre led the trees,
Led the wild beasts of the wilderness."
Orpheus and Eurydice

In a metaphorical landscape where the greatest achievement comes from sharpening one's reasoning skills, we explore a culture famous for their myths because of their influence on Western art and science. The Greek deities interacted with the human realm on a daily basis. At the same time, the philosophers looked upward, finding ways to lift humanity above their natural condition.

The Greeks transformed a world of superstition into the beginnings of rational thought. We have explored the repressed symbolism of motivation, and self-worth, now we explore how intellect can trap us in our growth. We can spend the day going through the *motions* of believing everything around us acceptable. When we dream however, our *real* feelings have expression.

The Negotiator's Labyrinth is explored in the appropriately clever and intellectual setting of Greek mythology. The Greeks held reason to be more important than the animal passions, which kept one in an *uncivilized* state of vice and their myths offer many representations of *depersonalization*, where characters are turned into inanimate objects. In the same way, the Negotiator intellectualizes feeling to depersonalize experience. This is a detached and yet, highly clinical and imaginative approach to everyday interaction.

In the shadow of the Negotiator, we also discover how a fear of intimacy will be *projected* onto our relationships. Since we *do not own* our inability to be intimate, we *experience* rejection. Along the way, feelings are bypassed. We think them into abstraction where they cannot threaten our sense of well-being. Through *intellectualization* or the over use of the thought processes, we can rationalize anything.

The Greeks encountered the world through the mind and sought rational answers for experience. Logic consists of opinions and assumptions, rather than an ability to be *moved* by experience. Aristotle used logic and syllogism to expose the form of an argument independent of its content. The Sophists avoided the search for truth altogether, and sought merely to win debates. These mental gymnastics can create a strange Labyrinth as the mythology of the Negotiator.

The Greeks used drama to portray life and dreams too, seem to affect us in the same unspoken way as cinema. We explored how the setting reflected our state of mind, now we look deeper into the landscape to detect emotion. One of the first things I note when working with a client is how the dream *made them feel*.

In public life, the Greeks strove to be virtuous and image was everything. *Shame* or *dishonorable behavior* was considered far worse than merely being found *guilty* for a crime *opposed by law*. After all, laws were man-made structures and weakness could be detected through any diligent reasoning process. This clever approach personifies the reward system for a fear of intimacy, where we merely *evade being caught*.

Greek mythology reveals deities with humanly inspired characteristics of passion, greed and lust. Since they developed a culture where passions were believed to be a disease of the soul, perhaps they displaced their more human qualities upon their divinities. Like the Negotiator, their imaginative and intellectual life was profound and truly gifted.

In Homer's words, the gods were "like a young man at the age when youth is the loveliest." Chiseled into the pages of history, we find an image of humanity at its most graceful, like a sculpture. Similarly, the Negotiator often retains the grace and enthusiasm of a child, with intellectual gifts and humor far surpassing the rest of humanity.

The Sophists, which means clever, endeavored to popularize scientific learning. The term *sophistication* has come to mean the lessening of our naturalness and simplicity. It suggests an almost artificial charm or wit and likewise, we often use humor to mask our discomfort with our natural feelings. The Sophists believed knowledge was, at best relative, and that the truth was unattainable.

Logical reasoning and syllogism consisted of three statements with two premises and one conclusion. As an example: a) a bird is a living creature; b) a lark is a bird; c) therefore a lark is a living creature. Or, a) a dog is not a biped; b) all humans are bipeds; c) therefore a dog is not human. This is an interesting way of keeping experience at surface level.

The Mythical Setting of the Negotiator

"Julie" is a renowned artist who struggled with a heroine addiction. She described a past of abusive relationships that always ended in drama. She had many years of recovery under her belt when we began dream work. She was in her mid thirties, lived with a man, but was having difficulty opening up to this relationship.

Initially her dreams revolved around her dogs and how tending to them caused her to be late for something. The dog is often a symbol which appears when we are exploring the idea of *unconditional love*. Being late is reflective of not meeting expectations about where we should be in terms of life stages. The landscape and setting of her dreams were often snowy, reflecting her sense of coldness and isolation.

She described how prior to working with me, her dreams always revealed something ugly about herself or grotesque body parts. Her artwork too, portrayed similar subject matter where beauty was juxtaposed with weapons that released tiny drops of blood. Dreams of blood bring feelings to the surface, while decapitation, or a head separate from a body, merely shows how we disconnect from our ideas. If it is another person's head, it can symbolize how we reject the ideas associated with this person. The point is that dreams do reveal crisis and conflict, although even grotesque images are always trying to help us uncover our beautiful nature.

As Julie and I worked together I noticed her dreams began to portray strange, slow motion movements, which always followed a situation of being intimate with someone. She described how she moved in "slow, break dancer spins," or "I pull myself down the hall using the door jams and moldings. Sure enough, my legs weren't even touching the ground, so now I'm pulling myself down the hall like an astronaut in space." This was a productive representation of how she was beginning to focus more on her actions and *reactions* when meeting her fears.

Her dreams then involved *portraits* of men, as a symbol of the distance she kept from being intimate. Then she dreamed she and her mate were looking at comics on the bed. This common dream portrayed a lighter way of exploring her sexuality. Finally she dreams of an attractive male grabbing her in a headlock. She feels sexual stirrings, breaks away from him in slow motion and laughs. She mentioned she was surprised at how her dreams had become funny and not so grotesque.

Julie was learning to see her mental gymnastics as a simple fear response and not crisis and calamity. Like the backseat male in Cathy's dream, this attractive male was a symbol of her growing sense of self acceptance. He embodied the transformation or the empowerment `necessary to move fearlessly toward intimacy. Moving beyond the male negativity of her earlier experiences, she is seeing herself through the eyes of this *new* male character. In the end, she said, "I had a dream that someone told me I was pretty and I caught a glimpse of myself in the mirror and I was... pretty that is. This is hugely different from my usual mirror dreams where I am discovering something really ugly about myself and trying to fix it."

The remedy I prescribe for a fear of intimacy is to find ways of exercising vulnerability. She gave a presentation to other artists of her life and work, holding nothing back. Sharing her drug experience was cathartic for her because it enabled her to give full expression to her shadow life. By revealing the shadow's *creative dimension*, she was better able to see that something fearful can also heal. When the lights came on after her presentation, she said, "I was surrounded by people telling me bits and pieces of their life. While there were no ex- drug addicts who made themselves known to me, there were many who knew the feeling of unworthiness in their life and the creativity it inspires. They know what it is like to troll for a sugar rush in the middle of the night, which is akin to what a drug addict wants."

Shortly thereafter, Julie got married and has a newfound respect for her muse. The mythology of the Negotiator often brings us in front of the public because of our gifts. Wellness, however, requires we understand the *real nature* of what is driving us.

The Minoans

The Minoan's of Knossos, Crete were thriving around 1600BC. In their history, we find the beginning of the tales that would evolve into Greek mythology. King Minos married the daughter of the sun, Pasiphae. Her illicit union with a bull produces a monstrous offspring, the Minotaur who was half human and half bull.

King Minos hid the Minotaur in the Labyrinth. This beast received the tributes of sacrificial youth sent from mainland Greece and the hero, Theseus embarked on an adventure to free them. He was given a ball of string for use in finding his way of out the maze by Daedlus, its architect. When Theseus entered the maze, he secured the string to the entrance. As he went forward, he unwound the string and this allowed him to find an exit from the maze. He came upon the horrible Minotaur and killed it, thereby releasing its prisoners.

When King Minos discovered how the Greeks had escaped from the Labyrinth, he knew it could only have been through the aid of its clever architect. Daedlus and his son Icarus were captured and imprisoned inside the maze of his own making. From the feathers of birds and wax, he made two pairs of wings to aid in their escape. Both father and son flew out into freedom, above the rocky shore of the Mediterranean. Daedlus urged Icarus not to fly too high, and warned him the sun would melt the wax holding his wings together.

The delight and power of flying went to Icarus' head and of course, he did exactly what his father told him not to do. He was exhilarated and flew as high as his wings would carry him. As he approached the sun, his wings melted. He crashed into the rocks below and sadly, Daedlus flew to Sicily. The Sicilian king received him with great kindness and admiration but King Minos devised a clever trap to find the escapee. He offered a great reward to anyone who could pass a thread through an intricately spiraled shell.

This news traveled to Sicily, and Daedlus assured the Sicilian king that it could be done. He made a hole at the closed end of the shell and fastened a thread around an ant. After placing the ant inside the shell, he sealed the hole and when the ant came out of the other end, everyone cheered.

Minos knew only Daedlus could have devised a way to thread a seashell. He immediately set off for Sicily to capture the crafty architect. Upon his arrival, however, the Sicilian king refused to turn Daedlus over and in the interchange, King Minos was slain.

Around 1500BC, the Minoan palaces were ruined and the major towns on the Aegean islands were destroyed by fire. An eruption on Thera may have caused tidal waves and earthquakes as a cloud of thick ash blighted the fields, and destroyed the early Aegean civilization. Thereafter, the Minoan culture was transferred to the Achaean people in mainland Greece.

The Mycenae people lived in city-states ruled by individual kings. They colonized the shores of Asia Minor, most notably Troy, located at the entrance to the Black Sea. The epic of the Trojan War took place about 1200BC near what would become modern day Turkey.

The Creation Story and the Greek Pantheon

Before the earth, sea and heaven came into being, there was only chaos, existing as a confused and shapeless mass. In this heaviness were the slumbering seeds of all that would manifest. Earth, water and air were combined into one mutable substance that stayed in a state of flux. This was a time, when the earth was not yet solid, the air was not yet transparent and the sea was not yet fluid.

From this lack of permanency, all things flowed and nothing was constant. A process of strife created opposites in a ceaselessly changing system. Everything moved and grew in a state of *becoming*. *Being* was just a transitory snapshot of each passing moment.

The cosmic matter called *Apeiron* was the boundless and infinite. Within it, were the basic substances which were sometimes *fluid* and at other times *air* or *fire*. The Originator or *Arche* made use of heat and cold or *motion* to derive earth or matter from this basic substance.

Over time, the earth was separated from the sea and the heavens. Fire, the lightest of the elements, sprang up to form the skies. Next, air took its place between the heavens and the earth. Since the earth was heavier, it sank below and came to buoy itself upon the water, heaviest of all.

In this beginning, was Gaia the earth and Uranos, the sky. When Gaia gave birth to the Cyclopes, Hekatoncheires and Titans, Uranos grew alarmed because of their enormous size and monstrous form and forced them back into Gaia's womb. Kronos was the last conceived Titan, so she persuaded him to castrate his father the next time the two had intercourse. This killed Uranos and thereafter Gaia was able to give birth to the rest of the Titans including Prometheus, Atlas, Epimetheus, Iapetus, Themis, Tethys and Okeanos.

Kronos became the ruler of heaven and took as his wife, his Titan sister, Rhea. Fearing he too, might be overthrown by his offspring, he devoured every child as soon as Rhea gave birth. She concealed the sixth child, Zeus and instead, wrapped a rock in swaddling clothes to present to her husband. Kronos didn't notice this trickery and quickly swallowed the rock.

Zeus married Metis, the daughter of Tethys and Okeanos. She helped to overthrow Kronos by serving him an emetic potion that made him spew up Zeus' brothers and sisters. These were the twelve Olympians: Poseidon, Hades, Hestia, Hera, Ares, Athena, Apollo, Aphrodite, Hermes, Artemis, and Hephaestus. Together, these children overthrew the Titans and created Olympus.

The Olympians resided above the mountains, behind magnificent gates, guarded by the Seasons. Feasting on nectar and ambrosia, they wore white gowns and wreathes made of golden laurel leaves. They found serenity and comfort listening to Apollo play his lyre. This was a place where the wind, rain or snow never trespassed into their divine space and only the white gold light of the sun danced upon its palace walls.

Stealing the Fire

A prophecy claimed Zeus' wife Metis would bear a goddess equal to him in wisdom. He devoured Metis in an effort to prevent such a birth. One day, he had a raging headache and asked Hephaestus to split his head open with an axe. When he did, Athena, his daughter, sprang forward, fully armed, dressed and formed. She was the goddess of intellect and rivaled her father in wisdom. Athena could be seen wandering through Olympus with an owl perched on her arm.

After devouring Metis, Zeus took his sister Hera as his wife. Zeus' lustful adventures and Hera's jealous retaliations occurred almost daily. Many innocent mortal women would feel her wrath for simply being beautiful and catching the eye of Zeus.

Prometheus (foresight) and Epimetheus (hindsight) were two of the overthrown Titans. They were charged with making all of the earth's creatures, including man. As Epimetheus worked, Prometheus brooded over the defeat of his Titan siblings to the Olympians. They were to endow each creature with gifts and Epimetheus chose courage for the lion, the gift of flight for the birds, gills for the fish, great claws for the eagle and the wild cackle of laughter for the hyena. When he had finished dispersing these gifts, he realized he had saved nothing for man.

Epimetheus consulted his brother about what gift they might give to humans. Prometheus resented the gods and sought to spite them by promoting the interests of man. He knew exactly the gift that would make humans superior and consulted with Athena. Since her mother, Metis had also been destroyed by Zeus, she agreed to help Prometheus ascend to heaven and light a torch upon the chariot of the sun. They brought this burning torch back to the earth and gave the gift of fire to humans.

Endowed with fire, the animals were no match for humankind. Able to live anywhere, regardless of the climate, they shaped tools with fire, and eventually subdued the earth. The gods conspired to punish both man and their helper, Prometheus. They created the first woman as something sweet and lovely to look at. She would come to earth as a shy maiden of radiant beauty and a veil of flowery garlands adorning her head. They named her Pandora, which means the gift of all.

Aphrodite gave her beauty, Apollo taught her to sing and Hermes taught her how to be coy, clever and even deceitful. In this way, the first woman was created from the most alluring elements of heaven. She was sent to Epimetheus to become his wife.

She was described as a *beautiful disaster* because although her beauty was captivating, she was endowed with calamity. She was sent with a box which the gods had filled with toil, sickness and conflict. Before closing the box, Athena had added one last ingredient: *hope*.

When beautiful Pandora arrived with her box, Prometheus could only warn his brother not to trust any gift that came from Zeus. Epimetheus put the box away and told Pandora not to touch it. He used her as a model to create mortal women, although while he worked, her curiosity got the best of her. She opened the box and released its contents, allowing all the sorrows and torments of the world to pour out. When she looked into the empty box, only *hope* remained.

After punishing men by creating women, Zeus turned on their helper, Prometheus. He had him bound to the rocky peak of Mount Caucasus and each day, an eagle would feast upon his liver. Every night, his liver would regenerate only to have the eagle descend upon him again each morning. This was his punishment for giving fire to man.

Prometheus and Io

One day Prometheus had a strange visitor. It looked like a white cow with horns, yet rambled nonsensically in a woman's voice. She appeared distracted and awkward as she ran up and down the mountains. When she saw Prometheus bound to the rock, she stopped immediately and said:

"Who are you,
Storm-beaten and bound to the rock.
Did you do wrong?
Is this your punishment?
Where am I?
Speak to a wretched wanderer.
I have wandered so long…so long.
Enough, I have been tried enough.
Yet I have found nowhere
to relieve my suffering.
I am a girl who speaks to you
but horns are on my head."

Prometheus recognized her at once and replied:
"I know you, girl. You are Inachus' daughter Io.
You enticed Zeus' heart with passion
And Hera hates you for it. She it is
who drives you on this flight that never ends."

Io was amazed that someone recognized her. She thought she was lost and now this stranger spoke her name.

She answered:
"Who are you, sufferer that speaks the truth
to one who suffers?
He replied:
I am Prometheus, who gave mortals fire."

She had heard his story too. Prometheus told her how Zeus had punished him and she recounted how it was Zeus too, who had been the reason she was changed from a beautiful princess into a wandering and starving beast. Zeus lusted after her beauty and seduced her while creating a mist to hide them from Hera's jealous eyes. Although the thick cloud blocked Hera's view of the earth, she was no fool. She knew quite well why this strange occurrence was happening down below, and Zeus could usually be found in the thick of it.

She descended immediately and when she found Zeus, he quickly made the cloud dissolve. He hid his unfaithfulness by turning Io into a cow. When the mist evaporated, he and Hera looked at each other and then at the cow. Zeus pretended to be surprised to see the creature and laughed. He told her how amazing it was, how the cow had just sprung up at that moment, newborn and beautiful the way it was. Hera wasn't amused. She pretended she believed him, and asked that he give it to her as a gift. Zeus had no choice but to turn little Io over to his wife. Hera knew exactly how she would keep this beautiful child from Zeus.

Argus was a sleepless giant with one hundred arms and one hundred eyes. Hera knew he would keep a stealthy eye on her. While some of his eyes slept, others stayed awake and so he perpetually kept a careful eye on the little cow. Zeus knew poor little Io was miserable and he asked his brother Hermes for help in setting her free.

Hermes flew to earth and removed his winged sandals, cap and anything that would reveal his divine nature. Pretending to be a shepherd boy, he played his tiny pipe made of reeds. Argus clapped along with the music, while another hand patted a place next to him for Hermes to sit.

The clever god piped a little and then began to tell the giant one boring tale after another. He talked as monotonously as he could and although he saw the giant's eyes growing drowsy, always some would fall shut, while others remained open. Argus constantly kept one searching eye upon the piper and the cow.

Hermes was up to the challenge and told Argus a tongue-twisting tale about Syrinx and her sister nymphs. It worked! The dreary tale finally put all one hundred eyes to sleep. Just as the last eye closed, Hermes took out his knife and killed Argus. Even though Io was now free from Argus, Hera sent a gadfly to chase and torment her. The pesky insect chased her up and down the hills where Io could only keep running in a cloud of dust.

In time, Io's journey would take her to the banks of the Nile. Zeus would return and change her back into her human form. She would eventually give birth to the god Hercules, the same hero who would come to free Prometheus from his chains.

Depersonalization and Intellectualization

The Greek myths present many characters that are either transformed into inanimate objects, or obsessed with them. Baucis and Philamon are both turned into trees. Daphne is pursued by Apollo and is changed into a laurel tree. Pygmalion rejects all women and later falls in love with his statue. Arethusa is pursued by Alpheus and becomes a spring, while Alpheus changes into a river. Narcissus falls in love with his reflection and even the moon pursues Endymion who is put to sleep on the side of a mountain where she can eternally embrace him. Ceyx and Alcyme change into birds, just as Io was turned into a cow. These stories personify the mechanics of depersonalization.

Like the Warrior's Tale and Survivor's Famine, the Negotiator's Labyrinth was constructed in an environment of hurt feelings and pain. Instead of developing a strong will or allowing anxiety to run unchecked, the Negotiator wards off the threat by *depersonalizing* the experience. In a sense, difficult experiences happen in the mind and not to *me*.

Unlike the Survivor, who allows anxiety to co-exist with the personality, as Negotiators, we create so much distance from crisis that we can live on the edge, while loved ones wonder how. By animating feelings into mental abstraction (ideas or humor), the uncomfortable energy that might come to hurt us is effectively transformed.

Abuse or extreme discipline in the early environment of the Negotiator is mirrored in how these mythical characters are punished unjustly by the divinities. The fire of Prometheus and his later punishment conjures the image of the manic-depressive artist, driven to process the internal fire of manic inspiration. Artists thrive upon the fire of unworthiness made beautiful through a work of art. Great emotion grows within only to be ripped out by an eagle each day, leaving a gaping hole of emptiness. During the night the fire regenerates anew as passion and divine vision. It is symbolized as *the addict's sugar rush* that seeks whatever medication can subdue it.

In dreams, fire represents anger, passion and feelings. Prometheus was punished for having fire (feelings). Like Odin's ravens, the eagle that descends on him portrays how "thou shalt" can replay the critical tapes and dysfunctional punishment of early childhood. It descends upon us daily to remove any feelings that might regenerate. Later, it can lead to a lifestyle of self-punishing/self-medicating behavior. The eagle tears out the liver, and many manic types resort to alcoholism to control their *dis-ease*.

Intellectualization is a way to experience something through the mind and not the feelings. This is accomplished without having to give proper regard to emotional considerations. We have an idea something happened, but we never actually felt it. In an environment of anger, emotional coldness or constant criticism, we may have begun to depersonalize negative feedback or pain. We develop as an *intellectual* or *comical character* unable to process feelings or using our antics to rescue one caregiver from another.

Rising energy finds dissipation through quick wit and intellectual gymnastics. We justify and laugh away any feelings that make us uncomfortable. This behavior belies a *fear of intimacy* where our inability to relate deeply to others becomes our shadow. Once we have established this way of interacting, we are emotionally unavailable.

Plato thought sexual or emotional desires were an inferior class of pleasures. He held that intellectual, detached love for another transcended all other forms of desire, leading to our idea of *Platonic* love. When we are unable to accept gratification through any type emotional interaction, we find abstract ways of gratifying ourselves. We know we are a Negotiator when we discover how we cash in pain for heightened creativity.

Feelings are the value our emotions give to perception and experience. Once we have de-valued our experiences, we become susceptible to losing all sense of value in life. Like the Greek pantheon, this displaced energy gives free reign to fantasy, imaginative life and humor.

Many gifted comedians, inspired thinkers and entertainers come to self-medicate repressed pain through painkillers and other drugs. Some of our best entertainers are in a sense, a Greek tragedy that has become our entertainment. Only when their star crashes to the earth, do we learn about their inner turmoil. We saw their gift although it was only the animated life of their shadow.

This type of lifestyle makes real fulfillment impossible because we have cut ourselves off from the ability to feel. We can't help but see a modern version of Pandora in the life of the actress, Marilyn Monroe who was graced with divine beauty, yet carried her box of woe. She personified the Pandora archetype that was called "a beautiful disaster." Marilyn however, looked inside her empty box to find even *hope* had escaped.

Prometheus also embodies the scientist, developing a sort of fire in the mind which keeps us one step ahead of real human interaction. When we travel into the inner recesses of the mind to escape intimacy, we never see how what is sought in theory can be discovered in the deeper layers of human interaction. Uncomfortable with feelings in any form, we can only intellectualize our experiences.

The unrecognized source of the fire within, or the pain we attempt to escape, is like the claws of an eagle tearing at our insides, everyday. Nothing is resolved and the liver grows back. The liver is also the organ which processes toxic substances and since processing does not occur, but is only medicated, the pain subsides, only to return the next morning.

We think and think, but can't find the answer, and the eagle descends on us again. The only person strong enough to free us from our chains will be powerful Hercules, who eventually rescues Prometheus. So, what are we feeling and what is the mountain that holds us its prisoner?

The puzzle the ancient Greek physicists studied in trying to understand the true nature of the universe still remains a mystery today. When we go out to measure the fabric of life, we find we somehow participate in the measurement by affecting the result. The fundamentals of our universe remain a mystery to us. On the other hand, a mountain of thought in a world of puzzles does offer a perfect *place to hide*.

We are trying to think our way out of something that was always a gut feeling. How many times does the eagle have to tear out our liver, before we feel alive? In the case of the Negotiator, the pain we are avoiding funds our gifted inner life. We are the ultimate performer, dancing on top of the fire, so we do not feel the flames.

As Negotiators, we recognize our inability to feel but no matter how hard we try, we can only think about what we are feeling in abstract form. The energy channeled into mental processes is oftentimes in direct proportion to the pain we are trying to escape. Through our mental flight, the energy goes underground and funds our inspiration. Like Icarus who thought he was invincible, not until our star crashes and our wings melt do we come face to face with our mortality.

The Hybrid of Self Punishment and Reward

There is a reason we are called Negotiators. This is because of the reasoning processes we master, even while we sell ourselves into denial. In some cases, we assume nobody can really see how our life has fallen apart.

Like the Warrior who is too strong to show weakness and manifests *physical* symptoms, or the Survivor with their unrestrained *anxiety* states, when we live on a type of self-prescribed pain medicine, we are expressing the *dis-ease* of our feeling nature (addiction).

This energy funds our shadow life where we encounter the unrecognized part of our nature through others. This is how a fear of intimacy projects itself as the *experience* of constant rejection. We do not seek help because we are intellectual geniuses or masking our pain with humor, but *because our relationships fail.* Even while we deny harboring an innate fear of intimacy or a problem experiencing our feelings, the first symptom is that we continually experience rejection.

For some strange reason we find ourselves attracted to unavailable, emotionally distant and non-committal mates. We resemble the ancient Greeks who had a passion for mystery and *unsolvable* puzzles. Possessing an uncanny ability to attract the type of character least likely to pull us into real intimacy, should we be mistaken and someone does get close to us, we have the wherewithal to negotiate our way right out of the relationship. In most cases, we don't even realize how we began undermining the relationship the moment it began. All we can say for sure is that our relationships continually fail.

To protect our vulnerability, the shadow acts as a master weaver and *projects* rejection. This is a difficult concept for us to grasp and yet, over and over I see this as a recurring theme underlying many dreams. To move toward a healthier type of interaction, we need to heal ourselves. Without the ability to love ourselves, we cannot truly love another.

It is as simple as Aristotle's syllogism: a) those who cannot feel cannot have a normal relationship; b) if this knowledge remains unconscious, we will attract people who also cannot feel and cannot have a normal relationship; c) therefore, while this knowledge remains unconscious, we will not have a normal relationship. We have exposed the argument independent of its content yet amazingly enough to a gifted Negotiator, the problem remains unsolvable and rejection remains a mystery.

In the case of self-medicating/punishing behavior, we believe we have found a way to hide our pain from everyone around us. While we believe we have truly learned to feel nothing, this lie is recognizable to everyone except us. If we didn't feel so deeply, we would have no reason to hide.

Locked within our self-created Labyrinth, we have devised one of the most difficult defense structures to penetrate. Anyone who has been on the tough love side of addiction knows just how difficult it can be to help someone who has repressed or medicated their ability to feel. Without the ability to experience pain or negative emotion, there is no way to establish exactly where the bottom is. In addiction, loved ones can see our life crumbling around us, even while we continue to justify our condition. Unable to feel, rationality and perspective begin to implode all together.

So how did the Labyrinth get constructed? It was built to hide *the monster* and since we constructed it, only we can find our way out. The ball of string becomes the lifeline for an addict who must take responsibility for their condition and ask for help. We retrace our steps back to where we began hiding from our feelings. Asking for help requires vulnerability, something inherently frightening to the Negotiator.

Yet this is the string which allows us to retrace those places we visited *without actually being there*. Before we can leave the Labyrinth, we must understand and kill the Minotaur. If everything represents an aspect of us, *what is the Minotaur?*

We know the Minotaur is half human with the head of a bull. It embodies an unnatural type of mask. Odin's ravens and wolves draw from *unfathomable essences* where Fenris grows from the energy trapped by depression. The Survivor wears the symbolic snake upon the forehead, signifying the *unfathomable essences* of anxiety when it takes over the personality. The Minotaur embodies how denying our passions and feelings gives life to a half human and bull headed character *trapped within*.

Unprocessed and unacknowledged, the unfathomable essences of the unconscious begin to stalk us. In this case, the Minotaur represents our *feeling nature* growing in the shadows. Like Fenris and Seth, the Minotaur develops as a *self*-destructive monster.

In this myth, the mother had mated with a bull to create the Minotaur. Often the parental dynamics of the Negotiator reveals an angry father and a mother in denial. "He gets angry sometimes, but he doesn't mean it." When the father sees this passion emerging in the child he hides the *monster* away. *"Do what I say; not what I do."*

Symbolically, bulls are said to *see red* and behave with extreme aggression. We begin erecting the maze of denial, initially to hide from an abusive and bull-headed caregiver. Even while we devised a strategy to hide, we also adopted the head (ideas) or irrational discipline of this angry or aggressive parent because we cannot help but identify with the caregiver. While we may have created a lifestyle and blame past experiences for our pain, healing requires we shed this mask and learn to access our *real* nature.

Our shadow is not the *frozen ocean of a giant person,* or the *usurper Uncle Seth and his wasteland* which must be transformed. The monster we must slay wears the *internalized* aspects of a sense of discipline gone awry.

72

Early influences may have led us to punish and criticize ourselves unjustly and the Labyrinth is how we have come to *tune it out*. Luckily, we know the Minotaur's head is not ours because it is not human. Therein lays the promise of renewal.

As a defense mechanism, we enact a mixture of self-medicating and self-punishing behavior. We may punish ourselves by remaining alone or allow our lives to crumble around us. Turning toward self-medication, we repress our feelings, or use humor and abstract thought to distance ourselves from intimacy, which for us, *leads to pain*. Non-committal intimacy may be the only way we can express love. Ultimately our relationships fail.

Like "Linda," an unacknowledged low self image can be *projected* in a way that we *experience* controlling and degrading relationships. When we deny that a fear of intimacy is *our* problem, rejection appears to come from *someone else*. The more we deny the issues that keep us stunted in our growth, the more these issues become the fodder of our dreams. We may dream of parasites, vampires and the type of symbolism that represents something preying upon the body to reveal blood (feelings) or *eating* at us. Without understanding our dreams, we may only wake up believing we have glimpsed something ugly or disturbing about ourselves. In reality, all dreams are *disturbing* to awaken us to how we are *not growing*.

Many recovering addicts dream of using, which is merely portraying how they are repressing this urge in daily life. When the root of why we self-medicate is recognized, the urge to do so dissipates. "Maggie" dreamed of bars before she came to acknowledge that alcohol was becoming a problem for her. *Dreaming* reveals the opposite of what we believe to be true about ourselves. That is why dreams can become a powerful catalyst in helping us through difficult transformations.

Whether or not we were allowed to express our emotions becomes the measure of how we express our emotions. How we were disciplined creates the tapes that shape our self-discipline as adults. If a caregiver was overly aggressive or provided discipline in an abnormal way, we can't help but play these tapes.

In the Greek myths, we find Zeus and Hera as merciless parents and somewhat self-absorbed, gratifying their unchecked emotions and punishing their children. Zeus throws lightning bolts and Hera looks the other way. In fact, Zeus sets out to punish man simply because he was *given* the fire (passion). The fire embodies the anger or passion bequeathed to us, while at the same time we are punished for having it. As we adopt the behavior of our role models, the punishment continues, although it is internalized.

73

Poor Io, she too has become a hybrid because she is the female version of a bull that still speaks like a human. In her exchange with Prometheus, we see both the simpatico of attracting like-mates, who are unavailable, and how she too, must acknowledge her horns.

"Where am I?
Speak to a wretched wanderer.
Enough, I have been tried enough.
I am a girl who speaks to you
But horns are on my head."

The mythology we carry from childhood emerges as symbols in our dreams as adults. If we are living in a Labyrinth or tied to a rock, chances are, we have not recognized the enormous power of the *unfathomable essences* that allowed us to hide our vulnerability. Regardless of our past or early experience, we come to realize our parents did not come with instructions on parenting. We can release the mask they may have given to us; a mask that can only keep us from actualizing our destiny.

The Healing Journey

Without the ability to feel, we are no longer responsive to life, whether it is a fear of failing, diminished self-worth, intimacy or the life of an addict We lose our ability to feel sympathetic toward others in proportion to our inability to feel sorry for ourselves.

Just as Metis used an emetic potion that made Kronos spew up the Olympians, we can purge our painful memories and ground our inspiration in more balanced ways. "Julie" was able to retrace her steps and demonstrate her vulnerability by sharing her experiences with her peers. Later, she was able to take responsibility for the reasons her relationships failed. Our animated, yet repressed inner aspects are not unlike the characters of the Greek Pantheon who had been swallowed. They are passionate, lustful and abundant in feeling and emotion. A potion like this would be worth its weight in gold if we have lost our ability to value life.

As we move toward intimacy, we may have dreams of being undressed in public or relieving ourselves in bathrooms without walls as a result of having our nakedness exposed. When we *get naked* or express ourselves, we reinvigorate other aspects of the psyche that had not found expression. The Negotiator's displaced feelings combined with a fear of intimacy can fund dreams of ferocious animals that draw blood in the image of bringing our feelings to skin awareness.

More than the gifted life which stirs in the mind, we can discover fulfillment in intimate relationships. Conversations that allow us to hide our weaknesses can transform into sharing our vulnerability so we can discover who we *might become*. When we are fearless in opening to others, the interchange will always teach us something about ourselves.

We have the opportunity to approach experience from a sense of scarcity or abundance. Negotiating from the scarcity of anything always tips the scales against us where we lose. We are creating tomorrow based on our beliefs of today. If we negotiate from abundance or fearless vulnerability, we will create a life of abundance. Consumed by scarcity, we can only create the experience of knowing scarcity.

Being unavailable for deep human interaction, we unwittingly create rejection. Instead of distracting ourselves from life, we listen to the words of Socrates: "the unexamined life is not worth living." Only by understanding what is creating our experiences, can we change them. If we cannot find the clues to our unhappiness, we need only start paying attention to our dreams.

Aristotle wrote: "we are what we repeatedly do." To experience life differently, we do things differently. Giving and receiving often go hand in hand. If we learn to receive, we are more able to give. Conversely, if we learn to give, we oftentimes increase our ability to receive. Exercising the opportunity to become vulnerable is the key to the Negotiator's healing journey.

The syllogism creates a different result: a) new experiences change us; b) only by being open to feeling can we have new experiences; c) therefore, if we learn to feel, we can change and continue to grow. Daedlus does more than help us out of our intellectual maze; he also gives us wings to fly. If we must fly, we must also wonder if we are simply escaping.

He teaches us that if we fly too high, our wings may melt and we will crash to the ground. We may have devised ways to lift ourselves above our humanity, but we are human, after all.

Chapter Four
Aeneas and the Protector's Empire

The Creation Story of Ancient Rome
The Subconscious Net and the Fear of Abandonment

> "I take courage. Here too there are tears for things
> And hearts are touched by the fate of all that is mortal."
> *The Aeneid* (Virgil)

"Joe" was in his late thirties and in a two-year relationship with a beautiful woman. They lived together, although episodes of heavy drinking and unfaithfulness revealed the lack of commitment his partner brought to the relationship. She had difficulty finding her way in life and sought to reinforce her low self-image through romantic conquests that validated a low self-image. Joe believed if he continued to show support and love for her, in time she would change. They built a life together which revolved around the fear that she might leave him.

Eventually she did leave, and he immediately found himself in a similar relationship with a neighbor. Dream work allowed him to recognize how he transferred his beliefs onto his relationships and he made a conscious choice to take a time out to become more observant. When we find ourselves repeating patterns in our relationships, we can no longer blame our partner for the issues we face. All we are drawn to serves us in some way, and we need to understand *what it is*.

Joe described a dream of a beautiful woman who stalked him in the shadows. She appeared with a syringe and injected him with a substance that made him vulnerable and under her spell. He interpreted this to mean beautiful women could actually cast a spell on him. The syringe however, revealed the guiding nature of dreams that usually present the *opposite* of what we believe. The syringe is a *cure* and is associated with healing. His dream captured how the *female character* appears to a man as the embodiment of *his* repressed feelings. His psyche cleverly combined the ideas of vulnerability, transference and healing.

Only when dreams are viewed from this ego-centric perspective can we *really* understand their healing message. In this case the dream portrayed the mind altering power *his* beliefs held over him, and how it is sewn into *experiential reality* through projection. The woman in his dream and therefore, the women in his life were merely the *representation* of how he "gives away" his disowned power.

The most fascinating aspect of dreams is how they also teach us about our relationships with others. Since everyone in a dream portrays aspects of us, relationships also teach us about ownership and transference. Situations do not happen *to* us, they happen *because* of us. Whether it is rejection or abandonment, both types of *crisis* have a way of reflecting *our* condition.

Being *injected* with a cure reveals the way in which the shadow can also become a healer. The dream captured how he was *projecting* this power onto his mates. Awakened by the healing power of his dream, he discovered the courage to speak openly about establishing boundaries.

What appears frightening in a dream can also be good, and because of this Joe found a sense of power which had eluded him. While he cannot control what others do, he *can* control what is acceptable. After better understanding his dreams, his perspective no longer revolved around a fear of hurting another or being hurt himself. He began to tap his dreams to understand why he was drawn to *the damsel in distress*. This is the mythology that spins the tale of the Protector.

We turn to the mythical story of ancient Rome to observe a *culture* created by *both* partners in a co-dependent relationship. This partnership is constructed by denial and founded upon the premise that conquest is the only way to ward off being wounded. A fear of abandonment is nothing more than a fear of abandon or liberty *for us*. Like the ancient Roman Republic, the relationship may deteriorate, even while we remain oblivious to the dysfunction that undermines it.

Ancient Rome's self-protective ruling style also models the motivation behind the subconscious net. This portion of the psyche constructs a defensive posture to ward off the invasion of foreign ideas, while holding tightly to its beliefs. Its goal is simple: *to uphold the status quo.*

Classical Rome existed for over 450 years and was at its height in 117AD, comprising most of the Western world known at that time. It included most of Europe, the Middle East, Egypt and North Africa. The Romans were the mass merchants of ideas which merely sustained their style of government. They adopted and spread the Greek heritage, the Christian religion and much of the philosophy, art and innovations of the people they conquered, but only if it upheld *Romanitas*.

As the civilization taking the world stage after the Greeks, Rome would make an impact on the West in engineering, organization and administration. Roman children grew up reading Greek classics and writers aspired to create prose and poetry on equal footing with Greek epics. Rome's renowned poet Virgil would accomplish this feat in writing *The Aeneid*.

The Etruscans

Rome's roots are found in a group of Etruscans who gathered south of the olive line along the hills of modern Tuscany around the eighth century BC. By trading with Greece and Phoenicia, they adopted much of the Greek culture. When the Etruscans were weakened by their struggles against the Greeks, a group revolted and broke free from Etruscan rule. By the end of sixth century BC, the last of the kings had been expelled. Opposed to monarchy in any form, these early Romans established a Senate government that would exercise the rights of the people.

They would come to *romanticize* or express *Romanitas* for the great Republic they were building. Subscribing to a type of mass delusion in a government *by* the people, their military power simply recreated another form of monarchy or dictatorship. Like the protectionist tendencies of the subconscious, they took offensive measures to defend themselves against the *possibility* of invasion.

Their innovations included contributions in the areas of law, government and engineering. They invented hydraulics, concrete, and revolutionized the shape of buildings with their vaulted domes. Town planning was an art and they recreated Greco-Roman cities that became a type of oasis in the barren landscape. Each city had a theater, bath, forum and temple, built in a customary grid pattern. Their goal was to perpetuate *Romanitas* or the Roman way of doing things.

Just as "Rome was not built in a day," the subconscious net is built over a long period of upholding an ideal, controlling the flow of new information and defending a territory. Their creation story was based on the celebrated heroes of the past in a blending of Greek deities, Etruscan ancestral beliefs, and the migrating warriors of ancient Troy.

The Creation Myth of Ancient Rome

By the twelfth century BC, the Greeks had defeated the Trojans in a battle was fought because Paris of Troy had fallen in love with Helen, the wife of a Greek king. Paris brought her to Troy where the Greeks soon followed to defeat them in their own land. Afterward, Aeneas, the son of Troy's King Anchises and Venus, led a group of Trojans to the tiny island of Delos. He consulted the oracle of Apollo that said: "seek your ancient mother. There, the race of Aeneas shall dwell, and reduce all other nations to their sway."

Believing the oracle had spoken of Crete, the island of their Trojan ancestors, they embarked in search of their future. Upon arrival however, they experienced only famine and disease. With no other choice, they were forced to push onward. In a dream, Aeneas was told to steer toward Hesperia or the land of the Tiber where Dardanus, the founder of the Trojan race had once come. Hesperia was ancient Italy and so they sailed past Sicily and along the coast of Lucania.

Juno was the Roman name for Hera of ancient Greece. She watched angrily as these Trojans made progress toward Italy. She was still offended by Paris' insult of awarding the prize of beauty upon Helen. She felt an old grudge resurface and asked Aeolus, ruler of the winds to toss the ocean. A terrible storm broke over the water and the waves took on monstrous proportions. The Trojan ships were cast about and driven against the rocky coast of Africa.

Neptune saw the sweltering waves and knew he had not commanded such a storm. He raised his head above the water and saw Aeneas and his men fighting desperately against the gale. This tempestuous storm could have only been the work of Juno, and he was angered that she had meddled in his domain. He calmed the waves and with his trident, pushed the battered boats away from the rocks and onto the shore of Northern Africa.

Dido, the Forsaken

As the Trojan ships washed ashore, Juno devised a plan to keep them there. No matter what, she would not allow these Trojans to make their way to Italy. She would use the charms of beautiful Dido to captivate and hold Aeneas right where he was.

Dido had been a princess in Tyre or Phoenicia, but when her husband was murdered, she had fled her home to found Carthage in Northern Africa. As its Queen, she had laid the foundation for a magnificent city which would rival Rome. She exuded elegance and grace, blessed with a beauty and a power equal to Aeneas. Juno knew if she led Aeneas to Dido, it would not be difficult to make the two fall passionately in love.

Uncertain of where they were, Aeneas and his friend Achates explored the strange countryside while their men made camp. His mother Venus was desperate to thwart Juno's plan. While the heroes wandered about the African coastline, Venus went straight to Juno's husband, Jupiter.

Tearfully, the goddess wept and reminded the powerful god of her son's destiny. Aeneas was to start the race of people who would found New Troy, along the Tiber River in Italy. He would build an empire that would come to rule the entire world. The beautiful goddess pleaded with Jupiter to return Aeneas to his fate.

Jupiter reassured Venus the destiny of Aeneas had not altered in any way. She returned to earth and disguised herself as a huntress. Informing the men they were in Africa, she showed them the path to Carthage. She knew Dido would provide for them while they recuperated from their perilous journey, confident Jupiter would make certain Aeneas didn't stay too long.

Dido proved to be an incredibly gracious and generous host. For a time, Aeneas and Dido acted as man and wife. Aeneas behaved as if he was the King of Carthage, and the people embraced him in this role. He was quite content to remain in the company of this elegant woman who had premeditated his every need. Leaving this attractive woman and her generous city was the furthest thing from his mind. In time, Venus began to worry anew.

Jupiter had also observed how Aeneas was growing too comfortable in Carthage. He dispatched Mercury to rouse the hero from his tranquility. As Aeneas walked alone one day in the outskirts of town, Mercury suddenly appeared in a mist before him.

"How long are you going to waste time here in idle luxury?" The tiny god appeared out of nowhere and Aeneas was jolted from his reverie. He immediately recognized the glowing god, with winged sandals and feathered cap as Mercury.

"The ruler of heaven himself has sent me to you," Mercury said. "He bids you depart and seek the kingdom that is your destiny." Just as suddenly as Mercury had appeared, he was gone. Aeneas watched the mist evaporating and stood in wonderment. The encounter had the desired affect of immediately awakening him from his infatuation. With renewed purpose, he grew anxious to fulfill his calling and assembled his men to prepare for their departure.

When Dido heard of their preparations, she couldn't believe Aeneas meant to leave her. She summoned him and pleaded: "Is it from me you would fly? Let these tears plead for me, this hand I gave to you... If I have in any way deserved well of you, if anything of mine was ever sweet to you..."

Aeneas assured her she had indeed been kind, but since they had not married, he was free to leave her whenever he chose. "Cease these complaints, which only trouble us both," he said.

How could he cast her away like this? She was devastated. He had come to her starving, lost and in need of every kindness she had provided to him. She cared for and healed him of his sorrowful wandering. How could he forget that she had given him everything within herself and her kingdom? Aeneas remained steadfast in obeying the command of Jupiter.

The Trojans set sail that night, knowing the Queen would have made their departure impossible. When they looked upon the walls of Carthage, they saw the flickering light of a fire, burning in the darkness. They could not have known it was the funeral pyre of Dido. She had watched him sail away and ordered a fire to be built. After stabbing herself with the sword the heartless lover had left behind, she threw herself upon the fiery flames.

> "Unhappy Dido, was thy fate
> In first and second married state!
> One husband caused thy flight by dying,
> Thy death, the other caused by flying."

The Journey to the Underworld

Eventually, the Trojan ships would reach Cumae, in Italy. Aeneas sought the abode of the Sibyl, a prophetess of Apollo who lived in a cave attached to a temple and a grove. On his arrival, she prophesied of the labors and perils he would be forced to endure, on his way to success.

"Yield not to disasters, but press onward the more bravely," she said. Aeneas assured the Sybil he was up to the challenge, but asked for her help in making the descent into the underworld. He wanted to visit his deceased father, King Anchises who would guide him further, in seeking his destiny.

"The decent to Avernus is easy," she replied. "The gate to Pluto stands open night and day; but to retrace one's steps and return to the upper air, that is the toil, that is the difficulty." She told him to enter the forest and seek a tree with a golden branch. This would be a gift to Proserpine and if fate were with him, the branch would yield and become free from its parent's trunk. Otherwise, no force could remove it.

Venus sent two of her doves, which flew before him to show him the way. He found the tree and removed the branch, bringing it back to the Sybil. They traveled to the volcanic region near Vesuvius where the sulphurous flames sprang forth through the great chasm. Immediately the ground began to shake. The earth roared inhospitably and the tops of the trees began to sway. The howling dogs announced the coming of the deities. It was a perilous moment, one in which Aeneas still had a chance to flee, but the brave Trojan remained undaunted.

"You must summon your courage for you will need it," the Sybil said as she led him into the infernal regions below.

The deities were indeed frightful. They passed by the characters of Grief and avenging Care, pale Disease and melancholy Age. Fear and Hunger hideously tempted men toward a life of crime. Toil, Poverty and Death were too horrible to view and Aeneas was forced to look away. Mad Discord had hair that looked like blood soaked snakes, writhing and twisting in a fit of confusion and pain.

Briareus lived there too, with his one hundred arms. Nearby, the Hydras were hissing and spitting into the flames the Chimaeras were breathing. The Sybil and Aeneas made haste to the boat of the ferryman, Charon. At first, he refused them passage but when they showed him the golden branch, he agreed to take them across the water.

In the land of the shades, Aeneas thought he saw Dido, holding her hand over her recent wound. He had learned of her sad fate and in the dim light, he wasn't sure if it was Dido. As he approached the apparition, he recognized her immediately. Tears fell from his eyes and he spoke affectionately:

"Unhappy Dido, was the rumor true that you had perished and was I the cause? I call the gods to witness that my departure from you was reluctant and in obedience to the commands of Jupiter. Nor could I believe that my absence would cost you so dear. Stop, I beseech you, and refuse me not a last farewell."

She stood for a moment, with her eyes cast sadly to the ground and then, silently passed on. Aeneas followed, until with a heavy heart, he turned and rejoined the Sybil.

They came upon his father, Anchises, and the two cried. When Aeneas went to embrace him, he found his father to be without physical form and his arms went right through him. When Aeneas pulled back, his father described the difference between the dead and the living and he said: "My son, you see the Creator originally made the soul from the four elements of fire, air, earth and water. Fire, being the most excellent part, became the flame and it was scattered like seeds among the heavenly bodies. Of this seed, the inferior gods created man and all other animals. They mingled the fire with various proportions of earth that came to reduce its essential purity. Thus, the more the earth dominates the composition, the less pure is the individual; that is why men and women with full-grown bodies lose the purity of their childhood. In proportion to the time the soul and body are intermingled does the earth overwhelm the spirit."

He also told Aeneas how to fulfill his destiny by establishing Rome. Aeneas would lead the Trojan soldiers as the most powerful army in the world. He was told he would win a bride and found the people who would be called the Romans.

The Triumph of Aeneas

The next day, the Trojans sailed up the coast of Italy, in search of their home. An aged Latinus, great grandson of Saturn, had been warned in a dream that he was not to marry his only child, Lavinia to any man of his country. She was destined to marry a stranger who would soon arrive. When the Trojans landed, Latinus received them with good will and felt certain Aeneas was the son in law of the prophecy.

Juno again opposed the Trojans and she incited the King of the Rutulians, the favored suitor of Lavinia, to rise up against them. His wrath required no prompting because when he heard about the stranger and Lavinia, he was enraged.

To excite the fury of the Latins, she arranged to have Aeneas' son Ascanius, mortally wound the cherished stag of the Latin farmers. He was a playful pet that returned each night to a farmer and his child. All of the Latin farmers cared for and protected it.

After the death of the stag, even Latinus' Queen opposed the marriage of Aeneas and Lavinia. The Trojans soon realized they were treading in enemy territory. In a vision, Aeneas was told to enlist the help of the Etruscans and a furious war ensued until the Trojans were victorious. In the end, Aeneas married Lavinia and he was accepted as the leader of the Latins. Together, they founded the Roman race.

As the years passed, a descendent of Aeneas, Rhea Silvia, was forced by her father to become a vestal virgin. In a sacred grove, the god Mars raped her as she slept. She bore the twins, Romulus and Remus and had no choice but to abandon them on the River Tiber. The divinely conceived twins were left to cast adrift in a basket.

A she-wolf suckled and cared for the boys until the shepherd, Faustulus adopted them. When the twins had grown, Faustulus told them the story of their childhood. They were determined to build a new city where the she-wolf had found them. Arguing over the exact spot, Romulus was inspired by the gods to mark out a boundary on the Palatine Hill. Remus jumped over the line, demonstrating how vulnerable the area proved to be as a defense. Romulus saw this as an act of sacrilege and killed Remus, becoming the sole ruler of the settlement in 753BC. He founded Rome and declared it to be a safe haven for runaways.

The Mythical Setting of the Protector

"Ann" always finds herself in relationships where she lives *under the rule* of her mate. She is quite unhappy and yet, remains in the relationship. When she does leave, she finds herself in a similar one. Her partners undermine her self-worth by focusing on her deficiencies, although she is actually *drawn to* this type of relationship. We can safely say she *wants* this experience because each relationship is a carbon copy of the previous one. Our lives are often the result of *what we repeatedly do.*

She described her dreams: "When I slept with Frank, I always dreamed we were sleeping, but when I sleep with Scott I dreamed I woke up and found another girl sleeping with us." *Dreaming* of sleeping suggests that we remain asleep or oblivious to something we are not facing while awake. When she dreamed of *waking up* to find another girl sleeping beside them, this was the first step in acknowledging an unknown aspect of *herself.* While she disowns her condition, she is able to thrive in a type of bondage. In her dream, the girl was intoxicated. Ann sugar coats the truth rather than facing it. Even when we sell ourselves into denial, the psyche ever attempts to wake us. This dream was the beginning of Ann's awakening.

The Senate was established to do away with imperialism and tyranny. Although their goal was to form a system of government orchestrated by the people, their defensive posture created another dictatorship. Established to exercise the will of *all* the people, over a short period, the Senate was represented by a small ruling class. An imbalance developed between the represented wealthier class and the diminishing power of the lower classes.

The free citizens, farmers and peasants represented the bulk of the population. Conquest increased its citizen base because it offered subjugated people citizenship. While the citizens grew as a class, their power to affect events within the government diminished. To maintain the republic's army, every male citizen who owned property had to serve many years in military service. Although the wealthier classes prospered by these conquests, the peasants and farmers experienced a decrease in wealth. This was due to military service away from home and the influx of goods from foreign lands.

As this army moved forward, subjected states committed additional troops, which gave it enormous power. They maintained a system of defenses to protect their growing territory. Eventually, this growing army became its own industry, and strong generals were needed as leaders. Beginning with Sulla and Julius Caesar, a shifting of power moved away from the government and to the generals. This forced the

Senate to cast their vote for the general's dictatorship, in an effort to retain what little power they could.

From a dictatorship, the empire evolved back into imperialism due to the succession of family members who ruled after Julius Caesar and Caesar Augustus. They continued to romanticize a government by the people, although it was monarchy in everything but name.

When we romanticize unfulfilling relationships, we can sell ourselves into denial and ignore the internal politics of its dysfunction. The enormous defenses we build to protect ourselves can also become a trap to *our* freedom. Like the Roman army, we initiate conquest out of a fear of what *may* transpire if controls aren't in place.

The Subconscious Net

Consciousness is an *awareness* of thoughts and feelings. They can remain unconscious and still influence our behavior. The function of consciousness that directs, inhibits and censors the exchange of information between the conscious and unconscious realms is the subconscious net. In the *hypnotherapy* model, this net is believed to act as a gatekeeper. It takes a defensive posture to ward off the *foreign invasion* of new ideas that are inconsistent with what has been adopted as beliefs. It also employs a defensive posture to keep the *empire* of repressed ideas from rising.

These beliefs, established in early childhood, can be either positive or negative, although they remain just outside of conscious awareness. Without realizing it, we tend to dismiss any new information that contradicts these beliefs. During dreaming however, this mechanism is inactive.

Utilizing suggestibility, hypnotherapists can influence autonomic functions where suggestion can actually increase body temperature and heart rhythm not normally under active conscious control. When our feelings operate from this *underground*, we respond as if our partner is the reason we feel the things we do.

The complexity of our emotions are believed to have evolved from the sense of smell, designed to elicit either a positive or negative response in nocturnal mammals searching for food in the dark. Since facial expressions were the original form of communication among hominids, we can understand *emoting* as how we express our feelings. Responses, however, can arise without any sensory input and stimulation to certain areas of the brain can evoke an emotional response, revealing triggers that are activated by memory alone.

In essence, it is as if we perceive the world around us, not from the innocent perception of discovery, but by *taking in* information at the same time that we *project* beliefs upon events. Experience becomes a shifting percentage of actual perception and associative patterns of memory and feelings. This funds the defense mechanisms of *transference* and *projection*.

A *defense mechanism* allows us to block incoming information that may arouse painful or threatening feelings. The subconscious net allows incoming information to be passively rejected because *we came to believe* that the opposite was true. *Projection* allows us to bestow on others what we believe we are lacking. *Transference* is the unconscious coloring of someone by association with another, probably a parental figure. Both are at work in generating the shadow life of the Protector.

In dreams, we observe these processes at work clearly in how other characters portray *our* condition. In daily life however, transference and projection happen unwittingly. When our relationships fail or cause us to live in a subordinated condition of bondage and abuse, we can be certain we are failing to see how we are transferring our beliefs. Once we have bestowed our power onto another, the partner becomes *the orchestrator* of our feelings. They become *the reason* we feel anything at all.

Ambivalence and Monarchy

The Protector's early mythology can be viewed as a type of monarchy. We may be born into a type of *government* where the rulers are above reproach and established by heredity. The early environment may have subjected us to *the ruling elite* where organizational discipline abounds, while affection and intimacy is lacking.

When parents behave like rulers who arbitrarily lay down the law and remind us of our lower stature, a child comes to adopt a unique way of reading emotions. *We can interpret what appears to be love in ambivalent behavior or negative feedback.* This is especially true in instances where the emotions of the caregiver have been under the influence of drugs or alcohol. Mood swings and the erratic behavior of alcoholism usually amount to emotional or physical abuse. Thereafter, we are attracted to this type of emotional dynamic in our relationships.

Like Dido's emotional tirade, the caregiver's message may have made us feel guilty for exercising our autonomy. "You should be grateful that I..." and "if it weren't for me, you would be..." Later, we find ourselves *emoting* a similar message. Our fear of abandonment is a fear of letting go, or allowing autonomy and liberty to exist in the *culture* we perpetuate.

Females who experience distance or alcoholism in a father, and a mother who is weak and enabling, may pattern this relationship forward by choosing mates upon whom they may *transfer* or bestow the coldness of the father. From the role modeling of the mother, they may also become an *enabler* or someone who covers, protects and believes they can heal an addict.

Males who are raised by an emotionally cold, unavailable or weak father and a strong or colorful mother can also experience ambivalence in their relationships. They are drawn to strong, colorful mates like the mother, while they interact with emotional distance, like the father. However the relationship may manifest, it can produce dysfunction.

The characters of the Aeneid give us a snapshot of this ambivalence. Like the father, Jupiter has expectations of the hero, although he remains aloof and distant. Representing ambivalence in the mother, the real hero's mother, Venus guides her son to achieve, while Juno, *in the role of Jupiter's wife,* works at cross-purposes to what the hero is trying to achieve. His faithful partner, Dido then carries on the mantra, lamenting all that was done in the name of love in an effort to keep the hero from leaving. If our loved one's ability to actualize their destiny is a threat to us, we are probably living the mythology of the Protector.

Emotionally, we tend to recreate familiar situations. We re-establish opportunities to process feelings in the only way we have come to interpret and understand love. Although we set out to establish something different, unaware of our defensive tendencies, we simply replicate another form of tyranny.

The dynamics between the Senate and generals personify the *cooperative dysfunction* that exists in the Protector's relationships. What should have been a partnership of independence becomes merely a guarantee of security for one and a form of manipulation for the other.

When a relationship, which began as spontaneous attraction deteriorates into a sense of bondage and a loss of independence, it results in resentment and a sense of obligation. Like those conquered by the Romans, both the Protector and the codependent are mutually subjugated, taxed and drained of emotional resources. It is only the fear of abandonment that keeps them together. If either should talk about leaving, the other presents the overly dramatized abandonment tragedy of poor Dido.

Romulus and Remus were also abandoned, although Romulus founded the city of Rome as "a safe haven for runaways." This would be a perfect sign to hang on the front door of the Protector.

To be independent means to rely on our own resources. To be interdependent means to function as two independent people sharing resources. Codependency is not unlike a cooperative, where members own something collectively, and *share* in its benefits. We cannot call either party a victim because both are attracted to, or *served by* the dynamics.

The first question we must ask ourselves when we are unable to leave a dysfunctional relationship is: *how is this relationship serving me?* There is a benefit, and we must understand *what it is.* Sometimes it is deriving value from *fixing* someone. At other times, it is reaffirming the familiar tapes of childhood beliefs. In either case, the obsessive focus on another allows us to keep the focus of attention off of ourselves.

The Peacekeepers

Like the Roman peacekeepers who sought to replicate their own city in the countries they subjugated, transference allows us to recreate familiar dynamics to satisfy our comfort level. Without being aware of converting others to our system of beliefs, we unconsciously establish our organized city, and regulate quarrels by keeping the peace. The *Romanitas* we thrive on is more important than the truth.

After conquest, subjugated countries were treated like resource pools to be administered and tapped. Mirroring the exit strategy around dysfunction, revolts only lead to being forced back into the empire on harsher terms.

Defense mechanisms can lead us to conquer, employing a type of passive aggression. The first threat to the Roman Empire would come in the form of a Carthaginian general, Hannibal. He is famous for his march over the Alps in the winter, with 40,000 seasoned troops and a band of elephants. After the wars with Hannibal and the Carthaginian threat, the Romans would begin their famous battle cry: "Carthage must be destroyed!" Similarly, we defend ourselves by undermining the power and autonomy of another. If we believe our mate's independence is a threat to us, we take them prisoner.

There is a strong element of denial at work in this relationship. What started as romance erodes into a type of non-spontaneous, calculated withholding of that part of us initially used to attract the other person. We know there is an *addiction* at play anytime we continue in a type of behavior that diminishes our quality of life. Addiction, denial and codependency always seem to manifest together. Addiction doesn't always relate to chemical or substance abuse. Even if we have remained in denial about the addiction in whatever form it may take, we will usually discover it when we recognize we are unable to leave a situation in which we are unhappy.

We have the unique ability to hear the words *I love you* in conversations about how we need to change. Our partner hears *I can't live without you*, while we storm around the house, wearing suitcases for shoes. We would prefer to continue in superficial conversations that allow us to exist in an alienated, subordinated condition. We romanticize the idea of the relationship we are building. Even while it crumbles around us, we are oblivious to the internal politics of its dysfunction.

Perhaps we finally admit our partner has a problem when *we* become symptomatic of their denied condition, and cannot understand why we just can't leave. *The hardest thing we must face is that we are also to blame for the dynamics that exist in the relationship.* We came upon it through transference and projection.

We cannot help but recreate the mythology of our childhood. If we were told or believed we couldn't measure up, we will find a partner to carry on this mantra. Unable to process positive reinforcement, we feed on negative ambivalence. Ultimately the environment continues to validate the idea that we are *not good enough*.

When we look for something, we will find it. In a relationship, we will always blame our partner for *making us feel* like we are not measuring up. If not being good enough isn't in our bag of childhood tapes it doesn't come up in the relationship.

We might as well arrive with a letter from home stating: "thank you for taking care of Susie. She is not good enough although you can try to love her because she believes this love will make her feel better about herself. Please be especially sensitive to this, because no matter what you do or say, she is going to interpret it as *she is not good enough*." To the Protector who provides a shelter for runaways, a letter like this might as well be posted on your forehead. *"At last, here is somebody who will never leave me. If ever I am afraid they will leave, all I have to do is replay this tape."*

Meanwhile, we look at this great Protector with our bright eyes confirming: *"finally, here is somebody worse off than I am, and so I will fix them."* Immediately a character flaw is identified and together, a lifestyle is enacted.

We discover in the Protector, all we fail to acknowledge about ourselves. In subsequent relationships, we do not see how we carry this projection tendency forward. We continue to experience new relationships as a representation of all we have seen before. Without owning the life that stirs *in here*, we cannot see how we project it as drama *out there*.

Establishing boundaries, we overcome the need to blame our mate for *our feelings* of insecurity. By taking active responsibility for what we experience, we can move toward independence even if it means taking a time out. If we do not allow ourselves to be *pulled into* someone else's drama, we can own what is ours and let go of what undermines our self-worth. Just as "Rome was not built in a day," erasing our tapes will not be an overnight process.

Elephants Never Forget

Carthage was always the nemesis of Rome. We find this state at the center of their battle cry, in the abandonment story of Dido and as an important part of Rome's history. What we remember most about the Carthaginian general, Hannibal was his use of elephants during battle. It was shocking and heroic, if not intimidating.

In dreams, elephants are symbolic of an enormous source of emotional power that is disowned. Their massive size reflects the *unfathomable essences* that can trample over us as we give our power away. Since dreams reveal what is repressed, if we are dreaming of enormous emotional mammals, unacknowledged emotion is growing in a way that threatens to stampede over us. While we do not own the powerful source of our feelings, we project them onto someone else and *allow* that person to become *the reason* we feel them.

Like the subconscious, it is said that elephants never forget. In fact, research has shown elephants experience post-traumatic stress, memory and share in emotional pain just like humans. In an effort to thin growing elephant populations, older elephants were exterminated. This practice led rogue juvenile males to embark on angry rampages, destroying towns and killing people.

Two factors were at play in creating this problem. The first was that in all cases the rogue males were orphans who had perhaps retained the traumatic memory of witnessing the slaughter of their mother. Without guidance, they were also left unchecked by older, dominant males who had also been killed. Once older males were reintroduced into the population, the juveniles began to settle down. It was a clear example of how human interference had created disastrous consequences.

We know we are creating a situation when it is repetitive. In the same way *our unrecognized* fear of intimacy creates the *experience* of rejection, *our unrecognized* fear of where autonomy and independence might lead creates the *experience* of bondage. All healthy relationships require the freedom of autonomy and self-actualization. Conquest and subjugation are unnatural and sow the seeds of its own demise.

If our self-image is strong however, nothing anyone else does or says can change it. Like the elephant appearing in our dreams, there is enormous potential for power and feeling that can be actualized. The protective body armor of the Roman soldiers is not unlike the protective covering used to hide our feelings.

An enormous amount of energy is wasted in serving a lifestyle that perpetuates highly charged drama and bondage. Love and hate can exist simultaneously in a way which leaves us feeling confused. They can be intertwined so deeply that exciting one actually increases the capacity for the other. There is something inherently irrational when we keep doing the same thing over and over and expect a different result.

The power we bestow upon another is ours and subjugation is an illusion. When we own this power, we can self-actualize and trample over any barriers that stunt our growth. We've proven our endurance; we need only apply it productively. Only by taking the opportunity to heal, can we experience new relationships without transference and projection.

The Healing Journey

The healing journey revealed in this myth captures how we re-create the same situations. Like Aeneas, we must put the present in proper perspective, find our new home and actualize our destiny.

Hypnotherapists begin work by accessing and altering behavioral tapes, and often lead subjects through a guided meditation process. Traveling in a descending pattern, down steps and into a cave, they cross a meadow to locate a forest. This process is also used in Shamanic work. Aeneas is guided by a Sybil who lives in a cave attached to a grove of trees. Like dreams, she leads him into the underworld where the hero seeks information about his destiny.

When Aeneas meets the Sybil, she says: *"Yield not to disasters, but press onward the more bravely."* We know the potential loss experienced by our fear of being alone and autonomous evokes overly dramatic emotional responses. If we want fulfilling relationships, we must press bravely forward, either beyond the relationship or beyond our own defense mechanisms. In this case, we are traveling to the underworld to reclaim our lost power.

We are to meet the deceased father who will guide us in seeking our destiny. This is symbolic of the death of the transference process and negative projections that no longer serve us. *He is dead when Aeneas meets him yet, he is told about creation and of the power of the spirit.* It is more powerful than life itself. Symbolically, this is an appropriate way to put our tendency to project the *lost wanderer* archetype to rest. Experience may have diluted the spirit although it holds the power to transform.

"The decent to Avernus is easy," the Sybil says. *"The gate to Pluto stands open night and day; but to retrace one's steps and return to the upper air, that is the toil, that is the difficulty."* Pluto not only rules the underworld, but he is also the keeper of the precious treasure that resides in the underbelly of the earth. We know our beliefs descended below the subconscious net quite easily. However, in retrieving these internal tapes, we find the toil and difficulty. Once the tape is created, it is difficult to access and erase it.

"Seek the tree upon which grows a golden branch," said the Sybil, *"to gain access to the underworld and if fate is with you, the branch will yield and quit its parent's trunk. Otherwise, no force can remove it."* This tree is symbolic of our family roots and by removing our branch we "quit the parent's trunk."

In our initiation into the underworld, we follow steps to become more autonomous. *Venus is Aeneas' mother who sends two of her doves to fly before him to show him the way.* The doves symbolize making peace with the caregiver through forgiveness. This is not something that happens from a religious sense, but something which takes place from a rational perspective. We must truly find empathy for those who cared for us in whatever form it may have taken. We also must recognize our parents as unique individuals with their own strengths and faults. *Forgiveness becomes paramount in releasing us from the past.*

They traveled to the volcanic region near Vesuvius. The sulphurous flames sprang forth through the great chasm and immediately the ground began to shake. The next step requires that we establish boundaries so we are no longer pulled into another person's drama and pain. At such times, the immediate lack of our *normal response* may invoke hostility from our partner. Oftentimes when we feel helpless, we too, will demonstrate anger when we are forced to acknowledge how *we* are responsible for our condition. Instead of finding sympathy, we are forced back upon our own devices.

A volcano in a dream symbolizes the release of long held emotional pain. Its eruption from the earth is symbolic of *allowing energy to rise up after years of keeping it below the surface.* It is unlike a hurricane for example, which represents an impending emotional storm threatening to destroy the *inner architecture* built by our belief structures. When the ground shakes in a dream, it portrays how our footing and all we have taken for granted can give way at any time. This is the beginning of realizing that what appears concrete and unchangeable is, in fact, malleable. This is actually a positive message about releasing our frustrations, if we can overcome our fear of the unknown.

The earth roared inhospitably and the tops of the trees began to sway, and the howling of the dogs announced the coming of the deities. As described in

93

Chapter One, dogs and wolves represent the *free flowing* feelings of aggression, sexuality and hunger. These natural urges can be repressed in the image of the "the coming of the deities." They represent the regulating influence of conscience and how it holds our real nature at bay. The next step requires that we descend below the subconscious net to reconnect with the core of who we are. We discover a type of hybridization of distorted emotion locked beneath our tight subterranean structure.

Dogs are known for their expression of unconditional love and companionship. We may believe we demonstrate the ultimate picture of unconditional love when we exchange autonomy for what we believe is expected of us. We will discover that our demonstration of love was indeed, conditional because it is always given *on terms*. We must experience well being and unconditional love for ourselves before we can truly offer it to another.

This repressed and hidden part of our nature is activated through projection and witnessed in our dreams. If we were to dream of meeting the character of *Grief and avenging Care*, it would tell us much about our arrested condition. Grief is the depressive state we are in that leads us to create defensive structures. *Avenging care* reflects how we can care for someone in a way that might actually be punishment. When we rescue someone, we disempower them. When we disempower another, we punish them. Care would be better demonstrated through emancipation.

We tend to treat others in the same way we treat ourselves. When we jump from one dysfunctional relationship to another, we do not take the necessary time to understand the dynamics at play. Sometimes a retreat *to the underworld* is necessary for lasting empowerment.

Mad Discord had hair that looked like blood soaked snakes, writhing and twisting in a fit of confusion and pain. Discord is derived from the Latin words *dis* (apart) and *cor* (the heart). In myths, the heart is the divine access vehicle that inspires us toward actualization. The heart is the core of who we are; without it, we lose direction. Dis-cord is not unlike the confusion created when we are not connected to our heart.

Mad Discord offers a snapshot of *how we move away* from our center. When we identify what we feel as *something orchestrated by another*, we give away control of *our* heart and center. The blood soaked snakes personify feelings (blood) and the regeneration (snakes) required for healthy growth. Disconnected from the *real* root of our feelings, the snakes symbolize arrested energy turned back upon us, when its symbolic growth and rebirth aspects are thwarted.

The Hydras were hissing and spitting into the flames that the Chimaeras were breathing. Hydras are dogs with the heads of dragons. Like the Minotaur, their merging can personify our wild, and unconditional loving nature (dog) as it seeks expression, while the head symbolizes how it is trapped by adopted ideas and beliefs. In this story the head is a dragon, representing how our flight and fight mechanisms take over the personality. They dramatize anger by spiting fire and the *unfathomable essences* become reptilian in the personification of anxiety and fear.

And the chimaeras thrive on the fire. Chimerical is a figment of the imagination. By breathing the fire, they feed on excited feelings, bringing the past as an active illusion onto the present to personify *transference*. These characters reflect how *inner* turmoil is projected as the drama we experience *out there*.

Finally, we see a classic image of *ambivalence* in the exchange between the Chimaeras and Hydras. This final step allows us to see how we can have simultaneous and conflicting feelings that reveal the mystery of how we become trapped. Love and hate can be intertwined in a paralyzing fixation where exciting one, stimulates the other. Reclaiming our center however, where *another's words and deeds cannot affect us,* we resurrect self-love, exchange hate for forgiveness and release our fears.

These fantastic creatures personify the dynamics of repressed autonomy. It is not our partner that has trapped us; it is the fear of letting go. Like Aeneas, we can discover our *real* destiny and return to the upper world to claim it.

The Fall of Rome

The enormous energy required to maintain a defensive posture can be reclaimed. Regardless of Rome's internal political dysfunction, it is recognized as the greatest empire the world had ever known. The fact that it is called the Roman Empire underscores a government run by an Emperor or supreme ruler, regardless of how they idealized the power of the people. In a relationship, we may often fail to see the Emperor or Empress behind the mask of the beneficent Protector.

When the empire collapsed from barbarian invasions, a folk or more natural culture took form as the roots of what would become the diversity of Europe today. Only when the shadow of Rome receded into the pages of history did creativity and cultural variety emerge in its wake.

Just as the Roman walls gave way to the adoption of new ideas and technologies, strong defensive walls can be loosened. The psychic energy that funded these defense mechanisms and the impenetrability of the subconscious wall, when redirected, can give life to enormous individualistic and creative potential. Instead of perpetuating *Romanitas*, a renaissance can occur within.

Fearful of the independence required to grow, we may dream of losing baggage (identity/self-worth), being late, or being left behind. To understand the message of the dream, we observe that whatever we are *losing* is actually holding us back. At the same time, if we disown our subordinated condition, we may dream of waking during sleep, being drowsy or under someone's spell.

At the end of our dream work, Ann dreams of attending a wedding, although she does not know the bride and groom. Wedding dreams symbolize the marriage of what had previously been conflicting aspects of our nature. For example, we may dream of marrying an unknown person as we adopt or allow for the merging of *our* unknown potential. Attending the wedding of this unknown couple signified the release of boundaries that allowed for independence in her relationship.

Hybrids too, occur frequently in dreams and are the mind's way of presenting complex ideas in a clever way. "It seemed like a horse, but it had purple fur," or "it seemed like a guy in my sixth grade class, but he was a banker." The horse embodies the natural spirit, while purple could be associated with religious doctrine. Based on the other symbolism, one may be at odds with the other. The guy from sixth grade personifies an aspect that was associated with him or characteristics developed long ago, while the banker suggests how the issue has to do with finances in the present.

Dreams portray the pathway to self-discovery that is necessary to activate fulfilling relationships with others. Because we have difficulty establishing boundaries, we may manifest the symptoms of another's denied condition as a form of illness. When we are unhappy in a relationship, we must step back to separate our condition from another's.

By unleashing the power of diversity or evolving aspects of what we may become, we stop recreating the past and evolve colorfully into the person we were meant to be. *Our fear of being abandoned or left out in the cold can be relinquished when we realize that we were always meant to exist independently.*

The past does not have to continue influencing our future, and like Aeneas, we can reinterpret sorrow and move on. We can experience events for what they can teach us here and now.

When one door closes, another always opens. The vicissitudes of life always lead us toward new opportunity for growth. We have the power to view our experiences in anyway we choose. Our experiences can become either negative or positive, depending upon how we interpret them. This ability to believe in anything is our gift. *It teaches us that anything is possible as we apply ourselves toward our future.*

Tales of Ancient Europe
Imagination, Intuition and the Cauldron of Inspiration

> "And near him stood the Lady of the Lake
> Who knows a subtler magic then his own,
> Clothed in white samite, mystic, wonderful.
> She gave the King his huge, cross-halted sword
> Whereby to drive the heathen out."
>
> *King Arthur* (Tennyson)

The stories of King Arthur, the Knights of the Round Table and their quest for the Holy Grail evolved from the ancient tales of Celtic and Welsh legend. The ancestors of the Celts once occupied a large part of Europe, and were at their peak during the fourth century BC, prior to the Roman expansion.

One group had reached the British Isles and before Old English was used in Britain, a form of Welsh was spoken. Rather than trading, the Celts were a culture of warrior tribes, and their languages date back to 1200BC. They were called keltoi or *barbarians* by the Greeks of the sixth century BC, which simply labeled them as being *different*.

Later, the Romans were able to conquer most of the warrior tribes of Europe, with the exception of the people in Ireland and North Britain. The French and English crowns too, would seek to conquer them, and were successful against the Anglo-Saxons. The stories of King Arthur, Rob Roy, Braveheart or Scotland's William Wallace, and Ireland's King Brian Boru developed from the wars of resistance fought against these colonizing armies.

Like many pagan stories during the Christianization of the tribes of Europe, ancient legends were infused with the ideas of this growing religion. Christianity was carried upon the back of the Roman army and laid the foundation of the countries that evolved into Europe. Prior to the Christian version which describes the Grail as a vessel or chalice, this symbol underwent centuries of metamorphosis. It was augmented by the various tribes who respected it as vessel that held the healing power of the unknown.

The Grail evades historians as it shape shifts and remains just beyond the reach of interpretation. It is appropriate the Grail or Cauldron, as it was once called, should become our symbol of the inspired realm that provides insight through dreams. In this sacred Cauldron, we explore the creative source of our dreams as a *guiding source within.*

Central to the myths of this region is the search for the Holy Grail. At the same time, we meet Kings who are overthrown when their towers are destroyed. "Jake" dreams of being in a beautiful house while a *man-made*, limestone wall threatens to crash down and destroy everything. Since a wall is a defensive structure and he used the words "man-made," the dream reflects his inner defensive structure. The dream offers the symbolic idea of how the walls he builds must come down, regardless of how the foundation is reduced to rubble. In the wake of this *disaster* is the promise of rebirth.

"Patricia" dreams of being in a house and everywhere she walks, the house tips in that direction, as if it may fall to the ground at any moment. She describes how *negative* the environment feels, and how she wants to get away. Since the house represents her *inner architecture*, the dream is helping her identify how her negative ideas weigh against, and actually create all that she experiences. She too, is being guided to understand how all that appears solid and unchangeable can crumble with a subtle shifting of belief.

In both cases, the Grail is *that thing* that comes to light from the dream to guide the dreamer through a transformation. Dreams often revolve around a story line of searching for something or not being able to go somewhere because we have misplaced an item. Focusing solely on *this item* often reveals powerful clues about what traps the dreamer's growth. It usually portrays a subtle shift of where we place emphasis in our lives, so we might be more fulfilled.

The man-made wall is the treasure of Jake's dream. It helps him understand how *he has built* what keeps him from experiencing fulfillment. For Patricia, the Grail is *the tipping point* or the change achieved when a situation reaches *critical mass*. In the final cycle of her dream, she said, "I made everyone get into the middle of the house because it was coming down. After it fell in slow motion, everyone in the house fell to the ground." The people in her dream represented different aspects of her. Getting everyone into the middle and having everything come to ground level is another symbol of finding our center, and letting go of the past to achieve rebirth.

The Grail and the Mandala

The Cauldron or *greal*, later called the *sangreal* was originally a Welsh or Druid symbol. It first appears as a Cauldron, offering access to the underworld as described by the Welsh poet, Taliesin of the sixth century. Like inspiration rising from the unconscious, it provided timeless vision into the dimension of darkness. What we call the Self also provides this type of vision. Jung described the Self as being composed of the ego and all other aspects of our potential. It is often called the *"one that knows within"* and is believed to be the purveyor of our dreams.

To the Druids, the Grail was a cornucopia of plenty and the *greal* was the spicy contents of the *Sangreal*, guarded by deities. Later, Bran's Cauldron of Rebirth became fused with the talking head of Bran the Blessed, a deity of Welsh mythology. Perhaps that is why, in some tales, the Grail is said to speak. To the ancient French, it was a platter. Wolfram von Eschenbach described the Grail as a clear stone, or garnet-hyacinth, representing paradise. Other stories relate it to a stone, but one that had fallen to the earth. It resided beneath the waters protected by the Lady of the Lake.

By the twelfth century AD, the stories of Arthur and the Grail merged and take on a distinctly Christian flavor. It evolved into the chalice from the last supper said to have caught the blood of Christ, and brought to England by Joseph of Aramathea. In every case, the Grail always speaks of spiritual or philosophical nourishment and the quest to seek all that exists beyond the grasp of everyday experience.

The Celtic religion was presided over by the Druids, an order of priest-poets. The sun god Lug was the most prominent deity, along with Cernunnos, the stag-horned Shamanistic Lord of the Animals. Among the female deities, the mare goddess called Epona in Gaul, Macha in Ireland, and Rhiannon in Britain, ruled along side of the crow goddess Morrigan. The mare was a fertility goddess, while the crow goddess, like the crow in many mythologies, personified death and rebirth.

The search for the Grail or Cauldron allows us to explore creativity and the images that bring us to our center during dreaming. In its evolution, it becomes the vessel from which inspiration is both drawn and given form. From Wagner's opera *Parsifal* to Dan Brown's modern interpretation of the Holy Grail in the *Da Vinci Code*, it would appear this ever-elusive Grail continues to provide timeless inspiration and spiritual mystery.

The Round Table was said to have been inspired by the constellation of the Great Bear, of which Arthur derived his name. The Round Table is also thought to be a re-creation of Stonehenge, said to have been brought to England by Merlin. Both are manifestations of ancient circle worship, which contrasted the movement of the sun with the human journey, as a type of *mandala*.

This sacred circle is found in many cultures as a vehicle that enables one to compose chaos into order. The mandala captures and illuminates spiritual awareness and removes the confusion created by the manifestations of our complicated lives. It is used as a guiding intelligence or supernatural structure in Hinduism, Buddhism and in astrology. In the same way, dreams compose an image of the *Self* out of the complicated world in which we thrive. Both provide a pathway to enlightenment.

Dream analysis involves identifying the aspect of the dream, around which, everything else seems to revolve. The lost item, the falling wall, the tipping foundation, the unknown child, teeth falling out, are all themes that describe the hero and what they need to acknowledge. We can live each day unhappy, but dreams are continuously working to make us *wake up* to happiness. Teeth falling out can signify how we say things that are not true. We open our mouths, our teeth fall out and suddenly our credibility is in question. The dream cycle often presents many symbols and landscapes that give the dreamer a repetitive message. This message is inspired by *something* and dream analysts label it the Self. In the dream work I do, I see it as the *great treasure* or Holy Grail of our awakening.

The discovery of the mandala, which appeared in many cultures with no prior contact, led Jung to conclude that we may be inspired collectively. He explored the similarities of our ancient myths, and set about deciphering the wellspring of inspiration he believed came from one source called the *collective unconscious*. He believed that in addition to our personal unconscious, we are inspired by primordial images common among the world. When I am doing dream work with an individual, I too observe archetypal patterns where personal images will give way to common scenarios of accompanying a child as a sense of rebirth, or meeting the Wise Man or Wise Woman once a transformation is underway.

Upon a setting when the world religions, chivalry and the blossoming of creativity occurred, we can see a representation of how something natural can become *sublimated*. When we channel energy toward something believed to be of higher value, it usually comes at the price of our wellness.

The purpose of celibacy is to achieve heightened spiritual awareness. *Sublimation* can transform sexual and aggressive energy into inspiration, visions, and the uncanny experience of otherworldly visitations. We can observe it active in those driven to approach philosophy, art and religion with the same passionate devotion which would have been bestowed upon a lover. This is not necessarily a negative process. On the contrary, it has provided a richness of dimension to life and world culture.

Like the individual, civilization is the awe inspired recipient of these applied energies of self-diffusion and sacred vision. The process only becomes negative when any one aspect of our nature overwhelms and represses another. In civilization too, balance is necessary for our well-being. Repressed energy can erupt into psychic conflict as in the case of a celibate performing immoral sexual acts.

The Peak Experience

To any artist or seeker of enlightenment, a *peak experience* describes an event greater than everyday awareness. It is the *apprehending of wakefulness beyond the borders of time.* This mysterious process encompasses more than the mere ego, revealing the totality of who we might become in whatever way we come to define it.

We use many labels to describe areas of the mind, although the Self allows us to identify an aspect within, which inspires us with an awareness that already knows who we may become. In these stories, we see how the Self is embodied as the *Wise Man or Mysterious Woman, Spirit, Inspired Guide* and is often called the *One Who Speaks Through the Heart.* Jung's *Collected Works* describes how the ego approaches knowledge of this higher aspect. When the Self makes its presence felt within the psyche, he wrote: "it is a defeat to the ego as if the recognition of something more powerful than the ego will somehow lead to its annihilation."

The stories of Arthur and Percival personify different ways the ego finds guidance from the Self. They portray the wounding which leads the ego on a quest to uncover this guiding source, and the eventual assimilation that must occur.

The Self is more than the tiny ego that penetrates its searchlight into the darkness to build its small island of consciousness. Jung believed enlightenment came when one relocated the focus of the personality from its gravitational orbit around the ego, toward the empowerment of the Self.

In *The Process of Individuation,* M.L. von Franz describes the Self as the organizing center and creator of dream images. He defines individuation as the recognition and incorporation of this Self-awareness into our existence. He wrote: "Its subjective experience conveys the feeling that some supra-personal force is actively interfering in a creative way. " He described it as the unconscious leading the way in accordance with a secret design, unknown to us in daily life. "It is as if something is looking at me, something that I do not see but that sees me – perhaps that *Great Man in the heart* who tells me his opinions of me by means of dreams."

Water always represented something otherworldly and was symbolic of the mystery of life. Similarly, the Celts would make sacrifices of prized possessions by ritualistically throwing treasure into rivers, lakes and streams. In these myths, we meet the Lady of the Lake and the Fisher King, both who appear from a mysterious realm to guide the hero,

Symbolizing the great treasures which reside deep within the unconscious, water dreams often occur at the onset of the ego's wounding. Dreams of choppy seas will eventually give way to dreaming of seeing creatures below the surface. When we are more aware of our motivation, we may find ourselves on a vessel moving over calm seas. The treasures we discover gives shape to the internal guidance of dreams that appear to have its own direction, input and sense of time.

The Growth of the World Religions

The period between 600BC to 600AD is called the axial age because of the offshoots of world religions influenced by spiritual leaders in the form of Buddhism, Christianity and Islam.

In 1750BC, a nomadic and warrior group of people called *Aryans* arrived in India bringing horses, chariots and the *Vedas* that laid the foundation for the Hindu religion. The Aryan people are believed to have descended from the steppes of central Asia, migrating into Persia, India, China and parts of Europe.

From the northernmost region of the Indian cultural zone of modern Nepal, Siddhartha Guatama was born into the religion of Hinduism in 563BC as a prince of the warrior class. After a comfortable upbringing, he left this world behind to live the life of an ascetic. Eventually he would evolve as the *Buddha* or the enlightened one. As an offshoot of Hinduism, Buddhism promoted an eightfold pathway, shedding the demands of the flesh in search of enlightenment. Through moral and spiritual discipline, he created a revolution in the Hindu religion. While Hinduism continued to flourish in the Indus Valley, Buddhism would combine with the Shinto religion of Japan and Taoism in China to become the primary religion of the Far East.

In 6BC, Jesus of the house of David was born into the Judaic world in the Near East. He was called *Christ* or the anointed one and would lay the foundation for Christianity. He emphasized the coming of the end of days and offered a pathway to understand the mysteries of creation. As one of several mystery religions appearing at the time, his teachings revealed the relationship between things, both visible and invisible. He taught how one could transcend the flesh through spiritual awareness.

After his death, he was believed to be the manifestation of God on earth. This was against the Jewish laws that forbade idolatry, and the commandment, "thou shalt have no gods before Me." There was no place for this type of teaching inside of Judaism and this new religion was forced outside of the Temple to develop separately.

The third religion of the axial age was born in an area of central Asia, landlocked from access to any oceanic contact. A group of nomadic people skilled in the use of horses and bows became the Bedouin civilization of the modern Arabs. Like the Hebrews or Habiru (wanderers), they were a tribal society that wandered the desert.

The Prophet, Muhammad was born in 570AD into the monotheistic religions of Christianity and Judaism. He worshipped the one God of Abraham and followed the teachings of the Jewish prophets, of whom the last was believed to have been Jesus of Nazareth. To his people, the one God was called Allah. Muhammad was born in Mecca, an oasis and center of pilgrimage as Arabs traveled to this great city to worship a large black meteor that had fallen to the earth and was venerated.

Contemplating in a cave outside of Mecca, Muhammad heard a voice that told him to record the words of the Creator. For twenty-two years, the voice inspired the graceful body of text that was recorded into a book called the *Koran*. These writings laid the foundation for the religion of *Islam*, which means surrender or submission. He and his followers believed he was the last prophet, and that his words were to be the last message to mankind.

Muhammad defined the necessary observances that would lead to salvation and stressed a social and personal code of conduct. When the leaders of the tribe turned on this new religion, he and his followers moved to Yathrib, later to be called Medina or city of the Prophet. Eventually the Arab world embraced Islam and this religion dominated the Near East, conquering Persia (Iran), Syria and Iraq. Within a century after the Prophet's death, Islam had conquered Jerusalem, Egypt and the southern shores of the Mediterranean, including the North African coast and parts of Spain. Muhammad had traveled from Mecca to Medina in 622AD and like the Christians who observe a division of time after the birth of Christ time is differentiated by the people of Islam by this pilgrimage event.

At one point, the Arabs had successfully entered France but were ultimately beaten back. They were powerful and for a time, it appeared Islam would conquer the entire world. The adoption of Christianity by two classical powers of the Mediterranean however, would lead Europe in a different direction.

The Dominance of the Church

During the second and third centuries AD, Clement of Alexandria, a Christian Neo-Platonist and his pupil Origen found ways to reinvigorate the Stoic philosophy of the Greeks into the teachings of an emerging mystery religion called Christianity. In this way, Christianity was adopted and promoted within the Hellenistic or Greek world of the Mediterranean.

The first time military shields were painted with a cross was on the eve of battle
312 years after the birth of Jesus. The Roman Emperor Constantine had a dream and ordered the Christian monogram to be painted on the shields of his army. The next day they won the war, and thereafter, Constantine became instrumental in driving the Christian religion toward adoption throughout the Roman Empire where the Church and papacy were centered in Rome. At the "command of God," he founded a new city called Constantinople in 330AD on the site of old Byzantium or in modern Turkey, straddling the gateway to the Middle East.

By 500AD, the Western Roman Empire had collapsed, although its papacy would continue to influence Europe from Rome, while the last surviving remnants of the classical Roman civilization thrived in the eastern city of Constantinople. Constantine could not have known creating Constantinople ultimately created a division in the Christian Church. From Rome, the Roman Catholic version of Christianity would flourish in Western Europe, while the East would follow the Eastern Orthodox version and Constantinople would become its hub. The result would be a growing tension between these two great cities and its rulers.

After the decline of Rome, the abandoned provinces of ancient Europe faced many barbarian invasions. The Norsemen or Scandinavians moved from the North while the Magyars or people from Hungary conquered from the East. The Mongols attacked on horseback from the steppes of Central Asia and conquered savagely, instilling fear into the hearts of the Europeans. In historical terms, they were all called *barbarians*.

The invasions of the Norsemen laid the seeds for the first nations of Europe. To the North, were the Saxons, Angles and Jutes. They formed the Anglo-Saxon kingdom called Britain. Celtic colonies also formed Wales, Scotland and Ireland. In the Rhine valley, France and Germany would emerge.

In addition to the Celtic tribes in Northern Europe, the Norseman had established colonies in Novgorod, Kiev and Moskovy as the roots of Russia. In 980AD, legend describes how Vladimir had the various religions debated for their merits. He chose Christianity for Russia, although he adopted the Eastern Orthodox version from Constantinople. Poland would come to adopt Roman Catholicism because of their close proximity to Germany.

During the middle ages, the Church was the center of civilization for Europe and ultimately became the hub of all aspects of society. It functioned as the deliverer of culture, truth and thought. Most of Europe existed as a feudal society where local chiefs who had developed as wealthy landowners, protected the humble classes in return for labor and military services. The local chiefs aligned with the Papacy, and there was little separation between Church and State.

The Age of Chivalry

Out of this barbaric, yet highly moralistic society grew a movement that sought to right the wrong, protect the weak and demonstrate courtesy and bravery. Chivalry produced knights who were devoted to the Church and set the model for honor, loyalty and self-sacrifice that would shape the centuries to come.

Chivalry comes from the French word cheval, which means horse. To become a knight meant one had obtained the privilege of bearing arms. After successfully completing the proper training, one became a mounted warrior or a man of rank. At the age of seven, noble children who were candidates for knighthood were sent as *pages* to the castle of their future patron. They were taught religion and the proper ceremonies of court. Initiation included spending nights fasting and in prayer where they would confess and receive the sacrament. Dressed in white, they knelt before a presiding knight to state their request for admission and to take the oath of knighthood.

In leisure, knights could be found fulfilling pledges of love to damsels, or attending banquets in the castles of the nobility. These knights-errant were cherished guests and were on a quest for adventure to redress wrongs and to enforce rights.

Jousting tournaments had the objective of unhorsing one's opponent with a lance. Each knight proclaimed the name of his *servant d'armour* or the lady who cheered him to victory, and had bestowed her favor with a scarf or piece of jewelry. In Italy, Troubadours recited poetry and love songs. The age of chivalry produced knights who dreamed of rescuing fair maidens, while armies marched against the enemies of religion.

The Crusades took place from the 11th to the 13th centuries and sought to recover Christian holy places from the Muslims. Wars were fought that were believed to be favored by God, yet were instigated by the Pope. The Crusades sought to aid the Christians of Constantinople in their fight against Islamic invaders. For his efforts, a knight could receive a reduced time in purgatory. What he found in this world however, was the opportunity for conquest and to partake in the spoils of war.

In Moorish Spain, Christianity, Judaism and Islam coexisted and Spain would become an important learning center. The Islamic culture promoted education and tolerance for other's beliefs. Eventually Christianity and Islam would develop ideological conflicts that became unbridgeable after the Crusades. The Reconquest was a time when Granada fell as the last Islamic capital and the Moors were expelled from Spain. The Spaniards fought this as a religious cause and were able to attract many warriors hungry for land.

The Mythical Stories of England

It was said that Brutus, son of Silvius and great grandson of Aeneas, founded London. He had the unfortunate accident of mortally wounding his father during a game of chase. Banished by his relatives, he led a fleet of 320 ships to Devonshire on the coast of Britain. Called Albion, the Trojans found this land inhabited by giants and fought great battles to rid the land of these terrible creatures.

Cornineas demonstrated great bravery during this assault and founded Cornwall on the place where the enormous Green Giant had been slain. Brutus established his city in a town called Trojanova or New Troy, later to become London. After ruling for twenty-four years, he died and his sons Albanact founded Alba or modern Scotland, while Camber established Cambria in the middle part of the island.

Arthur was the prince of the tribe of Britons called Silures, from South Wales and was the son of Uther Pendragon. His name means Great Bear and he was named after the constellation of Ursa Major. Merlin is said to have brought the great bluestones of Stonehenge from the Prescelly Mountains in Wales, across the Severn Estuary to Wiltshire. Originally erected in Ireland as the Giant's Ring, Merlin transported it whole, in a simple feat of magic, for he was endowed with many gifts.

The child of a virtuous woman and a Spirit, Merlin's father was not mortal but inhabited the air, and was given to the mysteries of the unknown. Knowing of his unusual origins, Merlin's mother entrusted him into the care of a priest. Although his baptism ensured that his father's influence would be good, Merlin had unusual powers and became a prophet and seer. He retained many of his father's gifts and could see the future.

During this time, a usurper named Vortigern reigned in Britain. After killing the rightful king, the usurper drove the king's son, Uther Pendragon into exile. Vortigern erected a tower and lived in constant fear that the rightful heir would someday return to overthrow him. Three times the tower fell to the earth, without any apparent cause and so Vortigern consulted the astrologers to learn of the cause. He was told the cornerstone of the tower needed to be bathed in the blood of a child born without a mortal father.

Vortigern sent his men out in search of such a child and they came upon Merlin. Once they learned of his unnatural childhood, they immediately brought him to Vortigern but Merlin quickly pointed out how the tower was unstable because of the pool of water beneath it. He told them that in the depths of this water, two immense dragons battled. When they did, the earth shook, causing the tower to crumble.

The townspeople dug beneath the tower and uncovered the dragons, much to their dismay. Unfurling great wings, the dragons flew above the onlookers, breathing flames that scorched the earth below. They resembled something otherworldly, with a thin skin membrane covering a sinewy structure of bones.

Trumpeting with a sound like mad elephants, they swooped above the heads of the terrified people. They flapped their wings until the town was covered in darkness. The townsfolk ran but Merlin remained, merely clapping his hands. He cheered the dragons into combat against the usurper, Vortigern.

Merlin told the onlookers how the dragons represented the battling Saxons and Britons. At that very moment, the rightful prince was returning with a very large army. Upon Uther Pendragon's arrival, Merlin watched Vortigern burn alive in the tower of his own making.

When the dragons appeared, Vortigern was too afraid to climb down. Once the usurper had died, Uther Pendragon ascended to the throne. Merlin won the admiration of the king and became his close advisor. He would often transform himself into a dwarf, stag or other animal while at court. At night, he would return to his home in a cave, below the earth.

> "There the wise Merlin lived they say
> To make his home, low beneath the ground
> In a deep crevice, far from the view of day
> That no living light should be found." -*Caer- Merdin*

Merlin entertained the king with his clever humor, inspiring the practice of employing Fools or Jesters in the court. These characters would often appear comical or deformed but they were endowed with the gift of prophecy, knowing things no men could know.

Arthur was only fifteen when his father, Uther Pendragon died. He became king but not without rivals. Spending many years proving his right to rule, he won battles with Merlin acting as his chief adviser.

One day as Arthur was riding in the woods he came upon the scene of three ill-bread peasants chasing Merlin as if they would kill him. Arthur immediately accosted the churls and when they saw that he was a knight, they fled.

"Merlin, you would surely have been slain had I not come. Your sorcery proved futile in your time of need," said Arthur.

"Not so, for I could have protected myself," Merlin answered, "but you are more near death than I."

As they spoke, they came upon a knight positioned on his horse in a way that blocked their passageway.

"Sir Knight," said Arthur, "for what purpose do you abide there?"

"There will be no knight that rides this way unless he jousts with me. Such is the custom of this pass," the knight responded.

"Then I will amend this custom," Arthur said as he ran against the knight. They clashed together at great speed and met with such intensity that both their spears were shivered. Drawing their swords, they resumed their battle until the knight split King Arthur's sword in two.

"Now it is within my power whether to slay or save you! Unless you admit that you are overcome and surrender, you shall die," said the knight.

"I welcome death," said King Arthur, "if that should come upon me, but to admit defeat to you, I will not do." He leaped upon the knight and threw him to the ground. The knight was more powerful however, and he wrestled Arthur until he was pinned below. The knight raised his sword and was about to slay Arthur when Merlin stopped him.

"Knight, hold your hand, for this is a man of worship, more than you could know."

"Why, who is he?" the knight asked.

"He is King Arthur." The knight would have slain him for dread of his wrath, but Merlin cast an enchantment upon him and he fell to the earth, asleep.

"Alas!" said Arthur, "why have you slain this good knight with your crafts?"

"Care not," said Merlin, "he is more whole than you will be and is only asleep. He will wake in three hours."

They found a hermit who was known for his salves and healing abilities. For three days, Arthur rested and when his wounds were healed, they departed.

"I have no sword," declared Arthur.

"Without force," said Merlin, "we shall find a sword that shall be yours."

They came upon a Lake and Arthur watched as an arm was thrust upward from its center. Clothed in white samite, the arm held a great sword.

"That is the sword I spoke of," Merlin said. A lady appeared by the sword and began to walk upon the water.

"What damsel is that?" Arthur asked.

"That is the Lady of the Lake," said Merlin. "Within the Lake is a great rock and riches as fair as any on earth. When this damsel approaches, you ask and she will give you the sword."

"Damsel," said Arthur, "what sword is that held above the waves? I would have it, should you give it to me, for I have no sword."

"King Arthur," she said, "this sword is mine but I will give it to you if you return this gift when in time, I shall ask it of you."

"By my faith I shall give you any gift you ask."

"Well," said the damsel, "take this boat and retrieve the sword and scabbard. I will ask for it when I see my time."

Arthur and Merlin rowed across the water and when Arthur took the sword called Excalibur, the arm sunk below the water and the Lady disappeared.

Guinevere, Lancelot and Gawain

Merlin arranged for Arthur's marriage to Guinevere and selected the thirty-nine knights who would assist Arthur in his battles. Together they would become the Knights of the Round Table and their kingdom was called Camelot. Gawain was said to possess enormous strength but only during a certain part of the day. From nine o'clock until noon and from three until sunset he demonstrated remarkable strength. During the other hours, his strength diminished although he was certainly stronger than most men.

King Ban, faithful ally of Arthur was attacked by Claudas and forced to flee with his wife Helen and his infant son, Lancelot. When he turned and saw his castle in flames, he was overcome by grief and died. Helen left the infant at the shores of the Lake and attended the last sighs of her husband. When she searched for the child, she saw that he was in the arms of the Lady of the Lake. Upon seeing the queen approach, the Lady and the infant descend beneath the waters.

The Lady of the Lake lived behind a mist which reflected what appeared to be a real lake. It was an imaginary copy however, positioned to serve as a barrier to her true residence. She schooled Lancelot in the ways of knighthood and when he was eighteen, she gave him to the court of Arthur. The young man was graceful and skilled in arms, and made an instantaneous impression upon the heart of Guinevere. Their mutual attachment would lead Lancelot to achieve many conquests in her honor. Their love would also lead to the undoing of Camelot.

Percival the Fool

Percival of Gales was the son of King Pelenore. When his father and two elder brothers were slain in battle, his mother was determined this fate would not befall her remaining son and so, she hid him in the woods. Although they were royalty, she brought him up in a rural and ascetic setting. The only other person who knew they were in the woods was a deaf-mute man. On certain occasions, he would bring food and clothing but most of his life Percival saw no other human beings.

Percival amused himself with the toy javelin his mother had brought from their home. He hunted small animals and brought down flying birds after he became adept with the weapon. While his mother would never allow him to be skilled in warfare, she could see no harm in allowing him to hunt.

One day, while Percival played next to his mother, he saw a metallic figure flying through the woods on a beautiful horse. The magnificent sight left him awestruck.

"Mother, what is that yonder?"

"That is an angel, my son." Percival watched as the strange image disappeared behind the trees. The next day, he saw several more and this time he felt courageous enough to approach them when they stopped beneath a tree.

"Tell me, good lad, have you seen a knight pass through here?" One asked.

"I do not know what a knight is. I cannot say whether it has passed this way or not." Percival answered innocently.

"A knight is one, such as me." Percival eyed his appearance and remembered the image his mother had said was an angel. "If you will answer my questions, I will tell you what I have seen," Percival replied.

"I will gladly answer any questions you ask," said the knight.

Percival fingered the saddle and asked: "What is this?"

"It is a saddle."

"And this?" he said as he knocked upon the metal suit.

"A suit of armor," the knight said as he brandished his flashing weapon. "And this is a sword." It was heavy and powerful and yet, the knight swung it effortlessly through the air. Percival asked about every little detail of their weapons and accoutrements until he had satisfied his curiosity. He then told them how indeed, he had seen a knight who looked like them ride through the forest the previous day.

Later, he told his mother about the knights he had met: "They were not angels, mother. They were honorable knights." His mother began to weep because her worst fears were coming true. She knew his curiosity would eventually lead him from safety.

Percival went to the stable and chose the best horse, albeit a bony horse, but it was the strongest among the horses there. He found a pack used to carry firewood and formed it into a saddle. Bending twigs into the shapes of the stirrups and making reigns of twine, he fashioned them into the dressings he had seen on the knight's horses.

When Percival's mother realized she could not control her curious and headstrong child, she gave him his father's ring. "My son, if you must ride forth, you must go to the court of Arthur," she said. "Show him this ring and he will know you are the son of Pelenore. Ask him to bestow knighthood upon you." She offered what little instruction she could on how to behave honorably. With only his javelin and a few sticks in a packsack, he rode away, leaving his mother weeping in his wake. All he could do was promise he would return to her one day.

Percival believed he had become a knight. He rode through the forest undereducated about the life he was about to live. He had fashioned a suit of armor out of leaves and moss, and as he rode through town, people laughed and pointed at him. Percival smiled and waved back at the jolly people.

A few knights drew around him in amusement. One came forward mockingly, and called him to joust, while his friends gathered around laughing. As the knight assumed the position, Percival copied his every movement, but when the knight charged him, Percival threw his javelin right through the knight's eye. Of course, he could not have known the ways of knighthood and jousting. The other knights rode away in shock, and Percival continued his search for King Arthur.

As he approached Arthur's court, a Red Knight named Ither had insulted Queen Guinevere. A page was serving wine to the queen, and the Red Knight had knocked his arm, purposely splashing wine into the queen's lap and face. He grabbed the golden goblet and declared, "If any of you have boldness to avenge this insult to Guinevere, let him follow me." The Red Knight escaped into the meadow.

None took the challenge because they feared one brave enough to cause such an insult must be endowed with great power. Just then, Percival approached with his uncouth trappings and twigish strappings, riding upon the back of his bony horse.

"Tell me, good men," said Percival, "is that Arthur over yonder?"

"And what would you want with Arthur?" Sir Kay, a very tall knight, eyed the youth in amusement. The others simply laughed at his appearance. Just then, a mute woman of the court approached Percival. It was said she would not speak until one arrived who would represent the flower of chivalry. When she told Percival that he would someday be the bravest and best of all knights, the court was stunned.

"You are mad to say such things," Sir Kay said as he slapped the woman, knocking her to the ground.

"If you be the flower of chivalry," Sir Kay told Percival, "then you must ride after the knight who has insulted the queen. If you can retrieve the goblet, possess his horse and arms, you shall have knighthood."

Percival galloped away gallantly. After he left, Sir Gawain remarked how it was wrong to send such an innocent boy after the knight. Either the boy would be killed or considered an honorable member of the court, bring disgrace.

Percival came face to face with the Red Night who asked, "Young lad, did you see anyone coming from the court to pursue me?"

"The tall man told me to overthrow you and take the goblet, your horse and armor," Percival replied.

"Silence!" roared the knight. "Go back and tell them to send Arthur himself, or some other worthy of fighting in his place."

"You must choose whether you will give these things to me willingly or unwillingly," Percival answered, "for either way I will take them."

The knight ran at him furiously and struck Percival between the neck and shoulder with the shaft of his spear.

"I was not taught in these ways but will fight you in like kind." Percival took one of his sharp sticks and threw it, piercing the eye of the Red Knight, who fell lifelessly from his horse.

Gawain went into the meadow to see what had befallen the youth. He found Percival dragging the dead man about and Gawain asked him what he was doing. "I cannot get this iron coat off of him," said Percival. Gawain chuckled and unfastened the armor from the dead knight.

"Here my good boy." Gawain said as he handed the Red Knight's armor to Percival. "This horse and armor are better than my own. Come with me to Arthur's court to receive the order of knighthood, for you truly deserve it."

Percival replied: "I will not return to the court until I come to avenge the injury of the maiden by that tall man. Take the goblet and tell Arthur I will be his vassal."

Over the next few days, Percival overthrew sixteen knights by jousting with a branch. He did not kill them; he told them he would spare their lives if they returned to the court to say it was Percival, who overthrew them.

"Tell them I will not return until I have avenged the insult brought upon the maiden by the tall man." In this way, Percival achieved prominence and valor, and Arthur soon relieved Sir Kay of his duty.

The Fisher King

Percival came upon Lake Brumbane to find men fishing from a boat. Amfortas, which means *he who is without power*, was also called the Fisher King. When he saw Percival, he invited him into his castle. Upon entering the great hall, Percival noticed several people partaking in a sumptuous feast. All of the knights in attendance appeared to be weeping. The Fisher King was helped onto a cushion and appeared very ill, yet he asked Percival to sit beside him. Someone whispered: *'the king's life is but a dying.'* Percival was told how he had been wounded in the thigh and in his regenerative organs. He had been rendered powerless, and his entire kingdom suffered with him.

The Fisher King told Percival that if he wondered about anything taking place there, he should not ask the meaning. If he were not educated about these things, the blame would fall on the teacher and not on Percival. All this information left Percival puzzled.

A squire walked into the room carrying a spear with blood dripping from its point. As blood ran down the shaft, the grieving knights began to weep anew. When the Queen entered carrying the Grail, the knights were healed of their sorrow, but the Grail did nothing to relieve the Fisher King's suffering.

The Grail was a clear stone of garnet hyacinth and the Queen placed it before the King. It resembled the perfection of paradise and only she was pure enough to watch over it.

The Grail magically provided all of the abundant food they were eating. Afterward the King presented Percival with the sword he had carried into battle. After they retired, Percival slept fitfully. He wondered about the things he had seen, but nobody explained anything, and he had not asked about them.

The next morning he awoke to find that the King, his court and castle had all vanished without a trace. He found himself on the ground, sleeping beside his horse. A lone squire chastised him for not asking the host the all-important question. Had Percival asked the King about the mysteries of the Grail, the King would have been healed. Percival felt ashamed, although he still did not understand what had taken place that day.

The squire recounted the story of the Grail. It had once been visible for all to look upon. However under the guardianship of young Prince Amfortas, both had suffered through his misuse of its power. Amfortas had become King, although his wounded thigh left him in perpetual pain and suffering. The Grail and King entered a mysterious realm, and while the King kept the Grail in his possession, it prevented him from dying. It was said a knight would come one day, whose unprompted questioning would salvage the Grail and bring an end to the King's suffering. The knight had come, but had failed to ask the question.

When Percival returned to tell the Round Table knights about the mysterious Grail, they embarked upon a quest to find it. Percival lost his horse in battle, although a woman presented him with a black horse. As he rode, he took no heed of himself and the horse carried him across the terrain. A journey which should have taken several days took only an hour, and soon they arrived at the edge of a raging sea.

At the shore of this ferocious sea, the horse appeared determined to cross, but Percival grew frightened. He prayed, and when the horse felt him charged in this way, he shook Percival to the ground, and galloped into the waves alone.

Percival rose to find a small ship sailing toward him. A woman came to the shore and offered him all the riches he could desire. She only asked Percival to swear his service to her. He was about to do so when his sword become a crucifix. He knew something was not right, and he prayed for guidance. With that, the possessions vanished and the woman sailed back into the dark seas.

Walking along the shore, Percival eventually arrived at a mysterious ship. Sir Bohort was told in a dream, to go to the sea where he would find Percival. When he arrived, he too, boarded the ship covered in white samite. He met Percival and both heroes embraced with joy. A woman appeared to Sir Galahad and led him to the ship where Percival and Sir Bohort were waiting. When they entered the ship, all recognized the woman leading Sir Galahad to be Percival's sister.

Hidden within the ship, they discovered the long sought after Grail. Percival returned to the Fisher King and was able to heal him of his suffering. The Fisher King died peacefully, and Percival became the Keeper of the Grail Castle.

The Death of Arthur

A rumor surfaced that Queen Guinevere and Lancelot were lovers. This caused a growing animosity between Lancelot and the other knights. Lancelot was forced to flee, pursued by Gawain and King Arthur.

During these battles, Lancelot tried in vain to make amends with the King. He loved Guinevere above all others, although he had not betrayed the King. Even while they made great strides to slay Lancelot, he never surrendered his loyalty and refused to do battle against his friends.

"Where are you, false traitor, Lancelot?" Gawain cried out before the gates of the city where Lancelot had been received with great honor.

"My lord Arthur, although I have suffered you and Sir Gawain to do what you would, now I must defend myself since Gawain has accused me of treason!"

As Lancelot rode out to meet Gawain, a covenant was established. Nobody was to approach either knight until one was either dead, or had yielded defeat. The sight of two great Knights of the Round Table riding to joust electrified the air, and everyone watched in silence. After crossing the appropriate distance, they turned and charged at each other. They came together with such force of strength and opposition that both fell to the ground.

They fought on foot and as they battled, Lancelot realized Gawain had doubled his strength. It was the morning hours when his strength was greater. Lancelot wondered if he had made a mistake in acting so hastily to defend his honor. For three hours, they battled while Lancelot held Gawain at bay with great effort. At noon, Gawain's strength diminished.

Lancelot doubled his strokes and wounded Gawain with a great blow to the head. The knight fell to the ground but instead of killing Gawain, Lancelot withdrew.

Gawain said, "Why turn around, traitor? If you leave me whole, I will return to do battle again."

"I shall endure you when you are well, but I will not smite a felled knight," Lancelot said as he turned and walked away. He entered the walls of the city and the gates closed behind him.

During Arthur's absence, a usurper named Sir Modred had taken over Camelot spreading rumors that King Arthur was dead. He had captured Queen Guinevere and although he pledged he would marry her, she escaped and hid in a tower. When King Arthur learned of this change of events, he immediately returned home.

A horrible battle ensued in which many knights were lost and King Arthur found Gawain lying near death, in a boat. Gawain said, "Know that my day of death is upon me, although it is from my own hastiness and willfulness. I know the wound Lancelot has given me will be the cause. Had Lancelot fought alongside of you, I know these tragedies would not have befallen the court."

Gawain told the king to send for Lancelot and cherish him above all knights. At noon, he gave up his breath and spirit. Arthur buried him beneath a chapel within Dover Castle. Men would come to look upon his skull to see the wound Lancelot had inflicted.

The eve before the second battle between Arthur and Modred, Arthur dreamed that Gawain appeared before him. The king was overjoyed to find him alive, and received him with great affection.

"I have come to warn you of your death if you fight tomorrow with Sir Modred. Make a treaty with him for one month. For, in time, Lancelot and his knights will return. He will rescue you worshipfully and slay Sir Modred."

Arthur called his advisors together and a treaty was reached where Modred would have Cornwall and Kent during the time Arthur remained alive. After his death, Modred would take all of England. Wine was served and all drank, although Arthur did not feel joyous. He knew Sir Modred was a traitor and the feeling of uneasiness between them was mutual.

Just then, a snake came out of a bush and bit one of the knights. When he felt the sting, he immediately pulled his sword to kill it, thinking nothing of it. When Modred and Arthur saw the drawn sword, both sides blew their trumpets and all unleashed their swords. Innocently, another battle had begun.

One of the knights tried to warn Arthur not to continue in the fight, anxiously reminding him of Gawain's vision. Arthur would not listen. Modred and the great king ran at each other. Arthur's spear went under Modred's shield and into his chest. Before Modred died, he mustered the strength to swing his sword one last time, and delivered a blow which went right through Arthur's helmet

The knights tried to move him, but Arthur was weak. His brother, Sir Bedivere wept at his side.

"Do not weep," Arthur whispered. "Take my good sword, Excalibur and go with it to the lakeside. When you arrive there, throw the sword into the water and then return and tell me what you have seen." Arthur remembered his promise to the Lady of the Lake.

Sir Bedivere obeyed. He immediately took the sword and traveled to the Lake. On the way, he fingered the precious stones that adorned the sword's hilt and could not bring himself to throw it away. Instead, he hid it under a tree. When he returned, Arthur asked what he had seen and the knight said he had seen nothing.

"You have deceived me!" The king was furious. "You must do it, or you put my life in jeopardy."

Sir Bedivere finally obeyed and threw the sword toward the middle of the Lake. Suddenly there came a hand and an arm. It caught the sword and brandished it above the water, before sinking back below the surface. The knight returned and told the king what he had witnessed.

They brought the dying king to the Lake. Arthur recognized the boat he and Merlin had used to obtain Excalibur. He asked to be put inside of it, and as it sailed from the shore, the faint image of woman sat by his side. She rowed the king away from the shore and into the mist.

Sir Bedivere left in great sadness as he walked along the side of the Lake, into the woods. All through the night, he wandered grief stricken. The next morning he came upon a chapel and hermitage. A hermit was praying next to a tomb that appeared new, with fresh wreathes still adorning it. Sir Bedivere asked who was buried there.

"Fair son," said the hermit, "I know not, but this night there came many ladies. They brought one who had died and asked me to bury him."

"Alas," said Sir Bedivere: "that was my lord, King Arthur."

Beyond Enchantment

There is a dreamlike quality to these stories, where strange events unfold and heroes are provided clues to solve a deeper mystery. We sometimes fall prey to enchantment by attempting to translate the great mystery. Something as natural as *the design* that tells a plant to grow purple flowers can be misconstrued to the extent that it actually stunts our growth.

Since the beginning of recorded history, we have had two ways of interpreting life. One reveals a world observable by our limited sensory apparatus, while the other suggests a more real world that exists beyond the senses. All cultures have interwoven the idea of duality into their beliefs and use myths as a way of describing the organizing or divine principle at work in life.

On a natural level, all living things are *self-organizing systems* that must thrive in universe that is moving toward *disorganization* or entropy.

Molecules left to do what they will inside of an empty box, demonstrate life's drive toward random disorganization. The natural world appears committed to randomness because of the variations that become possible. Yet, even a universe predisposed to randomness also appears to display a type of order or intelligent design.

Light shows us life's duality as it is measured to be both, particles and waves. It offers subtle proof we might exist beyond our physical manifestation. Beyond duality however, is a *third* aspect, and one cannot help but notice the repetitious theme of the number *three* in these stories. Merlin causes an enchantment to fall over the sleeping knight who is to wake in three hours. For three days, Arthur rested, and Gawain experiences power associated with the number three. Vortigern's tower falls three times and Percival makes three attempts at approaching the sea before discovering the Grail.

In dreams, three suggests completion and a return to the beginning. Three is a transcendental symbol that provides objectivity. We can understand *one thing* by studying the qualities of its *opposite*. The openness required to explore the place in between these two ideas brings these ideas together in innovative ways. This is the transcendental landscape which leads us beyond the known and is active during dreaming.

Numbers have always been viewed as symbols that hold a profound mystery. Dreams of numbers often depict where we stand in relationship to our environment. One is alone and expresses a beginning, while two is duality, representing a choice or the desire to strike a balance. Three is the transcendental product achieved by blending opposites into something new.

Like the birth of a child, sexual reproduction allows for the variation that leads life to become superior in its evolution. Three suggested harmony for Pythagoras and completeness for Aristotle. The bizarre behavior of nine in mathematics has given this number an enchanting quality, although it is simply three in its triple form. We find this number symbolized in many mythical and religious groupings, describing the freedom to move within the transcendental landscape of change.

In the previous chapters, we traveled to the underworld to reclaim power, instinct, feeling, and our ability to see how we create experience through projection. As we move toward the transcendental realm of inspiration and intuition, we approach a mediating platform that gives shape to our dreams. While we sleep, some aspect continuously wakes us to explore change. When we apprehend this mysterious wakefulness during the day, we call it a peak experience or an epiphany.

The nebulous openness required to transcend the known is captured best in the symbolism of water. Since we explore change in our dreams, the behavior of water often reveals *how we feel* about these changes. We thrust our arm below the surface, and it changes color and dimension. We know it is our arm, and yet, *it looks different* somehow. Going below these depths always presents us with the danger of becoming quite lost.

Within these depths, we discover the treasure of self-knowledge. We are offered direction when we delve into the nebulous realm of the unknown. Both Arthur and Percival are empowered by traveling to the water's mysterious shores. Because it is a boundless realm, the possibility for disorientation is always present. Just as the Lady of the Lake and the characters surrounding the Fisher King appear otherworldly, bringing any experience back from this inspired realm into the mundane, always loses something in the translation.

The Search for the Grail

The search for the Grail, like the mystery that emerges from dream symbols, allows us to discover *our* way. We use the word soul to describe an aspect of our nature that transcends ego-awareness. The idea of soul as the fully realized potentiality of the body evolved from the Greeks. As it tumbled through the hands of religion, it became associated with words like *Spirit*, and takes on a *thou shalt not* somberness that makes it rather different from the original Greek concept.

Ideas of science, philosophy and art can't help but shape each other as they coexist through time. The early Greek idea that *potentiality* is inherent in each individual somehow split off to become the image of man's dual existence. One part of our nature (soul) was believed to be good and attempts to repair the second, which has fallen and was born into a world that had become fundamentally bad. Three however, provides an objective landscape. Transcending the idea of duality and absolutes, we may find that the Grail is how we are natural creatures in a natural world being led by natural processes.

The *positive* forces inherent in life cannot be called good, any more than the negative forces would be called bad. Electricity shows us how a *positive* force travels through metal and is brought forward by the *negative* pulling fields that are also generated. In actuality, they are variations of one force. Our dreams continuously wake us to explore our *beautiful* nature, which can often be hidden beneath the trappings of *our idea* of bad. *Dreams appear to be leading us toward continuous development, activating self-knowledge and direction in life.* We are not bad and the world is not evil. Ideas of this nature often cause us to lose our way.

Religion, like art, attempts to present reality from a perspective that we may not have considered. While art offers momentary participation in another's enchanted vision, organized religion demands more from us. When the budding of our inspired awareness leads us in search of answers, what we find instead is somebody else's interpretation of why we shouldn't allow it free reign.

The Lady of the Lake attends to the mysteries of her deeper realm, while projecting an image of the Lake to act as a barrier to her true residence. There remains a mysterious quality to life that no amount of measuring has been able to uncover. Both Arthur and Percival encounter mysterious events, and are given a sword. While Arthur takes his sword to conquer the world of everyday experience, Percival is more contemplative and yet, becomes the ultimate hero. Beyond Arthur's realm of ego-awareness and mundane conquests, Percival must travel into the heart of the mystery.

The Imagination

Most artists will attest to the experience of creating something which took on a life of its own. Characters lead writers in their stories, and the gifted actor sometimes gets lost within the gap created by forgetting who they really are. Mark Twain once said he could only write if the book wrote itself. Like dreaming, this ability to let go of the known heightens our ability *to discover.*

An artist's level of discovery is usually relayed in direct intensity to the observer. The more one is moved by their own creative processes, the more the work becomes profound to others. Moving away from ego, the performer must relinquish self awareness to allow inspiration to flow freely to engage the audience. Any sense of ego only interferes with their performance.

Intuition is the direct or immediate apprehension of something without reasoning. The imagination is the platform where inspiration and intuition come forward. We are inspired passively in dreams, but when we actively apply inspired images to what we experience, we call it intuition and synchronicity.

The artist experiences a state where time is suspended and ego awareness dissolves. They are able to perceive with some other apparatus. Like the mystic, the process is exhilarating and leads to participation in something that transcends a sense of time. This ability to achieve a perspective aside from the gravitational tug of the ego is our first

120

introduction into what is called the Self. From its perspective, we are free to observe phenomena in very different ways.

This *transcendental perspective* is not limited to creative or spiritual types. Bertrand Russell described working with mathematics in a way that equations possessed a "beauty, cold and austere, like that of a sculpture." Even physicists are inspired by the perfection and symmetry that emerges to give shape to their discoveries. This process is oftentimes described as being a witness as the mind is leading and being led at the same time.

Applied toward science, the imagination supplements the rational intellect as it approaches a specific problem. Einstein believed the imagination was more important than knowledge. He discovered his innovative theories about gravity as a phenomenon of geometry and space curvature when free falling backwards in a chair. As a clerk in a patent office, he was day-dreaming and had the sudden realization that in space, all things freefall until they succumb to the gravitational pull of other bodies.

The creative process can be explored by laying two unlike objects out on a table. By pondering their similarities and differences, a third or *new* idea emerges. Is there some part of one object that might crossover into the use of the other object? What exists in between these two concrete objects is a *question*.

This mysterious motif permeates the Arthurian tales. Two prominent kings, Arthur and the Fisher King are both initially wounded and at the mercy of a question. In the case of Arthur, he must ask for the sword, Excalibur. It is returned upon his death, describing the straightforward life and death of the ego. The Fisher King is also wounded, but he is at the mercy of Percival's *unprompted* question. Arthur takes the treasure to achieve increased power and potential in mundane terms. The Fisher King requires a healing which can only be achieved through the enlightenment and integration of another character.

Initiation

We can only access inspiration and intuition if we give ourselves *permission not to know*. Asking questions, we move into a space opposite from logical reasoning. Mystics achieve enlightenment by quieting the thoughts and the interruptions of the mind. They prepare a place where inspiration can come freely forward. If we want to access the inspired realm that guides us in our dreams, we must suspend our critical faculties and judgment. The same mystery guiding our dream life can be accessed by training the mind in this way.

Merlin is another guide into the transcendental realm. Geoffrey of Monmouth, in the *History of the Kings of Britain* describes Merlin as saying: "If I was to speak vainly or amusingly, the spirit that teaches me would fall silent and would leave me when need for him arose." The *spirit that teaches me* can be viewed as the guiding source of our dreams.

Like the Self active during dreaming, Merlin guides Arthur toward the shores of the mysterious Lake (unconscious). Portraying the inspiration of our untapped potential, the Lady of the Lake has a more real residence, deep below the water. It is guarded by a reflection or imaginary image just as the subconscious net keeps us recreating *our* version of existence. The strange events at the Lake resemble how this gate recedes as we drift off to sleep. This allows for the free exploration of our *more real* residence that remains deep below the surface.

In this story, Arthur portrays our movement toward inspiration. The knight guards his passage and similarly, something blocks our access to this transcendental perspective during the day. Whatever we might *discover* would only be lost when we hammer it back into the shape of the known.

While we dream, we are inspired by images from this realm. At the same time, we awaken and all we have discovered recedes back into the abyss. It is as if we have two ways of processing experience: through the events of daily life that shape our beliefs, and through the rehashing and hybridization of symbols that help us release them. The aspect of the psyche that blocks our access to this realm during the day is also stunting our ability to grow. This is why remembering a dream often requires patience and effort. If we can hold to only one symbol, initiation can begin.

When we make the decision to remember our dreams, we can do so by simply recalling how the dream made us *feel*. Connecting with the emotion allows us to capture bits and pieces of the dream imagery. The series of dreams that take place during the night are often repeating the same issue. Because of this it is not so important to remember *everything*. Re-capturing only a small portion will still offer amazing insight into one's current attempt at transformation.

Arthur and the Fisher King are wounded and similarly, initiation usually occurs because the ego is wounded or thwarted in its aim. Its smaller reality can only be relinquished when it is no longer working. After Arthur's recovery, he jousts with the knight, but the knight proves to be more powerful and almost kills Arthur. The ego often feels threatened by the prospect of something greater than itself.

Merlin, the Lady and the knight all personify the suppression and release of the unconscious regulating influence, which Jung labeled the *transcendent function*. The ego thereby gains insight into this mysterious world through a peak experience, dreams, or the sudden apprehension of inspiration.

If we were to identify the aspect of the psyche that experiences the reality of both conscious and unconscious processes, we would call it the Self. In very creative ways, it expresses itself upon the canvas of the imagination through dreams. It uses images gathered from experience or memory, and is sometimes said to pull images from its own inspired realm, which Jung referred to as the *collective unconscious.*

As the arm rises from the water to give us the sword, it allows us to cut through the illusions we create so we may discover a more authentic existence. Through dreams, the Self demonstrates creativity, wisdom and humor in very remarkable ways. When dreaming, the ego has no choice but to allow its concrete belief structures to be shattered. Just as Arthur rejects the omens and otherworldly guidance, we are generally so caught up in defending our beliefs against the drama *out there* that we fail to observe what experience may be teaching us about the world *in here.*

Arthur (ego) is drawn to the Lake (unconscious), takes the sword, seeks conquest and both he and the sword are returned to the Lake when he dies. Percival's interaction with the Fisher King reveals the deeper levels of initiation that will allow us to find our gravitational orbit around the Self. While Arthur experiences momentary enlightenment at the water's edge, Percival must integrate its contents.

The Fisher King's *entire life is but a dying* and captures how the ego dies and is reborn over time. It is only a temporary perspective in relation to whatever the Self might offer. The trials of experience Percival undergoes leads him to become keeper of the Kingdom as the empowered Self. Unlike Arthur, Percival must develop as more than the ego. He must begin to experience life from the center of the Self outward, if he is to become *Keeper of the Grail Castle.* In the language of myths and dreams, the unconscious speaks metaphorically and so, there is usually a puzzling quality to its message.

Regardless of the label we use to describe this guiding inspiration, we enter its mystery usually because we are called into a type of initiation. The Fisher King is *wounded* because he misused the power at his disposal. He tells Percival that if he wondered about anything taking place, he should *not* ask the meaning, and yet, asking a question is the key to curing his illness.

The Death of the King

Vortigern and Percival's father are both kings who ultimately die when their towers are destroyed. Sometimes the destruction of the *tower* of our beliefs is the only way we can be unshackled from the prison created by ego-awareness. *Vortigern was a usurper and had erected a tower.* In Freud's terms, this can be non other than "His Majesty, the ego."

Vortigern (ego) lived in constant fear that the rightful heir (Self) would someday return to overthrow him." This captures Jung's idea of how the ego fears annihilation at the prospect of meeting something more powerful. *"Three times the tower fell to the earth, without any apparent cause. Later it was discovered that a pool of water (unconscious) and dragons (fear) were hidden (repression) beneath its walls (defenses).* The dragons, like the snake, are symbolic of regeneration and transformation. While the ego attempts to rule from its castle, it is no match for the power of the psyche to topple it over.

Like Arthur, Percival is given a sword by the Fisher King. Arthur's sword allows him to express his physical nature in very grounded ways, although Percival was cut off from contact with others and finds his way only by internal clues. He personifies how dreams wake us to live our life from inner direction and not by following others. When the Fisher King tells Percival not to ask for meaning, he is coaxing him through *experiential* initiation.

From the moment we meet Percival, he moves through the world creating himself from only inspiration. He carries the javelin he has had since birth, which is symbolic of how we attempt to hit the mark in actualizing our destiny. Arthur is the best of what can be made of ego awareness. Percival takes the sword to cut through the illusion created by the ego, which only seeks conformity and acceptance. He does not turn away from action; he recognizes how action leads to inner wisdom, and he begins to measure outer events against his inspiration.

There is an obvious healing taking place in this story. The Grail heals the weeping knights as superficial spiritual nourishment. The healing of the Fisher King simply allows him to die. The word *heal* however, derives from the word *whole*. Upon the Fisher King's death, Percival is made ruler of the kingdom, representing the dying away of purely ego awareness and the awakening from the center of the Self.

We encounter a crisis in our lives and may wonder what we have done to deserve the punishment. Our friends gather around and offer encouragement, although they secretly wonder why fate has turned on us. Like the Fisher King, we too, are wounded and the world takes on a darkening gloom. As the light of the ego recedes, we find another light illuminating the darkness.

During depression, dreams speak most vividly and inspire us to make changes. Just as Percival used creativity to make the costume he wore into the world, these inner cues lead us to become authentically ourselves.

Dreams prove that everyone is creative. The imagination is the vehicle that allows children to interact with the image of the world that they are growing into. Somewhere in the process of growing, we forget this enormous power for self- creation, and become a reflection of what we believe is expected of us. *More importantly, we forget the enormous power that made us believe that anything was possible.* We may be unaware of the process, but beliefs continue to shape our experiences.

Where does this imaginative energy go? We have seen how the imagination can influence our perception. It can become either a positive or negative resource depending upon our willingness to grow. In the previous chapters, we identified the negative ways it keeps us recreating the past, through projection and transference. *We must assume it holds the power to create the future.*

I witnessed this first hand with "Mark" who had lost all respect for a weak and abusive father when he was young. He came to idolize an uncle with an arm deformity who had cared for him. As an adult, he experienced health issues with the same limb. I was unaware of his *dis-ease* when we began dream-work.

In his dream, the driver's door of a car was blocked by a wall and unable to open. On the body, this door would represent the left arm and so I asked him about it. He said he had developed cancer in that arm many years prior. Yet, in the dream, he was inside of the car worrying about where to hide his valuables. Symbolic of the Grail, it signified some unknown treasure that pointed to a wellspring of healing.

He described how he had not lived with his family, and held them in contempt, angry that the mother had never protected him from an abusive father. In our discussions about his father, the conversation kept turning toward this uncle, and it became apparent that he had acted as a role model. I asked him which of the uncle's arms was crippled and he said that it was the left one. Each time I asked about the father, he shut down and immediately shifted the discussion toward this uncle. This shifting captured the symbolic representation of why the door (exit of energy) was blocked.

If this was a form of repressed guilt stemming from his feelings about the parents, I wondered if it had manifested as a type of punishment (restraint) impairing the left arm. *"Honor thy mother and thy father."* He is devoutly religious and had he not repressed these feelings at the heart of an internal crisis, perhaps he may not have developed the dis-ease. In 1926, Elida Evans in the *Psychological Study of Cancers* wrote: "Cancer is a symbol as most illness is, of something going wrong in the patient's life, warning him to take another road." *Just as dreaming utilizes the imagination to explore what we have made of the past, we must assume that on another level, the imagination has the power to shape the future.*

Through dream work, the pathway to wholeness is revealed. Like Percival, dreams about drowning or succumbing to ferocious seas, often evolve into boarding a vessel on calm water to retrieve a treasure or to receive accolades. The fact that Percival never had a sister until the end embodies the integration of the introspective, feminine aspect of the psyche. Empowerment requires a balancing of introspection (feminine) and actualization (masculine). The search for the Grail is embodied in dreams of finding treasure or jewels. Like Mark, this lost treasure is revealed as the valuable part of our nature we keep hidden...even while it finds opportunities for expression and resolution.

As King Arthur, we may experience momentary enlightenment and develop as the powerful one, climbing to our position of respect in the world. As knights, we develop morality or conscience, seeking to do right and be courteous at the command of the superego. *Psychic balance requires that no one character become suppressed or overwhelmed by another.* In the process of enlightenment, should the superego and ego merge, our momentary enlightenment can become a crusade to convert others to our beliefs. Like Arthur, we assemble foot soldiers to fight in the name of our mandala or Round Table. Alternatively as Mark may have experienced, "honor thy mother and father" can be converted by conscience to reprimand and punish us in the unique mythology of our beliefs.

It was said that Merlin (imagination) was enchanted by the Lady of the Lake (unconscious) and disappeared into the deep waters, never to be seen again. Like Van Gough, Hemingway and Nietzsche, we have seen prolific creators dissolve backward into this watery abyss. In all cases, approaching inspiration requires that we do not abandon life, but maintain a concrete footing in the world around us.

Synchronicity

Jung believed when we are trapped in a transformative process, something rises from the unconscious, whether through dreams or events that will reveal the *way through*. He used the word *synchronicity* to describe the process by which we are inspired by these internal cues. Something rising from the unconscious links an outward event that appears *coincidental* with information that makes that event *personally meaningful*.

Its meaning is usually thematic in dreams, and as we connect inspiration to an outward event we find *active intuition* that validates our inner processes. These inner processes also come to validate our *pathway*.

An event might be dismissed because the individual is unaware of the symbolism currently manifesting in their dreams. Measuring dreams against outer events, we discover an uncanny correlation on a pathway of *waking up*.

As an example, we may be going through life in a state of panic and hurrying to appointments, as we travel further from our authentic center. We experience people honking and cutting us off while we are driving. Since we are *not* in control of where we are going, we may ignore dreams in which we are being driven by someone else, or losing control of our vehicle.

Perhaps we dream of police stopping us, and the next day our wristwatch stops working. The more we rush forward, the more life appears to slow us down. The police in the dream represent a regulating tendency rising from within: *slow down*. How can we be living our authentic life if we are constantly rushing to meet the future?

We may be holding in our anger and when an event happens, we explode and respond with more emotion than the situation warranted. Since we are repressing our feelings, we may dream of a bear or tiger (mammalian/feelings) attacking us as if our emotional outburst came *out of nowhere*. The next day, we may be drawn consciously to witnessing pure animal aggression or again, experience others attacking us in some way. *What happens around us has an uncanny way of reflecting the well being of our inner world. These repressed patterns of thought are usually thematic in dreams.*

The Healing Journey

Something drastic like a car accident or open-heart surgery doesn't have to occur unless our other cues have failed. Only then, are we planted firmly in one place to understand how our life may have become unbalanced, or how our heart had become closed. While we were running in circles, lost in the idea of what the future demanded of us, who were we? The *one that knows within* appears to take an active interest in promoting wholeness and wellness in this life. It promotes balance and demands that we stay connected to life *as it unfolds*.

Symbolism may first inspire our dreams and during the day, we may experience a synchronistic event where the same idea appears. Alternatively, a symbol in the outer world may appear in our dreams and then reappear the next day, giving it added emphasis. This symbolism may be repeated several times throughout the day or we may dismiss it and fail to see its message altogether. Usually the tower doesn't fall until the first two promptings have failed: first through dreams and then through cues in the outer world.

We see these three attempts symbolized in the story of Percival as he approaches the sea. First, he is on a horse, taking no heed of himself and the horse carries him swiftly on a journey that should have taken several days. Embodying how dreams transcend our sense of time, a swift black horse, carrying us on a frightening journey into a raging sea would indicate that our organic (dark) and spirited nature (horse) is trying to break free by leading us into the unknown sea (unconscious). Going there is usually a frightening prospect for the ego. Percival prays and the horse throws him off, as if knowing he is not ready.

Next, a woman comes from the sea embodying introspective qualities. She offers him the treasure that comes from turning within. Something in the outer world captures his attention as synchronicity. It is his *sword (truth)*, which suddenly looks like a *crucifix (death and resurrection)*. The black horse or unknown potential is now symbolized by a crucifix, again suggesting the death of the ego in return for the birth of the unknown Self. This time however, empowerment appears as resurrection and not annihilation. Percival believes that the power at his disposal is evil; the belief that leads to repression in the first place and he refuses. The woman sails back into the sea because Percival is still not ready.

Finally, Percival travels along the shoreline, measuring inspiration against his pathway. He meets his sister, representing the integration of introspection and action. He boards the vessel to bravely cross the water and is rewarded with the Grail or applied potential that emerges from Self-actualization.

Of course, the connection between the inner and outer terrain can be dismissed as coincidence. When the tower falls in a third attempt to get our attention we are usually called into initiation. The pain of dissolution is in proportion to how strongly the ego fights to ward off change.

What may have begun as a dream or the unconscious inspiring us toward *subtle* transformation can tapped as intuition or the vague sense that something is trying to get our attention.

We have many opportunities to strike a balance prior to requiring drastic life awakenings. Change, for which we are unprepared, is usually called *grace*, only when we look back to recognize how we were missing out on an important aspect of our existence. If we are too much in the world of thought, it will be a lesson about feeling. If we are pushing against a closed door, we find an open door only when we stop pushing. When inner and outer cues are measured against each other, we come to recognize and respect *the one that knows within*.

When we tap our inspiration and apply it to experience, we find ourselves on the pathway of our destiny. Whatever unfolds, we can be certain that it as special relevance for us.

It takes time to uncover the mysteries arising from our dreams. Whatever is guiding us is truly inspired and appears to abide by a different time sense. When awareness becomes centered in this guiding source, we become *Keeper of the Grail castle.*

In the same way we understand psychosomatic illness, we can activate psychosomatic healing.

As an inspired and guiding center, some part of us holds the mirror that reflects the road to wellness. It is more than the tiny searchlight of the ego which pales beneath its light. When it rises, it illuminates the inner landscape like the first sunrise. Instead of running off to wake the sleeping world, we come to realize that it rises daily.

It guides us nightly as the purveyor of dreams. Ultimately it embodies the direction that we are given as we travel through the darkness.

Regardless of whether it is guided by evolutionary mechanisms or spiritual processes, it is more than ego and comes to pull all of experience into its orbit. It offers us an opportunity to touch, if only for a moment, the center of eternity.

Chapter Six
The Zealot and the Trickster's Medicine

Mythology of the Americas
Morality, Conscience and Illness

"What is life? It is a flash of a firefly in the night.
It is a breath of a buffalo in the wintertime.
It is as the little shadow that runs across the grass
and loses itself in the sunset."

Crowfoot, (Blackfeet)

In the mind/body approach to wellness, therapists identify how lifestyle, including the inability to process anger, can lead to *dis-ease*. Like the Medicine Men of the Americas, there is a need to find, honor and process the confusion that has preyed upon the body. We may not know why we have become unwell, but we can be certain that we have been given a *time out*. As we slow down, we have the opportunity to put our lives back in balance.

Dis-ease can become a physical expression of internal conflict. Illness goes hand in hand with extreme self-criticism or the inability to express our vital nature and the inspired vision that drives us forward. At the same time, guilt can take root in conscience and orchestrate a type of self-restraint..

When Mark was unable to reconcile spiritual commandments with authentic feelings of disappointment, he may have required a time out in order to process and understand his internal crisis. Dreams ever push us beyond our ambiguous and *irrational* boundaries, where an intangible approach to the spiritual can sometimes lead us away from *natural* wellness.

The healing work of the Shaman and Medicine Men reveal that *where* the illness manifests is important to understanding *how and why* it was created. When unrecognized self-criticism or repressed anger festers, the primitive energy of instinct can be made subservient and is usurped. We have explored how vital energy can be converted in self-destructive ways. If energy is not flowing freely through the body, it must be gathering *somewhere*.

In time, repressed energy will find a way of making itself known because nothing in the natural world is stagnant. If we can understand illness as how added attention or a time out may be serving us, we can actually begin a pathway toward wellness. In a strange way, dis-ease is a less productive way of finding our way forward.

The Mythical Setting of the Zealot

When we believe that the world is fundamentally bad, we further increase our tendency to suffer. If we believe in a natural world that is in the pursuit of excellence and perfection, we find ourselves on a level playing field and suffer less. Energy in nature cannot function in a vacuum. Freud believed impulses of self-condemnation and guilt somehow turned vital energy back against the body. In the setting of conquistadors and missionaries zealously on a mission to subjugate the heathen in the New World, we can observe this strange energy mismanagement in personified form.

The Mythology of the Americas presents a more organic and holistic perspective of life. Their ideas were repressed by those who conquered in the name of *"all that is civilized."* The Zealot and the Trickster's Medicine reveal symbolic archetypes that allow us to re-discover our pathway to wellness.

We can imagine the superego as "thou shalt," dressed in its restrictive trappings, and moving across the psychic frontier like a missionary, wagging its finger at the id. To the superego, the id represents everything that is disgusting and uncivilized. The id is the primitive part of the psyche that wears animal skins and paints its face to express its naturalness. It has played the game of survival thus far and has won. The superego is a relatively new creation and travels like the missionaries who accompanied the conquistadors into the New World.

Growth, by its very nature requires a movement *away* from the status quo. Our idea of the present should not be dictated by the beliefs of others, and certainly not by those who are no longer living. Like the telephone game played in childhood, what may have been relevant in the beginning becomes quite distorted in the re-telling. In the hands of time, we find the stories of prophets and poets are intertwined.

When the characters of the *Zealot* or missionaries and the natives meet on the pages of history, we find the personification of guilt turned deadly. The natural vitality of id must now serve the strange disciplinarian tendencies of the superego. The uninhibited world of instinct is opposed, subjugated and forced to do the superego's bidding.

The power of the superego to subdue natural drives is demonstrated by how quickly and how enduring these moralistic ideas permeated the native cultures of the Americas.

In prior chapters, we recognized the importance of expressing our instinctual nature. Now we see what happens when its free expression is usurped by morality or conscience. As the charioteer drives the horses, conscience can take authority, interpreting dogma as *empowerment instructions* to punish the ego and convert the natural energy of the id. The word *discipline* and *disciple* derive from the same Latin root. The superego resonates to the idea of discipline, while the ego can become its oblivious disciple. Like a missionary and his conquistador, both go about conquering and exploiting the primitive energy of the id.

Repression at the hands of conscience can create confusion and misunderstandings among the characters. Both civilization and the psyche can subscribe to vague taboos, generating the boogeyman *out there* as a projection of what is being repressed *in here*. In the stories of the Americas, we find a healing pathway into the transcendental realm. We discover the *medicine* or way to become free from self-destructive tendencies.

Suggesting a middle road between absolutes, we meet the character that personifies natural mechanisms that keep us from becoming too ritualized. When our evolution and instinctual drives become inhibited, we find Trickster emerging on the psychic frontier.

The transcendental character that the natives called Trickster straddles the same psychic trading post where inspiration was packaged and sold as spirituality. After a peak experience, we may attempt to interpret spiritual vision with the rational intellect and somewhere in the left hemisphere of the brain, it gets distorted.

Trickster manifests at the psychic crossroad, pointing like the scarecrow in the Wizard of Oz. His antics reveal the ridiculous way we take life so seriously.

There are many roads and the right road is sometimes just the pathway exposing the contradiction inherent in absolutes. We find that the middle road between good and evil becomes our willingness *to let go*. Trickster teaches us that we must sometimes dance with ambiguity awhile to discover life's deeper mysteries.

The Clash of Cultures

During the first few centuries, philosophers had laid the foundation for the teachings of Christianity that would be transmitted to

133

the Western world. Adopted by both the Roman and Hellenistic civilizations, it came to define everyday life in Europe. Its importance in shaping Western thought is without question, but the equal contribution of Islam in paving the way to the Enlightenment is something rarely celebrated in the pages of history.

After the Crusades, the exotic goods of Asia were in high demand. Yet, the Europeans had developed only two things to offer in trade. They had produced a philosophy and culture that dictated the *absolute* meaning of life, and had developed superior weaponry. The conquest and colonization of Asia, Africa and the Americas proved that weapons proved to be a powerful marketing vehicle for selling any type of religion.

Once the Turks barred their access through Eastern land routes, they had no choice but to seek alternative sea routes to Asia. Along the way, they raided, slaughtered, enslaved and pillaged, taking what they believed God had put in front of them. One Spanish explorer would later describe their expeditions as a way to "serve God and his Majesty, to give light to those who sat in darkness and to grow rich as all men desire to do."

Their religious zeal kept them from understanding or embracing any contributing ideas of these conquered cultures. Had an equal exchange of information taken place, we may have avoided the environmental, health, race and religious predicaments of today. One glaring disparity arises between the mythologies of the Americas and the mythology of their conquerors: *somewhere in the evolution of thought in the Old World, there had developed a belief that men were born evil and required redemption.*

In contrast, the natives believed:
"Man's heart away from nature becomes hard;
he knew that lack of respect for growing, living things
soon led to a lack of respect for humans too.
So he kept his youth close to its softening influence."
Standing Bear, (Lakota)

When looking at Native American thought, we can appreciate ideas that respected the environment instead of exploiting it. This is something that we are only appreciating today. In the Native American writings, we also find that they understood the importance of dreams.
In the old days our people had no education. All their wisdom and
knowledge came to them from dreams.
They tested their dreams and in that way learned their own strength."
Ojibwa Elder

Transcendental access to an inspired realm was practically applied and supported by their culture. It provided a healing method for reversing the effects of those who had *trespassed* or committed a taboo. In the same way, there can be mysterious taboos, trespassing and severe judgments handed down by conscience. Sometimes we must air out our interior spaces to understand how our ideas have made us ill. Through Trickster, we find a path to the transcendental process that breaks down barriers to ensure our continual growth.

"Thou Shalt" in the Pulpit

The ego must negotiate between the needs of the id and demands of the superego. This back seat driver stands separate from the ego as that part of us that learned to do right and obey. Joseph Campbell called this aspect that can lead us away from bliss, "thou shalt." It develops from the tapes and discipline of early parental conditioning that controlled the child's unrestrained urges. The pleasure principle paints the id as wanting to have everything, anytime a desire arises. The superego grows alongside of the ego and its first expressions are heard in the "no, no!" of the toddler, repeating the voice that will come to track him on his journey.

Once the ego grows strong enough to direct the energy of the id, the superego remains in judgment of both. The relationship between the three and the ability to maintain an equal balance in expression remains at the core of wellness. The ego can sometimes make so much of a peak experience, that a long drawn out process of humiliation will be required before we can find our *real* way forward. As we have seen, the repression of our natural drives can lead to hybridization where energy is misguided.

In the case of the superego, it appears to want to bring scrutiny upon our natural drives, and behaves like the teacher's pet telling on a classmate. The id just wants pleasure and to feel its "oceanic connectivity to the natural world." The superego likes to establish boundaries and fosters self-discipline. As the psyche teeters in the direction of severe rigidity, something moves to strike a balance. Tottering in the other direction, an opposite tendency emerges as perhaps a dirty urge thrown out onto the table. "*See there!*" The superego is defiant because it has an arsenal beyond the ego's comprehension. Restriction is its only reality, and punishment is its sense of empowerment.

Where has the poor little ego wondered off to? Somewhere in the previous chapter, perhaps it misunderstood its peak experience. Instead of relinquishing control to the Self, a type of hybridization occurred and the ego and superego merged. Perhaps the ego, felt threatened by the Self, and hid itself under the robes of the superego. When we peak behind the curtain, we find the little ego dressed like the wizard, standing on a stool to make itself look bigger. When the superego and ego align, a strange hyper-management of instinctual energy occurs, and the imbalance can have disastrous consequences. Ultimately we will discover that the Grail is *not* the superego.

In the closet of denial, instincts are vacuum-packed and repressed into tiny packages. The energy remains the same, although at some point, it will express itself. We can imagine a Jack in the Box being pulled tightly into its coil. This time it is not aggression and fear that we are repressing, but the power of nature to inspire, renew and keep us earthy and sensual. If the ego and superego stand in opposition to our organic processes, the shift is achieved somewhat more dramatically.

If this bound up energy is not discovered and expressed as being *good* then it can only be labeled *evil*. At some point, the energy will reach critical mass and spring out of the closet in an overwhelming gesture of our instinctual conflict. Since we cannot recognize it as being our own, we come to call it the *boogeyman*..

When pleasure is forced into the closet of denial to be labeled repugnant, it has a strange ability to ferment back into pleasure of an overwhelming and frightful nature. We have seen the ways in which the closet of repression traps energy and how disowned power can then overwhelm us as addiction. Those shouting most vehemently about powerlessness in the face of evil are the ones least aware of their vacuum-packed closets.

When the inner landscape is usurped by the severe dictates of conscience, the sense of restriction is so profound that the most basic interpretation of right and wrong can be distorted. The molestation charges against religious leaders are one example of this imbalance, and the killing of innocent people in the name of religion is another. Nature abhors a vacuum and we always find that both civilization and the psyche require balance and free expression.

This fault finding internal critic can travel across the psychic frontier like the missionaries moving through the pages of history. *"We are on a mission to subjugate the heathen in the name of all that is civilized and divine. The entire world is evil and so we must all be punished. Any primitive instinctual creatures must be taught to give up their nature-worshiping tendencies!"*

In this vacuum of thought, it is always the natural world that suffers. The evolutionary and powerful id energy can then be turned back upon the body in self-destructive ways. When this energy comes out of hiding, we are often found in the wrong place, doing the unthinkable.

We compare the ideas of the *Zealot* with the ideas of those they called *heathens* to discover the medicine that *Trickster* brings to the landscape. The stories of the America's reveal natural healing mechanisms of transcendental pranks and looping. Their ideas allow us to change our perspective, restore balance and eliminate psychic rigidity.

The History of the Americas

More than twenty thousand years ago, Paleo-Indians believed to be of Asiatic origin crossed the Bering Land Bridge connecting Asia to North America. Because we have found no artifacts of this ancient journey, some believe they may have traveled in boats along the coastline. Moving throughout North and South America, by 2500BC, they had established agriculture and by 1500BC, the first civilizations appeared.

The Maya of the Yucatan, El Salvador, Guatemala and Honduras evolved into a civilization that was at its height from 300 to 900AD. This corresponds to the Dark Ages of Europe, after the fall of the Roman Empire. They had developed a hieroglyphic form of writing and demonstrated a remarkable knowledge of mathematics, chronology and astronomy, even producing the concept of zero. Their culture revolved around a civil calendar of 365 days, reflecting a leap year that was more accurate than the Gregorian calendar of the same period. Integrating the 260 days of a lunar calendar, they demonstrated an understanding of time more vast than any other civilization.

Studying astronomy, they predicted when eclipses would occur and even created a record of time that spanned from one day to 64 million years. Like the Egyptians, the Maya built pyramid style temples. When the Toltec of the Mexican valley seized Chichen Itza, the Maya civilizations of the southern jungles were abandoned. This occurred around 900AD, seven hundred years before the conquistadors arrived in the Americas. In Mesoamerica, the Toltec rule would give way to the Aztecs.

The Inca civilization thrived in Peru, Chile, Bolivia, Argentina and parts of Ecuador. Known for their brilliantly engineered roads and communication systems, they established a very complex form of government and had created a true state. Their conquerors were most impressed with the wealth of precious metal stored in these ancient empires. The Inca had established an efficient model for a complex social system where the individual was subordinate to the collective. To the European conquerors, this type of government proved to be an easy transition to subjugation.

In the Northern regions, natives had built civilizations founded on a common dependence and the cultivation of maize or corn. The sun or sky was Father or creator; the mountain was life-giver as life-sustaining water poured forth from the hills. The earth was called the Great Mother and treated with respect. Rocks, rivers, trees and animals were imbued with spirits and given supernatural meaning. Even shadows and the changing light of sunrise and sunset manifested a sacred presence. The dancing whirlwind, carrying dust across the desert took on the image of Man maker.

Ritual allowed for second sight or vision into a spiritual world. The natives sought *totems* or animal spirits to protect and guide them in daily life. Fertility ceremonies were practiced along with an annual ceremony of cosmic rejuvenation.

Each tribe had a Medicine Rite that the West would call *Shamanism.* Their rituals healed their people of negative influences or the consequences of breaking taboos. To the Indian, evil was not personified but came from shameful behavior like not asking permission prior to taking the life of an animal that was killed for food. They had developed spiritual beliefs based upon an appreciation and respect for the natural world.

The Indian was the child of the Sun and helped the Father daily in its rise and descent. When clouds hung low around the mountaintop or the pastel light followed the sun in its journey to the edges of the earth, they followed. They respected their interdependence with the earth and all of its creatures.

Like many cultures, they described the colors of the sky emanating from the four directions. When light was infused with gold, they were drawn to participate in the great mystery of cosmic renewal. Expressing their gratitude through ceremony, they danced in the costumes and antics of their feathered and furry companions.

Animals taught them how to hunt and soon the Indians adopted the same pre-hunting calls and rituals. Copying the mating sound and ritual of wild grouse and turkeys, they drummed, shook feathered fans behind them and danced. Moving in a strange state of ecstasy, they mimicked the creatures who they believed retained their connection to a more natural consciousness.

Cultivating this *instinctual* perspective was highly respected and exercised daily. Out of respect for their teachers, they understood the taboo against the wanton killing of game. Dressed in the costumes of wolves, bears or eagles they walked along side of these great hunters as equals.

Sometimes they followed the animals on a hunt and at other times, they led. Demonstrating a highly refined instinctual nature, they came to communicate in the mysterious language of the natural world.

Their rituals brought them closer to understanding their partnership with the earth and all of its creatures. Animals taught them about the Great Mystery of life.

The Arrival of the Europeans

In the fifteenth century, Spanish and Portuguese ships had set sail across the Atlantic, hoping to find an easier and more direct route to China and India. Instead of landing in Asia, they found themselves on what they believed to be an island, among people they could only call uncivilized. In modern Mexico and South America, the conquistadors sought the treasures buried within the Inca and Aztec civilizations. Their superior weapons allowed them to conquer huge populations while the missionaries unleashed their religious zeal upon the natives.

The Spanish found gold and silver in the South, and remained there. They had proven the value of conquest and soon France, the Netherlands and England started expeditions into the North. Although they sought the same riches, none were found. Instead, they developed colonies on the Eastern shores of North America where investors established companies to grow commodities like tobacco and tea, much in demand in Europe.

In the thirteenth century, the poet, Dante had given literary expression to New Testament images such as hell and the devil. From the mythical creature Hel, of Norse mythology, and the mistranslation of Venus, the Morning Star into a Lucifer character, the mythology of evil emerged Dante's literary descriptions inspired artists to begin painting spectacular biblical representations. Armed with an image, the Puritans arrived to discover people of red color who resembled their idea of the devil.

To make matters worse, the Indians demonstrated blasphemy by worshipping snake deities and a character called Trickster. In 1622, a letter from New England described how the natives were observed to worship an evil power: *"who as farre as wee can conceive, is the Devill."*

The Europeans may have appeared otherworldly with their flashing metal costumes and vast technological resources. Their arrival would leave a lasting legacy of pillaging and disease. Of the 20 million indigenous people living in the Americas when the Europeans arrived, 95% of them were killed, either by conquest or disease.

Long periods of evolution in one area gave the Europeans 10,000 years to develop immunity to some diseases. The trade and movement, occurring relatively rapidly across the earth during this period, transferred disease around the world before immunity could develop. While their weapons made them powerful, they carried germs in their arsenal that were far more destructive.

In the prior century, the Europeans had just recovered from the plague, which served two purposes. First, it gave them the opportunity to develop immunity to the bacteria transferred by flea-infested rodents. Secondly, it contributed to the growing skepticism against the Church, which had proved powerless in preventing the outbreak. The Spanish religious fervor and reinstated Inquisition can be viewed as a backlash to this growing dissent. This skepticism also generated the Protestant or Puritan exodus into the New World.

During the sixteenth century, Hernan Cortes descended upon the Aztecs in Mexico while Francisco Pizarro moved against the Inca civilization in the South. Montezuma was the ninth ruler of the Aztec civilization and was the last of the Aztec emperors. When the conquistadors arrived in Mexico 1519, he believed Cortes to be the white god, Quetzalcoatl, prophesied to return one day. Although the Spanish government declared the Indians to be subjects, not slaves, they were ultimately forced into labor and to adopt Christianity.

In Brazil, the Portuguese established similar Jesuit run plantations and set about converting the natives. The mission systems that developed in the New World had a devastating impact on the aborigines. Forced to abandon their territories and indigenous crops, the natives were moved into crowded and disease-ridden labor camps. During only three centuries of European conquest, ten million Africans were transported abroad to face a similar fate.

When the colonists fought the Revolutionary War in the 1770's against the British, they sought help from the Indians. Yet, within a few decades, the United States government would establish the Indian Removal Act of 1830. This culminated in the massacre of Indians at Wounded Knee in 1890 and the loss of their territory equaling 86 million acres.

Banning religious ceremonies in 1882, Hiram Price, Commissioner of Indian Affairs would write: *"There is no good reason why an Indian should be permitted to indulge in practices which are alike repugnant to common decency and morality. The preservation of good order on reservations demands of me active measures be taken to discourage -- and if possible, put a stop -- to the demoralizing influence of heathenish rites."* His message captures the misunderstanding and vague taboos that the hyper-critical superego can instigate against our natural tendencies.

Creation Stories of the Americas

"From the Great Spirit, there came a great unifying life force that flowed in and through all things—the flowers of the plains, blowing winds, rocks, trees, birds, animals. It was the same force breathed into the first man. "Thus, all things were kindred, and were brought together by the same Great Mystery. Kinship with all creatures of the earth, sky, and water was a real and active principle. In the animal and bird world, there existed a brotherly feeling that kept us safe among them. And so close did we come to our feathered and furred friends that in true brotherhood we spoke a common tongue. The animals had rights-- the right of man's protection, the right to live, the right to multiply, the right to freedom, and the right to man's indebtedness---and in recognition of these rights we never enslaved an animal, and spared all life that was not needed for food and clothing."

–Lakota

"Knowledge was inherent in all things. The world was a library and its books were the stones, leaves, grass, brooks and the birds and animals that shared, alike with us, the storms and blessings of the earth. We learn to do what only the student of nature ever learns, and that is to feel beauty. We never rail at the storms, the furious winds, the biting frosts and snows. To do so intensifies human futility, so whatever comes we should adjust ourselves by more effort and energy if necessary, but without complaint. Bright days and dark days are both expressions of the Great Mystery."

--Chief Luther Standing Bear

"In the beginning of all things, wisdom and knowledge were with the animals, for Tirawa, the One Above, did not speak directly to man. He sent certain animals to tell men that he showed himself through the beasts and that from them, and from the stars and the sun and the moon should man learn.... all things tell of Tirawa."

– Pawnee

"We should understand well that all things are the work of the Great Spirit We should know that He is within all things: the trees, the grasses, the rivers, the mountains, the four-legged animals, and the winged peoples."

--Black Elk

"All things emanated from Pachacamac, the all-pervading spirit who gave the plants and animals souls. He breathed life into man and said the creative word which brought humans into existence from nothingness."

–Inca

"The gods deliberated on how man should be created. From yellow and white maize, they made Balam-Quitze (Tiger with the Sweet Smile), Balam-Agab (Tiger of the Night), Mahacutah (The Distinguished Name), and Iqi-Balam (Tiger of the Moon). The god Hurakan who had formed them, thought that they would be too much like the gods themselves and so they once again took counsel. They agreed that these newly created beings should be less perfect and possess less knowledge so not to become like gods. Hurakan breathed a cloud over their eyes so they might see only a portion of the earth, whereas before they had been able to see the whole round sphere of the world."

–Maya

"Ometecuhtli and Omecihuatl made Tezcatlipoca
(Lord of the Smoking Mirror), Huitzilopochtli (Hummingbird of the South), Xipe Totec (Flayed Lord) and Quetzalcoatl (Feathered Serpent).
Each day, the sun draws the clouds around at noon.
The rain falls from the clouds with thunder and lightning. In this, we see the divine Feathered Serpent, Quetzalcoatl. It is said that Quetzalcoatl disliked the blood sacrifices demanded by Tezcatlipoca. He sailed away on a raft.
It was prophesied that he would return one day."

–Aztec

Coyote and Man Maker

Man Maker had made the world although he recognized that something was missing. "What could it be?" He wondered. "What could be missing?" He realized the earth was missing beings like him. Up to this point, there were only animals. "How should I make them?" He built a *horno* or oven. Then he took some clay and formed a shape just like himself.

Coyote was sniffing around like he always does, and when Man Maker went out to get more clay, Coyote grabbed the human shape and changed it with his paws. Man Maker returned and put the clay into the oven without looking at it. After awhile he thought: "He must be ready now." Taking it out of the oven, he breathed on it and it came to life.

"Why don't you stand up?" Man Maker was perplexed. "What is wrong with you?" The creature just barked and wagged its tail. "Oh my, Coyote has tricked me." He laughed when he realized what Coyote had done.

"Why can't you make more creatures like me?" Coyote asked. "Oh well, all right, but don't interfere again." Man Maker said. That is where the dog came from; it was Coyote's doing.

Man Maker tried again. "They should be companions to each other," he thought. "I shouldn't make just one. I should make two." He shaped more creatures like himself and made them identical. "What's wrong here?" Recognizing they could not increase, he pulled a piece of clay from one creature to leave an opening and assembled the extra clay so that it protruded from the other. "That's better." He put them into the horno to bake.

"They are done now," Coyote told him. Man Maker took them out and breathed on them and they came to life. "Oh my, what's wrong?" He realized they were underdone. "They are not brown enough. They do not belong here."

"They belong across the water someplace." He was angry at Coyote. "Why did you tell me they were done? I can't use them here."

So, Man Maker tried again and made a pair in the exact same way. He placed them in the horno to bake. After awhile, he said: "I think they are done now."

"No, they aren't done yet," said Coyote. "You don't want them to come out too light again. Leave them in a little longer."

"Well, all right," said Man Maker. They waited and then he took them out. "Oh my. What's wrong? These are overdone. They are burned too dark." He put them aside. "Maybe I can use them some other place across the water. They do not belong here."

Man Maker tried again and placed two more images in the horno. "Now don't interfere," he warned Coyote. "You give me bad advice. Leave me alone."

This time he took the images out of the oven when he thought they were done. He breathed on them and brought them to life. The two beings walked around, talked, laughed and behaved like him. They were neither, underdone or overdone.

"These are exactly right for this place." Man Maker was happy.

Raven as Trickster

Trickster descended into to the world to distribute fish and berries. However, the world was still dark and the people were distressed. He too, was perplexed and said: "How will I feed myself when it is always dark?" Everyone knows Trickster's most favorite past time was eating. He remembered how it was light in the heaven from which he descended. He decided to return to heaven and steal the light.

He put on his Raven feathers and flew upward until he found the hole in the sky. Upon arriving, he removed the Raven outfit and became a cedar leaf, floating in a pool of water. When the creator's daughter came to the pool for a drink, she swallowed the leaf and became pregnant. Later, she gave birth to a child.

Her family was pleased to have a grandchild and the boy grew and learned to crawl around the lodge. When he crawled around, he cried: "Hama, hama!" Nobody understood what he was saying. His cries grew louder and he pointed at the box on the wall where the daylight was kept. Amused, the creator pulled the Daylight Box from the wall, so the child could touch it. This made the child content and so they let him play with it. He giggled and rolled it around the room.

Crawling around the lodge, he pushed the Daylight Box here and there. As the days passed, he pushed it closer to the door until after several days, his family was less amused and soon paid little attention to him. When he saw they were not looking, he grabbed the daylight box, dashed out the door and toward the hole in the sky.

The creator and his daughter chased him but he quickly put on his Raven outfit and flew through the hole, toward earth. When he arrived back on the earth, he broke open the box and released the daylight.

Trickster was made chief of the village, but soon demonstrated behavior that was totally incompatible with the post. He set out on a warpath but during the preliminary feasts, he left early to have sex with a woman. When he returned to lead the war party, he began the journey without setting up the first night's encampment. He destroyed his canoe, stamped his Warbundle into the mud and threw his arrows into a canyon. Eventually his followers had no choice but to desert him.

One day, he encountered a buffalo standing at the top of a small hill. He made a scarecrow and the buffalo ran in fright into a muddy pond where Trickster killed him. Trickster no sooner began cutting up the carcass when his left and right hand began fighting one another over possession of the carcass. Before he had a chance to eat anything, he injured himself and had to stop to bandage his hand.

Many days later, Trickster jumped into the ocean, swimming aimlessly around because he forgot where the shore was. He asked one fish after another how to get to the shore, but they just looked at him the way that fishes do. Finally, he met a school of fish who told him that he was dogpaddling right next to the shore. He waded onto the beach and made a clay pail to catch a few fish to eat. After several attempts, he caught one, but it was already dead. He buried the fish to eat later.

As Trickster approached a lake, he found a man on the opposite shore pointing at him. Trickster thought it was funny and so he put on a black shirt and pointed back. Finally, he grew weary when the man didn't do anything else. He walked away and when he looked back, he realized the man was actually a stump with a branch jutting out.

Trickster decided to travel the world again. He cleared the Mississippi of all obstacles to make it a fit place for people to inhabit. He made the roads of the Waterspirits to be driven farther underground and when he encountered a waterfall, he ordered it to move. The waterfall refused, so Trickster made a stick and moved it anyway. After eating his last meal on earth, he returned to the heaven assigned to him by Earthmaker.

Hare, Bringer of Culture and the Medicine Rite

Hare brought culture to the Indians and stole fire from the fire people to aid man. The man in the moon was Hare, and it is interesting how the goddess Eastre kept rabbits on the moon in Norse Mythology. Both cultures would merge the Hare or Rabbit with Christian customs. As a savior of mankind, Hare was so important to their culture that when Christianity was forced upon the Indians of the Peyote Rite they represented the figure of Christ as the Hare.

Hare fought against greed and brought agriculture and tools to the Red Man. When Grasshopper selfishly ate all of the tobacco, something that Earthmaker gave exclusively to human beings, Hare hit Grasshopper so hard that tobacco was scattered across the land, allowing people everywhere to use it. Flint kept all the stone arrowheads to himself, so Hare smashed him, scattering arrowheads all over the place. A similar spirit had beheaded the Red Man and kept his living head in his fireplace. When Hare caught up to him, he gave him such a blow that flint again flew in every direction. Hare then reunited the head and the body of Red Man and he was brought back to his normal life.

Earthmaker gave him the mission of founding the Medicine Rite in which human beings would be able to attain as much life as they wanted through longevity and rebirth. Hare went to earth, and with the aid of Grandmother, he established the Medicine Lodge and all its rites and ceremonies. Thus, Hare was responsible for giving human beings much culture.

Hare lived in a lodge with his Grandmother and went hunting early each morning. No matter how early he went, he always found that someone with a very long foot had been before him, leaving a long trail. He would rise earlier each day in an attempt to discover this stranger, but always missed him. Irritated, he returned to the lodge to consult with his Grandmother.

"Grandmother," he said, "every morning I rise and set traps in hopes of snaring game. Someone always comes before me and frightens the game away. This time I will set the trap for the stranger."

"Why would you do that?" She asked. "In what way has he caused you harm?"

"It is enough that I hate him," he replied. That night, he set a trap in the place where the footsteps were. The next morning he went out to examine his snare.

He arrived at the spot and discovered that he had caught the intruder. It was none other than the Sun. He wasn't sure what he had caught and so he ran home to tell his Grandmother. She told him to return and watch how it behaved. Upon returning, he found the Sun in an angry rage.

"How dare you snare me?" The Sun cried angrily. "Untie me at once!" Fearfully, Hare crept near the trap and released the Sun. It immediately soared upward into the sky.

Redhorn and Storms as He Walks

Redhorn created heads on his earlobes and made his hair long and red. Thus, he was known as Redhorn and as He who has Human Heads as Earlobes. One day, he embarked on a warpath with Turtle and Thunderbird called Storms as He Walks.

On the first three nights of the expedition, Turtle helped them to kill bears by means of trickery. On the fourth night, Redhorn and Storms as He Walks scouted the enemy by walking in the clouds. The next day they attacked, and Storms as He Walks, Redhorn, Wolf, and Otter all won war honors, but Turtle abandoned the fight. They went on the warpath several more times, and were successful each time.

The sons of Redhorn decided to go on the warpath. The oldest son asked Storms as He Walks for the Thunderbird Warbundle. After some effort, it was secured from above, but the Thunderbirds demanded that it be put in a case to be brought to the earth. Their friend offered his own body for this purpose and allowed them to kill him for this use. He lay on the ground and the Thunder Beings ate him. They broke his bones and made him whole again. The boys took the Thunderbird Warbundle and with their followers embarked on a raid to the other side of day. There they captured two iron chiefs and resurrected their friend. After that, Storms as He Walks and all the spirits returned to their natural realm.

146

Flesh and Stump

An old man had a son and daughter-in-law living with him. One day he killed his daughter-in-law and cut open her womb where he found twin boys. One of these, he hid in a stump, and the other he left behind in the lodge before he fled. The boy's father returned and found him in the lodge. He called this boy Flesh.

The other boy, called Stump met up with Flesh. After playing all day, he disappeared with his brother's arrow. The father devised a way to catch the wild boy, and the next day as they played, he made the boys wear headdresses of inflated turkey bladders. When Stump, tried to escape into the lake where he often hid, he could not submerge. Stump had no choice but live with Flesh and his father.

The father of the Twins told them that in their wanderings over the earth, they should not visit a particular hill. In the eyes of boys, this must be an interesting place and so they went to the hill to play. There, they battled with a hoard of snakes that they killed and ate. In the process, the boys were killed several times, but each time they were able to bring each other back to life. When the father learned of their unnatural existence, he grew fearful and made numerous attempts to flee. Each time he would try to flee, he was frustrated by the strange powers of his sons.

The Twins went off to visit Herecgúnina who kept the book of life. While they were there, they decided to steal the book. Later, they visited Earthmaker who told them to stay away from Herecgúnina. Nevertheless, they returned and so, Herecgúnina tried to kill them by shutting them inside an iron sweat bath. Inside, they had so much fun banging around that they accidentally knocked down one of the iron walls. Fire escaped into the lodge and burst into flames and Herecgúnina barely escaped with his book.

At one point, the Twins had joined Redhorn's war party and were made scouts. They followed Storms as He Walks and came upon two Red Waterspirits. The next day, they were among those chosen to attack these Waterspirits and they alone succeeded in defeating them. During the fighting, Turtle was killed, but Stump brought him back to life. Redhorn expressed his gratitude by offering the Twins a place with him. They decided to resume their travels instead.

They found a beaver lodge and attacked its occupant. Instead of a beaver, it was really a Water spirit. Earthmaker sent Rucewe to bring the Twins to him. When they arrived at his door, he told them that they had become far too dangerous to creation and so he kept them in the heaven assigned to them.

Thunderbirds and Feathered Serpents

The four Thunderbirds are called *Wakinyan* and Storms As He Walks is one. The Thunderbird from the West is the most powerful and is clothed in black. The second is of the North and is white. The third is of the East and is red and the fourth is of the South and is yellow.

The four directions are sometimes described in different colors, which resemble the Jewish legend of when God created Adam. He gathered red, white, yellow and black dust from the four corners of the world. The holy man may see part of Wakinyan in his dreams, but its entire form will always remain a mystery. Nobody has seen a Thunderbird whole and so their description comes from piecing together many dreams and visions.

Everything in the world moves in a certain direction but the Thunderbirds move contrary to everything. That is their way. Their behavior inspires the antics of the *heyoka* or sacred clown. The Thunder beings are invisible because they are cloaked in clouds but they can be felt.

They test anyone on a vision quest or those crying for a dream. After several nights of fasting and staying awake, they may come to test the seeker's courage. Although they be frightening, they are good. To dream of Wakinyan makes one a *heyoka*: an upside-down, hot-cold, forward-backward man. You have power, although you cannot stay this way for long and through ritual, you are returned to your normal state. While heyoka is a sacred clown, the Thunder Beings are guardians of truth. Both reveal the 'other way.'

The Feathered Serpent of the Southern regions is the god of lightning. It flies to the earth with the power to ignite seeds and changes into a serpent to go into the underworld. As it passes through the earth, it sparks life into all living things. On wings, the Feathered Serpent is able to achieve flight into the realm of the gods. Only birds can reach these heights and the flight and songs of birds are omens. Being a snake, it provides a picture of cosmic rejuvenation.

Birds create the wind and water spouts, agitating the sky with their wings. Beating its wings, the serpent creates hurricanes, tornados and deluge. Thunder is the hissing of the great snake, while lightning is the scratching talon of the bird, breaking open the sky. Sometimes a white swan will sit at each of the four points of the earth to create the blasts of wind. From the West, the Wakinyan or Flyers send storms and create thunder and lightning, revealing their tracks. Sometimes the lightning is the flash of a Thunderbird's eye. When the sun draws clouds around itself, we see the image of the Feathered Serpent.

148

Original Sin and the Fall of the Serpent

We can understand the disparity existing between the nature appreciating beliefs of the Native Americans and their conquerors when we look back in time to trace the concept of original sin.

The Western world had spent centuries exploring the basic nature of man, where moral excellence or goodness was called *virtue*. If one was true to oneself; maintained integrity, and recognized useful acts, one was said to achieve genuine happiness. Socrates taught that the intellect equipped with knowledge directed the will on the right path.

Plato developed the ethical virtues of temperance, courage, prudence and justice. Later adopted by the Church as the *Cardinal Virtues,* courage was changed to fortitude. Courage describes overcoming fear, but fortitude is a firmness of spirit. The former describes moving beyond boundaries and the latter re-establishes them. This is the foreshadowing of the restrictive trappings to come.

The Stoics used the word evil to describe *vice* where evil was merely the inability of man to control his lower passions or animal urges, thus allowing them to rule over his reason. To the Greeks, passions were a disease of the soul and so one learned to expel them from the personality. Just as dis-ease was understood to be a disorderliness or uneasiness of the soul, the repression of our more natural impulses may actually cause a type of uneasiness or dis-ease.

During the early part of the Christian era, in the new, Greek capital of Alexandria, a trend had developed to reinvigorate Hellenistic philosophy with the emerging mystery religions. Neo-Platonism was established by Ammonius Saccas (175-250 AD) and his student Plotinus (204-269AD).

The idea that passion was a *disease* of the soul would evolve into the idea of original sin through the blending of beliefs from Middle Eastern and Hellenistic cultures. Zoroastrian myths from ancient Persia portrayed a good and evil creator, and contributed to how original sin found legs in the Christian version of the Hebrew texts.

This was a time when many mystery religions had taken root in these areas. Constant battle led some to be initiated into the occult or secret knowledge of a devotion centered on a particular god, like Isis or Mithras. By identifying with this divine being and undergoing a ritualistic death and resurrection, one could transcend death.

During the second century AD, the Gnostics taught this version of Christianity. This secret, esoteric tradition was not available to all Christians. Inspired by the teachings of Hinduism and Buddhism, they explored the conflict between matter and spirit. They taught that the sensory world had been created as a mistake and that Jesus had come to deliver man from Yahweh's error.

The intellectual work that was done in Alexandria to merge Greek philosophical ideas with Christian thought was undertaken in large part to combat the growing power of the Gnostics. They feared that Christianity might become just another mystery religion and adopted Neo-Platonism as the philosophical foundation for Christian theology.

In the hands of the Patristic philosopher, St. Augustine (354-430AD), Greek philosophy became subordinate to Christian doctrine. It upheld the idea that man had inherited corruption of his human nature and required redemption of original sin, since Adam had fallen from grace. "In His infinite wisdom, God had given man a free will, which man has so misused as to place him in his present predicament."

In the story of Genesis, Adam was said to disobey Yahweh and his punishment was the toil and difficulty of producing sustenance from the earth. Through death, it was said that man would return to the earth from which he came.

"Behold, the man is become as one of us to know good and evil." Although the couple was banished from Eden, they received their punishment immediately, as if to say that living with a belief in evil becomes its own sentence. The original writings of Genesis did not describe a corrupt nature that required redemption. Jesus had interpreted *sin* as something a man does, not something he was born into. The stories surrounding his martyr-like death would develop after he died.

Since the writings of the Old Testament did not include the concept of original sin, the New Testament that evolved over later centuries utilizes footnotes when referring to more literal translations each time it uses a word like evil, hell and the devil. Where evil was the idea of man's inability to control his passions, the other two words evolved from the adoption of foreign mythologies.

Somewhere in the numerous translations that led to the creation of the Bible and Christian theology, man became corrupt and the world would be punished for it. Like an unrecognized impulse forced into the closet of denial, the Gnostic approach that the early Church Fathers sought to repress is ultimately what Christianity has become. The Gnostic idea of an imperfect creation now requires a ritualistic death and resurrection to overcome mortality.

The Twins: The Reward for Being Bad

In the trying relationship between the Twins and Earth Maker, a similar relationship can be seen in the Genesis story of the twins, Esau and Jacob. It describes man struggling with and questioning the creator from the beginning. Flesh and Stump appear to demonstrate a lack of respect for Earth Maker. Jacob too, was deceitful, usurped his brother's birthright, and yet, won the favor of Yahweh.

Even while Jacob and Esau were in her womb, Rebekah felt their internal struggle and worried for her own life. In the same way that Stump is described as an outdoor child, Esau was a hunter and was described as a *man of the field*. Like Flesh who stayed indoors with his father, Jacob is described as a quiet *man of tents* who stayed near his father.

Flesh and Stump ignored the commands of their father, and Jacob too, deceived his father Isaac, in order to receive his blessing. He pretended to be Esau to receive the blessing, and had to flee to avoid Esau's wrath. On the way, Jacob dreamed of a ladder or ramp that led to and from heaven, similar to the Shamanic realm accessed by the Medicine Men. Although Jacob clearly recognized the dream to be a visit from Yahweh, he negotiated and demanded that Yahweh keep him safe on his journey before vowing his allegiance in return.

When Jacob returned home many years later, he wrestled with a *mysterious adversary* during the night. In dreams, all characters are aspects of us, and when Jacob touches the adversary's thigh, he feels his own thigh strained in return. In the morning, neither was winning and the adversary said: "Let me go for the day breaketh." Again, Jacob demanded a blessing before he was willing to let go. Jacob is told that he wrestled with Yahweh and prevailed. He was renamed *Israel*, which means *"he who striveth with Yahweh."*

It would appear that there is more to the Great Mystery than the shackles "thou shalt" places upon us. Our earliest stories reveal a relationship, not of punishment and piety, but of one that allows for the expression of our questions and natural curiosity. Even in a mythology of evil, we see how the hero gains the Creator's favor by striving.

Lightning: Grounding the Positive and Negative

Lightning was viewed as divine wrath in our myths. At the same time, it is described as life-giving and ignites the sleeping seeds below the earth. In dreams, lightning is the insight that can come in a flash to split the darkness. Just as the Thunder Beings move contrary to everything and symbolize how rigidity must give way, lightning can teach us much about balancing the idea of good and evil. Lightning is simply nature's way of redistributing the imbalance of positive and negative energy in the atmosphere.

At the molecular level, opposite forces generate movement and vitality where positive and negative forces are *equal*. Knowledge of good and evil altered our existence, although it would appear it was from the sense that unnatural absolutes *arrest* our growth. When we look back in time, we discover how the idea of evil was nothing more than the conflicting beliefs and political rivalries existing between religious sects.

Regardless of how we measure the landscape, the idea that separates good and evil is a place of ambiguities. Within these unacknowledged absolutes, problems arise. We use words to give contrasting ideas added meaning: up/down, sound/silence, good/bad, where one is simply a measurement of the other. Neither can describe the essence of *what is*.

Without understanding *how* we may have broken a taboo against conscience, we may only experience the unrecognized conflict as a disempowering situation. Just as ideas were manipulated to lead civilization away from an appreciation of the natural, the psyche can fall prey to a similar peril.

In the early centuries, the men of Alexandria set about creating what would become a handbook for the living. Greek philosophy along with various Middle Eastern and Gnostic beliefs were being translated, edited, added and deleted. By synthesizing the rational ideas of the Greeks with Christian teachings, the Bible was created. Its power to change the course of human events is unquestionable.

One important element of Greek philosophy however, would not have supported the idea of original sin. Its absence from the foundation of this theology would ultimately give rise to its instability. While the Bible was being assembled, there appears to have been a complete disregard for the writings of Aristotle. As Plato's gifted student, and the tutor of Alexander, Aristotle would come to be known as *The Philosopher*. More than eleven centuries would pass before his writings would be brought forward from obscurity to unleash the Enlightenment.

Resurrecting Aristotle

While we may never fully understand the true interpretation of Plato's evil, Aristotle provided an explanation for imperfection. He taught that the flaws in nature were due to the substance that the orchestrating force of life utilized to achieve perfection. The inability of matter to fully realize its form was similar to a sculptor using brittle or faulty material to achieve his vision. Nothing in nature is perfect; this is at the root of why it explores change.

At the beginning of the thirteenth century AD, most of the Western world was unfamiliar with Aristotle's ideas. All teaching, recording, and social regulation had been under the strict control of the Church. When universities developed, Greek texts became available from Islamic sources. Since Islam had promoted a tolerance for *all* ideas, Arabian scholars had continued access to the ancient writings of classical Greece. Jewish scholars translated these works from Arabic into Hebrew, while texts were also being translated into Latin. As direct translations from Greek to Latin became available, scholars could read for themselves the works of the classical Greek philosophers.

From the twelfth century onwards there was a change in emphasis that led to a re-birth of this long, lost tradition leading to *Humanism* and *Rationalism*. The Protestant Reformation against the Catholic Church took root under the teachings of Martin Luther and John Calvin. A movement began that promoted personal study of the Bible instead of blindly following ecclesiastical doctrines. In England, the Protestants were called Puritans and these were the people, who primarily settled the North American colonies.

In response to the growing crisis in the Church, a Counter-Reformation developed and in the fifteenth century AD, the Inquisition was re-established in Spain and Italy. Ferdinand and Isabella led the re-conquest of Spain as a Crusade. They set out to firmly establish Catholicism as its only religion.

Jews and Muslims had co-existed with Christians peacefully for many centuries in Spain. Their ideas were now viewed as a threat to security and they were eradicated through a mixture of ethnic cleansing and expulsion.

It was in this heated environment of defending the Church against a movement that sought the freedom of thought that the conquistadors and missionaries vigorously sailed across the ocean. Behind them, came the Protestants or Puritans in search of religious freedom. They held their Holy Book in front of them, believing it to be a work of faith and not reason. Whatever ideas had taken form in the New World prior to their arrival would be buried with the people they sought to conquer.

The Shaman, the Trickster and the Medicine

Those who approach alternative medicine to cure cancer realize that there is a need to break through a shell to resurrect hurt and anger. In many cases, it is the first time someone stops to explore *what they really feel.* Dream-work can reveal the symbolism behind its manifestation. Like the Medicine Men's healing methods, *how* and *where* someone is affected by illness is important in understanding *why.*

The Medicine Men utilized a type of second sight to cure illness. Recognizing an imbalance between the physical and spiritual, they could cure someone of what we might call *unrecognized guilt.* If a person fell ill, the Shaman uncovered how they had offended the clan's totem as a taboo in some way.

The beliefs that condemned mankind to the Dark Ages reveal how conscience can leave our more organic nature in the dark. Ideas that are incompatible with a strict order of beliefs can unwittingly establish incomprehensible or vague boundaries. The healing requires that we understand these inconsistencies. In the same way that the Shaman obtains a totem or animal guide to heal illness, our dreams of animals and reptiles attempt to resurrect our repressed and vital nature.

The Trickster stories that are so prevalent in the mythologies of the Americas activate the mechanisms of the Shamanic journey. Like dreaming, they offer a mysterious way *through* something that transcends a rational approach. We see this when the friend of Redhorn's sons allows his body to be eaten: "they broke his bones and made him whole again." This sacrifice of the physical body is a sacred initiation into spiritual Shamanism.

Raven and other Tricksters are always described as ravenous or hungry. Like Mimir in his exchange with Odin, transcendental initiation may require an eye and eventually consume the entire body in a Shamanic or alchemical ritual of rebirth. By releasing an attachment to the physical vehicle, participation with a holistic perspective is achieved to initiate healing.

In most cases, what Trickster does will start as the opposite of what is considered *sacred.* Through a ritualistic dance, mysterious steps unfold as the stories are interwoven with bits and pieces of truth and insight. Most myths tell a story of transformation taught in a non-rational way. Whether stories were told to exchange information in a cultural underground or to share the hero's tale of inspiration, like dreams, myths are a way of experiencing existence beyond rote and reason.

In the end, the guides return to their respective realms and the initiate is given the token of the experience or a *Thunderbird Warbundle.*

This commemorates the bolt out of the blue insight or inspiration that becomes the treasure as we begin to awaken.

The *heyoka*, like the Thunder Beings and Trickster, is a sacred clown in the clan who is also the guardian of truth. He turns ritual topsy-turvy to help others understand the self-limiting boundaries of rational thought. We recognize Trickster as both the artist and comedian who shake things up in society. Trickster personifies the opposite of ritual, where we can learn from the intangible. Similarly, the cryptic nature of dreams allows us to wake up to the obscure mysteries taking place within the psyche. In a lightning flash, or through the unexpected, Trickster coaches us beyond limitation and teaches us to laugh at ourselves.

Trickster is found in many cultures around the world, acting as both hero and clown. Most Trickster stories were told during winter, around the campfire to rouse the clan from stagnation. It was a way of disengaging fear and reactivating what lies dormant. Trickster invites the lightning to awaken the sleeping seeds of inertia. This character does more than make us laugh. He unleashes something more fundamental and primordial that would hoard our vital and instinctual energy. He points to the other way with the promise of insight from traveling the road *we have not taken before.*

Trickster plants a whoopee cushion within the psyche, triggering laughter when we know the time is not appropriate. Humor often arises when we perceive an incongruity. Cloaked as the Fool, he points to the middle way between absolutes or the conflicting ideas that stunt our growth. Presenting us with a wild card of possibilities, Trickster is not afraid to send us out with mismatched shoes during an important presentation. Teaching us a lesson of humility, we find this Jester of the inner landscape, making us laugh at ourselves in all of our serious attempts to be certain.

Symbolically, Trickster is the power of humor that makes us gasp and stop what we are doing. A burst of laughter allows us to experience a moment when life doesn't have to be so serious. Instead of finding our home in the absolute, we are forced out like a hobo in search of a train. Humiliated and riding in a boxcar, we encounter everything we believed we'd never experience. In our own way, we are forced to wrestle with the *mysterious adversary* that unleashes the blessing of our *real* identity. We have no choice but to shake our heads and laugh when the rug is pulled out from beneath our house of cards. *"Oh my, is this what life feels like down here in the gutter? I can't tell you why, but I suddenly feel human again."*

Trickster is the *Freudian slip*, or late night comedian who says what nobody else would dare say. He makes us blurt out the comical truth when in all gravity we have found ourselves trapped in our own illogical ideas. Popular comedy in culture coincides with periods of humiliation. All we do to *uphold truth and principles* is usually the opposite of what is required for natural growth and harmony.

Trickster inspires our dreams of going to school in our underwear when what we most want is to abide by the golden rule. It is Trickster, who removes the bathroom walls in our dreams where we have no choice but to of relieve ourselves in public. "Let go...live...find your human side and laugh." He is the breath of fresh air we find at the top of the mountain or sometimes, face down in a puddle, in our migratory journey across the psychic landscape.

The natives grasped a clearer picture of balancing an appreciation for all things, natural and divine. Their culture resembles a fabric spun of a more earthy texture, and their highly developed instinctual sense gave them access to uncharted territory. With a mixture of astute cleverness, refined instinct and a humorous approach to ritual, their tales provide a valuable contribution to our understanding of the psyche and our potential.

Personifying *abreaction*, Trickster is not unlike the sudden unconscious physical twitch or emotional response that can reveal *that thing* we try desperately to repress. This sudden gesture can point to a wellspring of healing. In the Indian tales, he is creator, hero and purveyor of access to the hidden realms. Comparing the Indian's Trickster to other Trickster characters, we find that he not only breaks structures but also becomes a guide, enabling us to move toward dynamic and flexible thinking.

Hermes, god of the crossroads, is another Trickster who confounds and regulates transcendental access. Trickster emerges as Loki of the Norseman, Monkey and Chen of China, Legba and Edshu of Africa, the Fool of the Tarot and the foolish character of Percival as he finds his way in the world by only instinct. These cunning and humorous characters push us beyond our self imposed restraints. Regardless of its form, Trickster is the rebel against authority and the breaker of taboos. Trickster teaches us that laughter is indeed, the best medicine.

Dreaming moves us back and forth to transcend our absolutes in a type of *transcendental looping*. As we dig beneath consciousness to resurrect the dreamscape, we capture inspired clues that reveal what we fail to recognize about ourselves. The looping in between different aspects of awareness provides us with a change in perspective. We are able to identify alternative views of what we take for granted. Trickster stories jar and re-position awareness, which is sometimes the only way in which we can be brought deeper into the Great Mystery.

Like Raven, we are oftentimes thwarted by the use of logic. We find ourselves swimming in circles where only the fish can tell us that we are dog paddling near the shore. When we attempt to nourish ourselves upon the fish we capture, we find that, like an outworn idea, it has already died. We must "bury the fish to eat later," or chew on the enlightenment awhile. Only by walking away, or disengaging from absolute thinking in an objective way, do we realize that the things we are afraid of are simply "a stump with its branch jutting out." All that grows and frightens us near the shoreline of a more holistic perspective can also be used to initiate our healing.

The Indians approached the Great Mystery differently than those who came to their shores because they respected the natural world as a place of benevolence. Although the Puritans worshipped the miracles of a long ago era, the Indians acknowledged how that miracle takes place everyday.

We discover the unusual, while standing in a familiar place, only when we remember that the world is fundamentally unknowable. In this way, we discover miracles because we weren't expecting anything.

The Healing Journey

To understand how mind might heal illness, we need to understand how mind created illness. We accept the idea of psychosomatic illness but shy away from a belief in psychosomatic healing. Just as the body knows how to heal a wound, mind is aware of illness and in some cases has created it. It is not punishment; it offers a time out that will allow us to get back on track.

The body has intelligence that transcends the knowledge of even our greatest doctors. We are born knowing how to breathe, blink, coagulate blood, heal wounds, sweat, shiver, circulate blood, pump our heart, digest food, combat illness through our immune system and we also dream our way to wellness *without doing anything.*

To move toward wellness is to recognize our relationship to what unfolds. Situations serve us and we need to understand how and why. All organs and tissues of the body are composed of cells. When the physician taps the leg, it jerks because sensations are transmitted along sensory nerves. The neurons in our brains are continuously eliciting action from our bodies and in this way, the mind communicates with the body constantly. *During illness, we forget that the mind holds enormous power over the body.*

Freud believed ritualistic ideas or critical judgments could become *dangerous*. In our effort to get the world just right, we develop a rigidity of thought that makes it difficult to flow harmoniously with new and evolving situations. To harmonize with change requires that we remain fluid and free from absolutes. A desire for perfection is an illusion of judgment that can only perpetuate our suffering.

On the way to our ritualistic prison, we have the opportunity to dance with Trickster. By revealing the contradictions apparent in opposites, we can arrive in the middle ground between absolutes. When we actively *wonder,* we can push beyond the boundaries that trap us.

Science has barely transcended the ideas of ancient times as if we swim in circles near the shoreline. The symbolism of fish in our dreams always offers the treasure of insight. They look at us the way that fish will do, amused at how we continuously dog paddle away from the earth. We could just as easily put our feet down and walk upon it.

"You have noticed that everything that an Indian does is in a circle," Black Elk would say. "That is because the Power of the World always works in circles, and everything tries to be round...The life of a man is a circle from childhood to childhood, and so it is in everything where power moves.

"You have noticed that truth comes into this world with two faces. One is sad with suffering, and the other laughs; but it is the same face, laughing or weeping. When people are already in despair, maybe the laughing is better for them; and when they feel too good and are too sure of being safe, maybe the weeping face is better." Laughter, tears, the ability to feel again, can break our defenses and remind us that we are natural creatures in a natural world.

Moving beyond the known, we encounter the opposite and eventually come to see it as the same thing only viewed from a different shoreline. Our journey there and back is always represented as a circle. This is because we need not go anywhere, but merely change our perspective. What we experience *out there* always reflects our inner growth.

Approaching the transcendental realm releases us from the illusion of certainty. When we seek to heal ourselves, something very fundamental and organic is available to us. As the repressed, but vital energy that can be observed as nature's evolutionary energy, we know its release will ensure our continued survival. Within the psyche, anything that would impede the free flowing expression of our nature will inspire the activation of Trickster. When structured thought inhibits our further evolution and instinctual drives, we meet Trickster somewhere on the frontier. As an aspect of the transcendental function, he demands balance and may actually be the Self, donning the animal skins of the id. In ancient snake worship, we recognized how shedding the old skin in our circular journey through life encouraged wellness. If we cannot understand Trickster as revealing something good, we will always travel to the opposite shore and call it evil. What is not owned and empowered can only be said to hold power over us. This is the illusion that changed the world into a place of victims.

The Indians celebrated Trickster as part of the Great Mystery, which displayed many faces. At the psychic trading post, we can trade our anger for compassion; we can exchange our robe for animal skins and we can release our pain for laughter. We can break the shell that holds us prisoner to the illusion of certainty, unleashing renewal that dances like the whirlwind across the inner landscape.

Guilt is nothing more than the misunderstanding occurring between our uniqueness and our need for conformity. Should we hold to unrealistic or unnatural absolutes, the natural drive for continual growth can turn back upon us in the form of illness.

On those shores long ago, we can imagine the missionaries and Puritans waving their bible at the natives. One Native American would write: "If you take the Bible and put it out in the wind and rain, soon the paper in which the words are printed will disintegrate and the words will be gone. Our bible is the wind."

Only through the free activation of all aspects of our nature, can we feel alive and participate in the mystery of life. Judgment is a shell that sometimes must be painfully broken and forcefully removed, if it would keep us from growing.

By learning to see with the heart and understand how it can lead us to actualize our destiny, we too, may appreciate the stories told by the trees and rocks. Their message is simple: access the inner design of whatever nature intended us to be. In time, we discover that even the wind can become our teacher.

Chapter Seven
Gilgamesh and the Shadow's Snare

Ancient Tales of the Middle East
The Victim and the Forest of Fear

> "I tried to think of some way
> to let my face become yours.
> 'Could I whisper in your ear
> a dream I've had? You're the only one
> I've told this to.'
> You tilt your head, laughing
> as if: 'I know the trick you're hatching, but go ahead.'"
>
> *The Least Figure*, Rumi *(Afghanistan)*

In ancient times, the shadow was believed to be a double that mirrored the soul of the individual. Therapists also view the *Shadow* as a double existence. Like the shadow that follows our every movement, we tend to project our disowned power and non-integrated qualities onto the situations we face. Perhaps that is why the lessons we learn from life attempt to release it. Life has more to do with teaching us about what is going on *in here* rather than *out there*.

"Everyone carries a Shadow," Jung wrote, "and the less it is embodied in the individual's conscious life, the blacker and denser it is." When these unrecognized aspects work their way into experiential reality, they can confront us in the guise of another. Through conflict, we are given the opportunity to learn from one masked as the enemy, but who has come to make our inner truth accessible.

If we observe nature, we see its tremendous power to renew itself, although we fail to realize that this same power is inside of us. The more we fight against change, the more our experiences become conflicted. Understanding how the Shadow is integrated is another aspect of waking to the healing power of our dreams.

In the stories originating in the Middle East, we come to the meeting ground of converging beliefs. The myths born of this region reflect a common thread weaving many of the world's religions together.

While we can observe the foundation of their unified beliefs, the same ideas have created many wars.

The Shadow as a Ballast

Ironically, we can see the Shadow at work in the relationship between the two men who gave it definition. Bitterness developed between Freud and Jung after they were originally drawn together by their mutual beliefs. The neurosis Freud observed in himself and his siblings led him at one time to question whether his father may have committed incest. Later, he would reverse this view to consider the harbored desires of the infant, leading to his concept of the Oedipal Stage of childhood.

Jung experienced a vivid imagination, remarkable dreams and powerful fantasies that were contrary to the religion of his clerical father. In light of his father's failing beliefs, he tried to communicate his inspired vision. The conflict that arose in the relationship between Freud and Jung can be understood by examining their childhood and early relationships. Each explored in the other, the attraction and repulsion dynamic of what their growing ego's had deemed unacceptable. They acted as ballast for each other where their individual differences allowed them to access their deeper insights.

Freud viewed the spiritual drive as the sublimation of repressed animal instincts, and described the devil as nothing more than our repressed and *projected* disowned power. After the break from Freud, Jung deliberately explored his fantasies and concluded that we are all inspired by what he termed the *collective unconscious*. In Jung's view, the obscure and neglected texts of ancient myths shed light upon dream symbolism. By analyzing thousands of dreams, similar symbols emerged from the dreams of different patients. These were ancient images of which, the dreamer had no prior knowledge and suggested an inherent source of primordial inspiration. He later helped clients to identify their *personal myths* through dream interpretation.

Freud described repression as "a shadow that falls over the ego," paralyzing its ability to perceive in the present. He recognized how repression arrested a way of being, which projected it as conflict and colored experience. One failed to observe experience objectively, but witnessed an "overlay where the past infused over the present through projection." As a type of defense mechanism, he believed repression *worked to keep the truth inaccessible.*

He also explored *fixation* and *fetishes* as ideas that evoked a sense of attraction at the same time that they activated repulsion, leading one toward a type of *hypnotic* compulsion. An urge that initially sought pleasure brought instead, displeasure as the pathway from urge to satisfaction became distorted. This convergence of feeling is at the root of the intense emotional response or *charge* created when we encounter our Shadow in another. Understanding the Shadow is central to our empowerment and wellness. When we can understand and transcend the initial displeasure arising in this type of encounter, we are able to access the truth that we keep hidden.

While Freud hinted at it, Jung pioneered the study of the *Shadow* and referred to it as the repressed and undeveloped aspects of the personality. Their diverging ideas over the nature of the unconscious created a schism between them. It demonstrates the enormous power the *Shadow* holds over us as our fear of *accepting* the unknown. Although they both explored the unconscious to understand repression, their personal experiences led them to describe its contents differently. Where Freud projected his sexual frustration into his interpretations, Jung came to project his strong need for spiritual freedom. Freud would have been threatened by Jung's sense of freedom and wholeness, while Jung would have bristled at the idea of such a limited system of interpretation focused only on repressed fantasies. They both were right.

Jung described *projection* as changing "the world into the replica of one's unknown face. The more projections are thrust between the subject and the environment, the harder it is for the ego to see through its illusions." He described the Shadow as those dark, unwanted, and unrecognized qualities of the ego that were deemed negative, and therefore, repressed.

Understanding the creation, repression and ultimate resurrection of the Shadow is another aspect of the healing journey. As Victims, we cannot acknowledge our fixation on conflicted relationships, and therefore fight against the *illusion* of our differences.

In this chapter, we explore the Shadow through the dynamics of our relationships with others. The current conflict born of religious beliefs embodies how the Shadow can take on the face of the enemy. The Hebrews were both *followed* and *persecuted* at the same time. The same cultures that embraced their beliefs are the ones that continue to persecute them. This demonstrates Freud's idea of the attraction/repulsion dynamic behind fixation. If we were to peel away the layers of *charge* or rising emotion, we would uncover the ways in which we are alike.

Long before the Hebrew stories were put into texts, there existed a more ancient work of literature called the *Epic of Gilgamesh.* It suggests the ideas behind the building of a tower, erected by mortals who wanted to become like gods. The story of the Tower of Babel describes how its construction led the gods to create different dialects to develop a type of confusion between the races. *Each time we definitively construct the right way, we build ritualistic prisons that can only separate us.* The story suggests that once, nothing was beyond our reach, as we attempted to explore our power as a species. The building of this tower put spiritual concerns above human kindness and was therefore, destroyed.

As a *Victim*, we are lost in a world of projection, casting our Shadow or disowned vitality upon others. Symbolically, towers are structures built and rooted in the past, although we climb into them daily to view the present. In mythical stories, the towers always fall or are destroyed because they embody how we lack tolerance and remain a prisoner to our fear of change.

We traveled to the underworld to explore our repressed landscapes. Now we enter a *forest*, surrounded by *mountains* and follow Gilgamesh as he goes to confront the Shadow, Humbaba. Instead of the underworld, we move into a landscape even closer to conscious awareness. Humbaba, the evil one is said to be the Forest's *Watchman*. Embodying any encounter with the Shadow, the heroes believe that Humbaba is evil and must be destroyed.

In the forest and in our dreams of trees we discover the roots of our heritage. They also symbolize the root within, where we can be fed by the germinating power of life. We dream of mountains when we are on the precipice of change. In this mythical Forest of Fear and upon the Mountain of Wider Awareness, we embark on a journey to understand the need to *resurrect* and *not destroy* the Shadow. It is not the enemy that threatens us, but our fear of unleashing the power, which takes form as the enemy.

Trees and mountains in dreams personify what Freud termed preconscious or hypnotherapists call the subconscious. They represent the region of the psyche that is associated with fear and projection. In this Forest, we meet the Trapper who embodies how the Shadow is created and sustained. Its close proximity to conscious awareness provides two possibilities: on the one hand, it is easily activated in projection, although it also suggests accessible vitality that can *easily* be brought back into conscious awareness.

As *Victims*, conflict becomes a meeting ground where we can explore our fear and projection tendencies. The inability to perceive projection as a mask to our unrecognized power, keeps us in the perspective of always being attacked.

When we encounter someone that pushes our buttons, we have the opportunity to learn something unknown about ourselves. By viewing conflict as a learning experience, we can discover the unrecognized, but valuable part of our disowned nature.

The *Victim* believes something must be defended or protected. At the core of any conflict is a voice seeking to be released from repression. Through the encounter, we oftentimes discover *our own voice*. Beyond our *every-day voice*, which defends our beliefs, is the voice that we are attempting to subdue. When we experience fear in any encounter, we can see it as a call to observe with an open mind; this front row seat allows us to observe the same type of healing that comes forward in our dreams.

The *Epic of Gilgamesh* comes to us from the blending of various cultures that traveled through the Mesopotamian Valley of modern Iraq. Its narrator invites us to: *"touch the threshold…it is ancient."* As if time is indeed, something without beginning or end, we find ourselves transported to this very threshold today. The *Shadow* portrays our potential for change and oftentimes becomes the *political enemy*. While we hold fast to our differences, nothing positive evolves. In a world of endless possibilities, we must ask ourselves why we continually recreate the past.

Through the adventures of this culture hero, we explore our passion to seek something meaningful in existence as we embark on a quest for immortality. His story personifies our yearning to reach the heavens to become like gods, although Gilgamesh learns about the boundaries of authentic power *here and now*. Immortality is simply a perspective, which releases time's hold on an ever evolving present.

In the nineteenth century, archeologists were resurrecting the buried and forgotten civilizations of the Middle East and came upon the tablets containing the stories of Gilgamesh. Deciphered from cuneiform, it appeared to give detail to the missing period between Noah and Abraham of the Old Testament. It tells us about the building of monuments to become like gods, and a place called Babel and we are also given the details of the Great Flood.

This ancient Babylonian king of 2700BC resembles the Hebrew characters of Nimrod of the empire of Babel, and Nebuchadnezzar who ruled Babylon. Gilgamesh is arrogant and defiant, ruling the people as a despot. This story was translated into many languages and was shared among the different civilizations occupying the Tigris-Euphrates valley.

First recorded in the Sumerian language in 2000BC, the best surviving version comes from twelve stone tablets written in the Akkadian language. This was a Semitic language related to Hebrew that was spoken by the Babylonians. One early version of this epic describes an army accompanying Gilgamesh, and it appears to be the inspiration for the Greek tale of Jason and the Argonauts. By piecing together the many versions, scholars were able to produce the translation that we know today.

Civilizations of the Fertile Crescent

The Fertile Crescent is an area of the Middle East that extends from the North coast of the Persian Gulf to the East coast of the Mediterranean. This area gave rise to the ancient Sumerian, Hebrew and Phoenician civilizations because of the natural irrigation occurring in this semi-arid land. Along the Tigris and Euphrates Rivers, Neolithic people began farming in Mesopotamia in 6000BC. By 3000BC, the Sumerians had settled there and developed cuneiform writing. Prior to being absorbed into the Persian Empire of modern Iran in 331BC, this area fell under Babylonian, Assyrian and Chaldean rule.

The Genesis stories of the Old Testament tell us of Abraham, born in Ur of the Chaldees, an area south of Babylonia in the Mesopotamian Valley. Zoroastrianism of ancient Persia personified good and evil as characters. While the ancient Hebrew texts do not mention a devil, the Persian Empire dominated this region for a time, and may have influenced the beliefs of its inhabitants. The historical interchange of Judeo Christian ideas with the mythologies of Assyria, Babylon and Persia became more apparent as the nineteenth century archeologists began deciphering the ancient cuneiform records.

We can imagine Trickster standing like a scarecrow upon history's great tapestry, teasing us with a shell game. The very devil that the Christians fight against *over there* was adopted by stories of this region, told so long ago that nobody knows how they started. Islamic fundamentalists fight against the idea of modernism as the devil *over here*, forgetting how they kept the lamp of reason burning during the West's darkest hour. When we attempt to identify who gave what to whom and when, we might as well put down our weapons and laugh.

The people called Semites are said to have descended from Shem, one of Noah's sons. They speak a Semitic language, which includes Arabic and Hebrew. Although these groups might be enemies today, their languages and stories reflect an ancient and common heritage.

In the Epic of Gilgamesh, we are told about a flood, a story which emerges from virtually every culture. Even as far away as China, we are told how a few mortals were saved because a god told them to build a boat. Since the beginning of time, we seem to share a *mythical rumor* of how a great body of water once engulfed us. This may be nothing more than the universal memory of our "oceanic connectivity" to the great waters of the unconscious.

Abraham, a descendent of Shem, became the father of the Hebrew people. He founded Judaism that records *one* version of history for this region. Abraham and Sarah were originally childless and Sarah

166

offered her Egyptian handmaid, Hagar to Abraham so they might conceive a child. Once Hagar became pregnant, Sarah grew angry, and Hagar was forced to run away in fear. An angel comforted Sarah and told her that she would give birth to a child, named Ishmael.

After Ishmael's birth, Yahweh established a covenant with Abraham, requiring the circumcision of all males. He told Abraham how Sarah would also have a child in her old age, named Isaac. While Isaac would carry on his line, Abraham inquired about the well being of his first son, Ishmael. He was told Ishmael would beget twelve princes and become a leader of men.

Abraham was commanded by Yahweh to sacrifice his son, Isaac. He obeyed, although Isaac was spared only after Abraham proved his willingness to do so. He led his people from Mesopotamia to the promised land of Canaan. While Isaac carried forward the covenant with the Israelites, Ishmael and Hagar migrated across the desert. Yahweh saved them and Ishmael was said to have fathered the nation of the Arabs. In this way, both Jews and Arabs find their roots as descendents of Abraham and Islamic tradition says Hagar and Ishmael settled in Mecca.

Arabs are descended from Bedouins or *badawi*, an Arabic word for desert. In its English form, it means one who inhabits the desert. The Bedouin values are respected by all Arabs and are based on generosity, emotional intensity, hospitality and the upholding of vendettas to protect honor. It was customary to send a city dwelling Arab youth to the *Nobles* or camel-breeding Bedouin tribes in the Syrian Desert. This gave them exposure to the values and mores of their ancestors.

Bedouins represent no more than ten percent of today's Arab population although most Arabs can claim Bedouin descent. Arabs are those who speak Arabic, and identify with the Arab culture spread abroad through the adoption of Islam. While Islam is often associated with the Arabs, there are Islamic people, like the Iranians, who are not of Arab descent. Additionally, there are Arabs who do not practice the Islamic religion.

Ancient Persia is the area of modern Iran, which means land of the Aryans. Like India, tribes from the North had migrated into its heartland, making their cultural heritage similar. In 1000BC, the Persian Empire began its rise to power and became one of the greatest empires of ancient times. Iranians pride themselves as custodians of the ancient Persian culture and many attribute this Persian influence to the Golden Age and growth of Islam.

Where ancient Phoenicia was strategically positioned for trade between the Fertile Crescent and the West, ancient Persia held the area where the Fertile Crescent traded with the Far East. Through the centuries,

Turk and Mongol invaders had conquered and assimilated into this region. The Persian Empire declined when Arab armies conquered Persia in the name of Islam, during the seventh century. Their refined culture was given over to the Arabs who had wandered the desert as Bedouin.

With the birth of Islam, a schism emerged that is almost as old as the religion. Two diverging sects, Shi'ite and Sunnite reflect a separate belief as to who had been the true successor of the Prophet, Muhammad. While the Sunnites honor the first three Caliphs, the Shi'ites reject them, recognizing Ali, Muhammad's son in law as his rightful successor.

All industrialized societies of the twentieth century need oil. Sixty four percent of the world's oil is found in the Persian Gulf, and Iran is strategically positioned to control its flow. In the stories of the *Arabian Nights*, we find magic oil lamps, housing powerful Jinn. The roots of the Jinn stories can also be found in the *Epic of Gilgamesh* where Humbaba pleads with Gilgamesh to release him, promising to bestow great riches.

To the Western world, finding black gold in your backyard is truly the magical stuff of which dreams are made. In contrast, Western cultural influences present their own temptations. The idea of modernism both attracts and repels at the same time. Western influences are considered evil by people of this region, and at odds with their traditional culture. This is because of the way their culture was suffocated and manipulated by Western influences during the nineteenth and twentieth centuries.

When Syria, Palestine and Iraq were under French and British mandates, oil was discovered, coinciding with the invention of the automobile. Iran's geographic location brought it into the center of the rivalry between Britain and Russia. Later Iraq, Iran and Afghanistan would become pawns for the growing conflict between the United States and Russia. Since September 11th, 2001, the greatest threat to the West is believed to be Islamic Fundamentalism and the development of nuclear weapons in Iran.

Representing the power we *believe* others hold over us, we portray the *Shadow* or Jinn for each other: "I swear if you will only let me out, I will not harm you. Release me and I will fulfill all of your desires." This plea is the message coming from both sides: One seeks the freedom to control their own resources, while the other attempts to bestow a different culture. In the meantime, neither side can be certain whether this Jinni is good or evil. Like any Shadow encounter, both just want to put *the power of the unknown* back into the bottle.

The Creation Stories of the Middle East

In the Akkadian creation epic, Apsu was the abyss or the primordial sweet-water ocean of creation. His female counterpart was Tiamat, the dragon of primordial chaos and the salt-water ocean. They coupled to produce Anu, the older deity of ancient Mesopotamia, called An by the Sumerians. His offspring, Enki of the Sumerians or Ea of Akkad and Babylon, both reflect the power of gods whose wisdom is associated *with water*.

Enlil was the greatest of the Sumerian gods and bringer of culture, along with Ninurta as the god of war. Female deities included Aruru, a goddess of creation, Ishtar or Sumerian Ianna, the goddess of love and war, and Ereshkigal, the Queen of the underworld. Similar to Kronos, Uranos and Zeus, Ea killed his father Apsu in a struggle that made his brother Marduk the most powerful god.

Ahura Mazdah was the supreme god of ancient Persia who embodied benevolence and wisdom. He created the dark lord Angra Mainyu, also called Ahriman who became his rival. These two deities personified the battling forces of good and evil on the earth. The most enduring deity to emerge from this region is the Hebrew creator who is said to be nameless. He is sometimes called YHWH, "Yahweh" or Adonai.

The Epic of Gilgamesh

His name was Gilgamesh and from the very day of his birth, he was two-thirds god and one-third man. The great goddess Aruru designed him, planned his body and prepared his form. Shamash, the glorious sun gave him beauty and Adad, the Storm gave him courage. His mother was Ninsun, a goddess noted for her wisdom. His father was Lugulbanda, the great champion and beloved king. And so, Gilgamesh surpassed all others. The form of his body no one can match.

Eleven cubits high is he, nine spans his chest as he turns to see the lands all around him. In Uruk he built walls, a great rampart, a temple for the god of the firmament Anu, and for Ishtar the goddess of love. These temples have no equal.

The Coming of Enkidu

He went out into the world, but there was none whom Gilgamesh could not beat. Armed, he returned to Uruk but in their houses the men of Uruk muttered: "Gilgamesh, noisy Gilgamesh! Arrogant Gilgamesh!" All the young men were gone, defeated by Gilgamesh, and no son was left to his father. All the young girls were made women by Gilgamesh. His lusts were such that no virgin was left to her lover! Not the daughter of a warrior or the wife of a noble. Yet, he is king and should be the people's careful shepherd, and the shepherd of the city. He is wise, handsome and firm as a rock.

In heaven, the gods heard the lament of the people and the gods cried out: "Strong as a wild bull is this Gilgamesh!" The great god Anu heard their cries and to the goddess of creation, Aruru – all the gods cried: "You created this Gilgamesh! Well, create him his equal! Let him look as into mirrors - Give a second self to him; yes, rushing winds meet rushing winds! Let them flow heart to heart against each other. Give them each other to fight, leaving Uruk in peace!"

The goddess of creation formed an image in her mind and there, it was conceived. Enkidu was made of material that composed the great god Anu, he of the firmament. Plunging her hands down into water, she pinched off a little clay. She let it drop into the wilderness and thus the noble Enkidu was born.

He had the strength of Ninurta, the god of war. His form was rough and he had long hair like that of a goddess. It waved like corn filaments, like Nisaba, the goddess of corn.

His body was covered with matted hair like the skins of cattle and like Samuqan's, the god of cattle. Enkidu was innocent of mankind and knew nothing of cultivated land. He ate the grass in the hills with the gazelles as they played together. Along with the herds, he loved the water hole and tasted the joy of the water with the herds of wild game. One day, by the water hole he met the Trapper. Face to face they met because the herds of wild game had strayed into the Trapper's territory. Three times they met and each day the Trapper was terrified, frozen stiff with fear.

He took the game home but was unable to speak and was numb with fright. In time, the Trapper's face altered; became new - a long journey does that to one, gives a new visage upon returning. The Trapper spoke with awe in his heart to his father: "Father, what a man! No other like him! He comes from the hills, strongest alive! A star in heaven his strength, and he resembles an immortal. He eats grass and wanders the hills with the beasts, grazing in your land and visiting the wells. I am afraid of him and have stayed far away. Each day he fills in my pits, tears up my game traps, helps the beasts to escape and they are able to slip through my fingers."

His father said: "My son, in Uruk lives Gilgamesh. None can withstand him and none has surpassed him. He is as strong as a star in heaven and resembles an immortal. Go to Uruk, find Gilgamesh and extol the strength of this wild man. Ask him to give you a hierodule or sacred slave from the Temple of Ishtar. Such a child of pleasure, she will use her feminine powers to subdue this wild man. When he goes to the wells, he will embrace the priestess and the wild beasts will reject him."

The Trapper went to Uruk to tell Gilgamesh about the wild man: "A man unlike any other is roaming now in my pastures; he is strong like a star from heaven and I am afraid to approach him. He helps the wild game to escape; he fills in my pits and pulls up my traps." Gilgamesh told the Trapper he should find a priestess from the Temple of Ishtar: "When they embrace, surely the wild beasts will reject him." And so, the Trapper returned with a priestess and waited next to the drinking hole. For three days they waited, facing each other. First day: nothing. Second day: nothing. Third day, yes. The herds came to drink, and Enkidu was with them because he loved the water too.

The priestess saw the wild man from the hills. "There, woman," said the Trapper, "bare your breasts now, to this wild man. Have no shame when you welcome his love. Let him see you naked and let him possess your body. As he approaches, take off your clothes. Lie with him and teach him the savage art of a woman. For as he loves you, then the wild beasts, his companions, will reject him."

She had no shame for this and made herself naked. She welcomed Enkidu's eagerness and enticed him to love. She taught him the woman's art. Six days, seven nights they lay together. Enkidu had forgotten his home, the hills, and was satisfied.

Then he returned to find the wild beasts and when the gazelle saw him, they bolted; when the wild creatures saw him, they fled. Enkidu tried to follow but his body was bound as though with a cord. His knees gave way when he started to run; his swiftness was gone. Enkidu had grown weak because wisdom was in him and the thoughts of man were in his heart. He returned to the priestess and listened intently at her feet.

She said: "You have wisdom Enkidu and now you are as a god. Why the beasts? Why the hills? Come to Uruk of the strong walls and temples. There you will find Gilgamesh. He is strong like a wild bull and lords it over all others." Enkidu heard her words and came to know his own heart.

He longed for a companion and told the priestess: "Take me girl, to Uruk where lives Gilgamesh of perfect strength. He who rages like a bull over all, I will summon him forth and challenge him. I will shout in Uruk that I am the mightiest! Yes, I will change the order of what is! Anyone born on the steppe is mighty, has strength over all others."

She replied: "Then let us go that he may see your face. I will show you Gilgamesh, for I know well where he is. In Uruk there are many ramparts and every day is a festival. Everyone is dressed, perfumed as they rise from their beds. To you who love life, I will find Gilgamesh who also loves life. He is beautiful, radiant in his manhood and exceeds you in strength, so do not be foolish. He was made by the gods with wisdom and will know you are coming before you even arrive. He needs no sleep by day or night, but will have dreamt of your coming before you cross the open plain."

When Gilgamesh rose from his bed, he told his mother his dream: "Mother, in my dream last night there were stars in heaven, and a star like an immortal descended upon me. I tried to lift it up, although it was too heavy for me. I tried to move it, but it would not be moved. Everyone had come to see it. My attraction was like that of a woman. All of my friends kissed its feet. I laid it at your feet and you said it was my equal."

Ninsun who is well loved and wise replied: "Your equal came like a star of heaven and descended upon you. You tried to lift it but it would not be moved. I called it your equal, comparing it to you. Its attraction was like that of a woman and I will tell you why. There is one that will save you and become your companion. He is the strongest of the land, reflecting your strength so that you are drawn to him overwhelmingly. He will never forsake you. Such is your dream."

Gilgamesh had another dream and said to his mother: "In Uruk of the ramparts was an axe and all were gathered around it. Although the people pressed towards it, I laid it at your feet. For me, its attraction was like that of a woman and you called it my equal."

She said: "The axe is a man and I called it your equal. You were drawn to it as a woman, for it was to rival you. It means a strong friend standing by his friend. Yes, he is the strongest of the land." Gilgamesh then spoke to his mother: "A friend, a counselor has come to me from the god, Enlil and now I shall befriend and counsel him."

Just as Gilgamesh revealed his dream, the priestess was revealing it to Enkidu. There came upon Enkidu's heart, the truth of what she said. He heard her words and they were good. She divided her clothing in two: one garment for him and one for her. Holding his hand she led him like a child into the shepherd's tent. When they came to the hut of the shepherds, all of them gathered around him. They pressed around him and were drawn to him; drawn to the wild man.

The priestess was proud of her instruction: "This is a man who is like Gilgamesh in form. He is taller and born of the mountains. Like the essence of the immortals, he is stronger."

Enkidu sat at their table so that he might eat their food. He knew only the milk of wild creatures that he had sucked in the wild. The shepherds placed their food before him and he choked on it. He stared at it, and then at them. Enkidu knows nothing of this; he knows not of eating food. "What is this drink? This strong drink?" He has not been taught it. Bread was set before him - he knows it not. Wine was set before him - he knows it not. Enkidu did not eat bread. Squeezing his eyes together, he simply stared.

The priestess spoke: "Enkidu, eat the bread, it is the staff of life. Drink the wine, it is our sustenance. Drink this strong drink. It is what is done here."

And so, Enkidu ate the food until he was full. He drank that strong drink, seven cups of it. He became merry, his heart exalted and his face shown. He rubbed down his matted hair and oiled his body. He put on the clothes like a bridegroom and became a man. He took arms to hunt the lion so the shepherds could sleep at night. He caught the wolves and lions so the shepherds could lie down in peace. Enkidu became their watchman and was a strong man without rivals.

One day, while at the table, he looked up and saw a man. He asked the priestess: "Girl, bring that man. Why is he here? I must know his name!"

She called to the man: "Sir, where are you going? Why have you taken this, your most difficult course?"

When the man spoke, he spoke to Enkidu: "Into the people's special place…their very own meeting-house, Gilgamesh has intruded! He sets aside the rules and laws for wedlock! On the city he has heaped shame! Strange practices he has imposed upon a city helpless to resist. For the king of fortified Uruk has altered the unaltered way. He has abused and changed the practices. Any new bride from the people is his; Gilgamesh, king of Uruk may mate with any new bride even before the lawful husband may have her! The gods have ordained this in their wisdom…by their will…it was so decreed from the moment of birth when his umbilical cord was cut out."

At the man's words, Enkidu's face paled. Fury grew in his heart and his eyes became frightful. He spoke in anger: "This cannot continue to be! I will go to Uruk and I will meet Gilgamesh. I will bring his excesses to an end!"

The priestess said: "You are exquisite Enkidu! You are like a god in your nature. Who is like you among men? Come Enkidu! Let us go to Uruk." She drew out a single garment and he clothed himself. She led him, holding his hand and like a god, his countenance shown. She led him to the place where the people were gathered together.

When he entered the fortress of Uruk, the people thronged around him. They spoke amongst themselves: "Look how he resembles Gilgamesh in his appearance! He is small in size but stronger in bone. He is a match for Gilgamesh! He is the strongest of the steppe and he once suckled the milk of wild creatures. There will be an endless clash of arms in Uruk!"

The nobles rejoiced: "Here is an honorable hero to match divine Gilgamesh! This is his equal!"

Even for the goddess of love the bridal bed was made ready! She was ready to receive Gilgamesh for his pleasures! As Gilgamesh approached, Enkidu stood in the doorway to bar his entrance. Gilgamesh stood opposed to the might of Enkidu. The divine Gilgamesh was face to face with his equal, Enkidu of the steppes. Gilgamesh recognized his equal who was smaller in size but stronger of bone. He had hair like Gilgamesh, although it was shaggy like animal hair. Gilgamesh thought his hair resembled the grass that sprouted on the steppes.

Gilgamesh drew himself up. He stood before Enkidu who blocked his way with his foot and would not let Gilgamesh enter. They grappled and wrestled like champions. Like bulls they held together as rushing wind met rushing wind. Heart to heart and against, yet they held fast and shattered the doorpost of the holy gate. The wall shook with this fateful act. They struggled in the doorway where the bride awaited Gilgamesh. They fought in the street and battled in the market. In the end, Enkidu was brought to the earth, even while his foot remained on the ground. Gilgamesh had won the contest and Enkidu's anger vanished.

As Gilgamesh turned away, Enkidu said to him: "As one single and unique, your mother bore you. She is the wild cow of the steer folds. Ninsun is wise and strong and you are raised above all others because your strength surpasses the strength of men. Enlil has given you the kingship above all men." Enkidu and Gilgamesh embraced and their friendship was sealed.

The Cedar Forest

Gilgamesh had a dream and Enkidu interpreted it. "The meaning of the dream is this: the father of the gods has given you kingship, such is your destiny; everlasting life is not your destiny. Because of this do not be sad at heart, do not be grieved or oppressed; he has given you power to bind and to loose, to be the darkness and the light of mankind. He has given you the power to conquer and rule. Deal justly with your servants, deal justly before Shamash."

Later, Enkidu's eyes were full of tears and he told Gilgamesh he was oppressed by idleness. It was then that Gilgamesh remembered the Country of the Living and the Land of the Cedars. He said: "I have not written my name on bricks as my destiny decreed. I will go to the Land of the Cedars and I will raise a monument to reach the heavens."

Enkidu sighed bitterly: "I have roamed the Cedar Forest when I traveled with the wild beasts, but its length is ten double hours in every direction. Enlil has appointed Humbaba to guard it and has armed him with sevenfold terrors. He guards the forest so well that although a heifer stirs in the forest sixty double hours away, he hears it. What man would willingly go there to explore its depths? Weakness overpowers anyone who goes near it and it is not an equal struggle, for Humbaba is a warrior and a battering ram. When he roars it is like the torrent of a storm; his breath is like fire and his jaws are death itself. Gilgamesh, this Watchman of the Forest never sleeps."

"Oh my friend," Gilgamesh said: "I have always wanted to climb the Cedar Mountain where fierce Humbaba dwells. He is evil and fearsome to look upon. I wish to slay him and banish the evil from the land. But he lives in the Cedar Forest and I do not know the way. Where is the man that can clamber to heaven? Only the gods live forever and our days are numbered. Our journey is but a breath of wind and already you are afraid. I will go first and you can call out 'forward there is nothing to fear!' Even if I fail, men will say: 'Gilgamesh has fallen in a fight with ferocious Humbaba and he fell fighting on Cedar Mountain.' In this way my name will endure."

The mother of Gilgamesh, who knows all things, lifted her hands toward Shamash the Sun to seek his protection. Shamash told the hero: "Gilgamesh, you are strong but what is the Country of the Living to you?"

Gilgamesh replied: "O Shamash, hear me. In this city, a man dies oppressed at heart. I look over the walls and see the bodies floating on the river and I know that will be my lot also. "Even a man tallest among men cannot reach the heavens and the greatest cannot encompass the earth. I would enter that country to leave my name stamped on a brick as my destiny decreed. Where no man's name is written, I will raise a monument to the gods." Tears ran down his face as he continued: "It is a long and perilous journey to the land of Humbaba. But if you did not want me to do this thing, then why did you stir me with the restless desire to perform it? How can I succeed if you will not help me? I will go and if successful, I will make a glorious offering of gifts to you upon my return."

Shamash accepted his sacrifice and made the winds his allies. He stationed the north wind, the whirlwind, the icy wind, the scorching wind and the storm in the cave to aid him on his journey. Like vipers, like dragons, like a scorching fire, like a serpent that freezes the heart, a destroying flood and the lightning's fork; such were they that Gilgamesh rejoiced. "I will ready my hand. I will fell the Cedar Trees and will make my name endure! I will commission the smith to cast weapons for us."

At the great gate of Uruk, the people gathered and Gilgamesh said: "Oh people of Uruk, I go to see that creature of whom, such things are spoken; the rumor of whose name fills the world. I will conquer him in his Cedar Wood and show the strength of Uruk so that all of the world will know of it. I am committed to this enterprise; to climb the Mountain, cut down the Cedar and leave behind an enduring name."

The elders of Uruk replied: "You are very young Gilgamesh and your heart has swept away your reason. You have no knowledge of what is involved. We are told how Humbaba is strange to see and terrifying. Who can possibly withstand his weapons? For ten thousand double-hours in every direction extends his Great Forest. Who would go down into such a place? Humbaba - his roaring is the Great Flood. His mouth is fire and his breath is death!"

When Gilgamesh heard the words of his advisors, he smiled to his friend: "Now, my friend, thus do they tremble and fear even to speak of fierce Humbaba. Oh Enkidu, together we can face him in his Great Forest of Cedars and gain renown."

Gilgamesh spoke to the people: "Oh elders of Uruk, I go with my friend Enkidu, he of the steppe who has strength. Together we will face fierce Humbaba."

The people pressed around Gilgamesh: "By the will of the gods may you return to the city! Trust not your strength alone! Let Enkidu walk before you, for he has seen the way and has traveled the road. He who leads the way saves his companion and he who knows the path protects his friend.

"Enkidu has seen combat, knows it, knows the way to the Cedar Forest. Over the obstacles and ditches, he will carry you. Let him penetrate and slip through all the passes of the Forest of Humbaba. May Shamash open the unopened path. After slaying Humbaba, which you are attempting, wash then your feet. When time to rest at night, dig a well - may the water of your water-skin be ever pure! And offer cool water to Shamash. And be ever mindful of Lugulbanda, your guardian! Enkidu, we the assembly entrust our king to you. Deliver him back to us!"

They went to Ninsun who offered up incense to Shamash. With the smoke offering in progress, she raised her hands: "Having granted me as my son Gilgamesh, why have you then given him such a restless heart? Why have you made him wish to go on a great journey to the place of Humbaba? He must face a battle strange to him and travel a road unknown to him." She prayed for her son's protection.

She summoned Enkidu and said: "Mighty Enkidu, you who came not from my womb, I have now adopted you; you are my other child like the foundlings they bring to the temple. Serve Gilgamesh as a foundling

176

serves the temple and the priestess who reared him." She placed an amulet around his neck. "In the presence of my women, votaries and hierophants, I entrust my son to you. Bring him back safely."

They departed and after twenty intervals, they broke their fast. After thirty more, they stopped for the night. Fifty were the intervals of each day and in three days they traveled a distance that should have taken one month and fifteen days. They crossed seven Mountains before they came to the Gate of the Forest and Enkidu called out: "Do not go down into the Forest; when I opened the gate, my hand lost its strength."

Gilgamesh thought to himself: 'remember your words when in Uruk? *Come, rise, that you may slay him! Are you not Gilgamesh, the progeny of Great Uruk?*' These words gave him confidence and he told Enkidu: "My friend - canny in combat, you are skilled in battle; only touch my garment and you will not fear death so that the limpness may leave your arm and the weakness may leave your hand."

After arriving at the Green Mountain, the both stood quite still. Silently they looked at the Forest and saw how high the Great Cedars were. They gazed upon the entrance and saw the tracks where Humbaba often tread. It was a fine path, straight and easy to travel. They saw also the Cedar Mountain where the gods lived. The Cedar rose aloft its great luxuriant growth; what cool shade, what delight! Mountain and glade were green with brushwood.

Gilgamesh dug a well before the setting sun and poured out fine meal onto the ground. He said: "Oh Mountain, bring me a favorable dream!" Taking each other by the hand, they lay down to sleep; and sleep that flows from the night lapped over them. Gilgamesh dreamed and at midnight he awoke to tell his friend his dream.

Gilgamesh said: "My divine sleep has been torn from me. My friend, I saw a dream - Oh, how ill omened! How terrifying and disturbing! I seized a wild bull of the steppe; He bellowed and kicked up the earth; he beat up the dust until the sky darkened. My arm was seized and my tongue bitten. I gave way before him. But he provided me fresh water from his water skin."

Enkidu said: "My friend, the god to whom we go is not a wild bull, although his form is mysterious. The wild bull that you saw must be radiant Shamash, the Sun. He will take us by the hand in our dire need and it was Shamash, who gave you the water to drink from his water skin. He is your special god who brings you honor and joins together with Lugulbanda, your father and familiar. In this way we might accomplish fame that may never die."

They took hold of one another and returned to their nightly rest. Sleep descended upon them as if it were the great surge of night. A

177

sudden sleep flew from Gilgamesh. He said: "If you have not waked me, then how do I wake? Enkidu, my friend, I must have seen a dream! Have you not waked me? Aside from that first dream, I now have seen a second dream. In my dream a great mountain fell and pinned me to the ground, trapping my feet beneath it. It was so large that by comparison, we were only small reed flies. A great glare of light overwhelmed me. From the blazing light, a man like none other - such a man as we have never seen - stepped forth from the light. His grace and beauty were greater than the beauty of this world. He freed me from the mountain and gave me water to drink. He quieted my heart and put my feet back on the earth."

Enkidu, the child of the plain spoke to Gilgamesh: "My friend, let us go down into the plain. Let us go take counsel together. Your dream is good. It is excellent. The mountain you saw was Humbaba. Now surely we will seize and kill him. We will throw his body down as the mountain fell on the plain."

The next day they traveled twenty intervals and broke their fast. After thirty more, they stopped for the night. Before Shamash the Sun they dug a well, and Gilgamesh went up the Mountain. He made offering of his fine-meal and intoned: "O Mountain, bring a dream for Enkidu; bring for him a dream of mine to interpret!"

And the mountain did bring a dream for Enkidu. It was an ominous dream; it caused a cold shower to pass over him. It caused him to cower like mountain barley under a storm of rain. Gilgamesh put his chin to his knees and the sleep, which falls upon mankind, fell upon Gilgamesh. He started, full awake and said to his friend: "My friend, have you called me? Why am I awake? Did you touch me? Why have I started so? Did not some god pass by? Why have I gone numb? Why are my limbs numb with fear? My friend, I saw a third dream and this dream was terrible in every way. The heavens were roaring and screaming and the earth was blasted with booming sounds. Darkness descended, like a shroud - a sudden streak of fire as lightning flashed. The clouds grew bloated and full and they rained down death! Then the fire-glow of the skies died out. The fallen fire of the downpour of death crusted into ashes. Oh, let us go down into the plain! There we can take counsel and decide what to do!"

When they went down from the mountain, Gilgamesh gripped the axe and with it, felled the first Cedar. Humbaba, hearing the sound raged with fury: "Who is it who has come - come and interfered with my trees? My trees that have grown on my own Mountains? Who has felled the Cedar?" He roared as he fastened his evil eye upon Gilgamesh: the eye of death.

Just then, the voice of the great god Shamash the Sun came from heaven: "Have no fear. Go forward!" Tears streamed down the face of

Gilgamesh and he replied: "Oh Shamash have I not trod the way that you led me. Have I not taken the way of heavenly Shamash but if you do not send succor, how shall I escape. Until we have fought this man, if man he be or this god, if god he is, the way I took to the Country of the Living will not return me to the city."

Humbaba said to Gilgamesh: "The fool, the stupid man – You should have taken better advice. Why do you now approach me with that Enkidu...that son of a fish? He knows not his father who was the companion of the small turtles, of the large turtles, Enkidu never sucked the milk of his mother." He looked at Enkidu: "In your youth I beheld you. Now should I kill you to satisfy my belly? Shamash brought you, Gilgamesh, and allowed you to reach me. It is through his assistance that you are stepping along thus. Gilgamesh, I will bite through the sinew of your throat and your neck. I will allow the shrieking serpent-bird; the eagle and the raven to eat your flesh!"

Gilgamesh said to Enkidu: "My friend, Humbaba's face keeps changing." Enkidu replied: "Gilgamesh why do you wail so miserably? Use the axe and seize the whip. Do not turn back! Strike with the axe and make your blow strong!"

Shamash in heaven heard the prayer of Gilgamesh and against Humbaba he stirred up the mighty winds: The Great Wind, the North Wind, the South Wind, the Whirlwind, The Storm Wind, the Chill Wind the Tempestuous Wind and The Hot Wind - eight were the winds that rose up against Humbaba. Lo! He cannot move forward! Lo! He cannot move backward! And so Humbaba relented. Gilgamesh said: "Now that I have discovered your dwelling, I will enter your house!"

So he felled the first Cedar and they cut the branches and laid them at the foot of the Mountain. At the first stroke Humbaba blazed out, but still they advanced. They felled seven Cedars and cut and bound the branches and laid them each, at the foot of the Mountain. Seven times Humbaba loosed his glory on them. As the seventh blaze died out they reached his lair. He slapped his thigh in scorn. He approached like a noble wild bull roped on the Mountain, a warrior whose elbows are bound together. Tears filled his eyes and he was pale, "'Gilgamesh, you, you know? My king? Let me say a word:

A mother who would have brought me into the world, I did not
know one. A father who would have raised me -
I did not know one.
The mountain begat me -
You...you will raise me."

Humbaba continued: "It was Enlil who made me Keeper of this Forest. Free me Gilgamesh! You will be my master and I will be your servant. And as for my trees that I have grown, they shall be yours. I will cut them down and build your palace."

Humbaba took Gilgamesh by the hand and Gilgamesh was moved with compassion. He swore by the heavenly life, by the earthly life, by the underworld itself: "Oh Enkidu, should not the snared bird return to its nest and the captive man return to his mother's arms?"

Enkidu said: "The strongest of men will fall to fate if he has no judgment. Namtar, the evil fate that knows no distinction between men, devours him. If the snared bird returns to its nest, if the captive man returns to his mother's arms, then you my friend will never return to the city where your mother is waiting, who gave you birth. He will bar the mountain road against you, and make the pathways impassable."

Humbaba said: "Enkidu, what you have spoken is evil. You are a mercenary, recruited for bread! In envy and for fear of a rival, you have spoken evil words."

Enkidu replied: "My friend, do not listen to him. Humbaba must die! Kill Humbaba first and his servants after." Humbaba scorned Enkidu for bringing Gilgamesh to him.

He pleaded with Gilgamesh: "Couldn't you have just married a wife and satisfied yourself with her voluptuousness? Why did you come here?" The great winds roared against Humbaba and the dust storms flowed perpetually on his head.

Enkidu pleaded: "I beg you to listen to me, Gilgamesh! Humbaba must be killed!"

Gilgamesh replied: "If we fell him, the blaze and the glory of light will be put out in confusion. The glory and glamour will vanish and its rays will be quenched."

Humbaba interrupted: "I should have lifted you up on high. I should have killed you upon your entrance into my forest! I should have let the shrieking serpent-bird; the eagle and the raven eat your flesh! But now, Oh Enkidu, it lies with you. Make limp your wrath and speak to Gilgamesh so that he might spare my life!"

Over Humbaba's roars, Enkidu shouted back to Gilgamesh: "Not so my friend. First entrap the bird and where shall the chicks run then? Afterwards we can search out the glory and the glamour, when the chicks run distracted through the grass. Kill him! Crush him and quickly before Enlil the Foremost hears his cries. The gods will be filled with wrath against us for this deed."

Gilgamesh listened to the word of his companion and with his axe and sword he struck Humbaba with a thrust to the neck. Enkidu delivered the second blow. From the third blow, Humbaba fell. Before he died, Humbaba screamed out a curse on Enkidu: "Of you two, may

180

Enkidu not live the longer, may Enkidu not find any peace in this world!" Then there followed confusion for this was the Guardian of the Forest whom they had felled to the ground. Across the Forest, the Cedars shivered when Enkidu killed the Watcher of the Forest.

It was Humbaba who struck fear in Mount Hernon and Lebanon. Now the Mountains were moved and all of the hills shifted, for the Guardian of the Forest was dead. They attacked the Cedars and all of the wonders of Humbaba were extinguished. Gilgamesh felled the trees and Enkidu cleared their roots. They set Humbaba before the gods and kissed the ground.

When Enlil saw the head of Humbaba, he raged at them. "Why did you do this thing? From henceforth may the fire be on your faces, may it eat the bread that you eat, and may it drink where you drink."

Enlil took the blaze and splendor that had been Humbaba's: he gave the first to the flowing river, the second to the lion, the third to the venerated stone, the fourth to the mountain and the remaining to Ereshkigal the Queen of the underworld who was carried off when the earth and the heavens were separated.

In the underworld, ordinary mortals sit in silence where dust is there food and clay their meat. They are clothed like birds with wings for their garments.

Enkidu had a dream and told Gilgamesh: "I dreamed that the gods took counsel and because we have killed Humbaba of the Cedar Mountain and Ishtar's Bull of Heaven, one of us would die." When she found out her Bull was killed, Ishtar climbed the mighty walls of Uruk and sprang upon the tower they built and uttered her curse.

When the gods came together, Shamash asked Enlil why Enkidu must die. Enlil was enraged: "You dare say this, you who went about with them, every day like one of them?"

Enkidu's adventure with Gilgamesh ultimately led to his death. Looking back, during the illness brought upon him by the gods, Enkidu cursed the walls of the city: "Oh, if I had known the conclusion! If I had known that this was all the good that would come of it, I would have raised the axe and split it into little pieces and set up here a gate of wattle instead." He cursed the Trapper and the hierodule and those who had destroyed his innocence.

Shamash, the Sun god, reminded Enkidu of all he had won because of his loss of innocence: "Enkidu, why are you cursing the woman, the mistress who taught you to eat bread fit for gods and drink the wine of kings? She who put upon you a magnificent garment, did she not give you glorious Gilgamesh for your companion. And has not Gilgamesh, your own brother, made you rest on a royal bed and recline on a couch at his left hand? The people of Uruk will mourn you and when you are dead they will let their hair grow long for your sake. Gilgamesh will wear a lion's pelt and wander through the desert." Upon hearing Shamash, Enkidu called back his curse.

As bitter as Enkidu's death was to both heroes, it would give meaning to life. When Enkidu had told Gilgamesh his dream of the Underworld, Gilgamesh responded: "We must treasure the dream whatever the terror; for the dream has shown that misery comes at last to the healthy man. The end of life is sorrow." In his rage and despair, Gilgamesh was forced to live with the death of his friend, and with this knowledge he realized: "What my brother is now, that shall I be."

The Great Flood

Refusing to accept this knowledge, Gilgamesh declared: "I will go as best I can to find Utnapishtim whom they call the Faraway, for he has entered the leagues of the gods." After the Great Flood, the gods took Utnapishtim to live in the land of Dilmun; in the garden of the Sun; and to him alone they gave everlasting life. On his way, Gilgamesh felled lions and came upon a mountain of Twin Peaks reaching to heaven and down to the underworld. At its gate were nineteen standing guard in a form that was half man and half dragon.

The Scorpions asked Gilgamesh why he had journeyed to this region. He told them he had thought his grieving would save Enkidu, but it had not. He wanted to find Utnapishtim to ask him about life and death. The Scorpions told him no man had ever gone there and the entire journey would be traveled in darkness. They agreed to allow him to pass through the Mountain Gate. He went through the darkness until he felt the North Wind upon his face. For many days he traveled in only darkness. Eventually the growing light appeared and the sun streamed out.

Glorious Shamash saw him dressed in animal skins and living off of the meat of his prey. He too, warned Gilgamesh that he would not find that which he sought. Gilgamesh replied: "Although I am no better than a dead man, still let me see the light of the Sun."

Beside the sea, Gilgamesh met Siduri, a Sybil who reminded him that his lot was to be human. "Gilgamesh, where are you hurrying to?" she asked. "You will never find that life for which you are looking. When the gods created man they allotted to him death, but life they retained in their own keeping. As for you, Gilgamesh, fill your belly with good things; day and night, night and day, dance and be merry, feast and rejoice. Let your clothes be fresh, bathe yourself in water, cherish the little child that holds your hand, and make your wife happy in your embrace; for this too is the lot of man."

She told him about Urshanabi, the ferryman of Utnapishtim. "Look at him well and if it is possible, perhaps you will cross the waters with him. If not, then you must go back." When Gilgamesh met Urshanabi, he persuaded him, not by charm but by force and broke his boat tackle. Without the tackle it would be a dangerous crossing. On the boat of Urshanabi, Gilgamesh crossed the waters of death.

When he arrived in the land of Dilmun, he saw Utnapishtim, the Faraway. He asked Gilgamesh where he was going and then reminded him: "There is no permanence." He took pity on Gilgamesh because he had traveled so far, and revealed the mystery of how he came to possess everlasting life.

Utnapishtim recounted the story of the Great Flood. It was a time when the gods, unable to sleep because of the uproar raised by mankind, agreed to destroy them. They would have succeeded had not Ea, one of man's creators, instructed Utnapishtim to build a boat: "Take up into it, the seed of all living creatures." When the rain subsided, Utnapishtim allowed his birds to fly free to search for dry land. When they did not return, he and his family left the boat.

Enlil was enraged because the humans had lived, and he directed his fury at Ea. Ea told Enlil that Utnapishtim had learned about the flood in a dream. Ultimately Enlil blessed Utnapishtim and his family. Thereafter, the gods bestowed immortality upon them.

After listening to the tale, Gilgamesh made ready to return home, empty-handed. At the urging of his wife, he revealed a second mystery of the gods. He told Gilgamesh of a plant that grew under the water of death. It could restore youth to all who ate it. It was a thorny plant, not easily removed but if Gilgamesh could retrieve it, the plant would give him everlasting youth. Strapping rocks to his feet, Gilgamesh jumped into the water and descended to the bottom of the sea. Carefully, he gripped the plant and pulled it out by its roots. He was determined to take it to Uruk to share with the elders.

Later, as Gilgamesh bathed in the cool water of a well, a serpent rose up and ate the plant. Immediately, the serpent shed its skin in rebirth and then, returned into the well. While the serpent had achieved immortality, Gilgamesh would find immortality in the stories told about him.

To the Sumerian, Ningizzida was the god of the serpent and "lord of the Tree of Life." Gilgamesh was forced to return to Uruk no different except for the way the journey had changed him.

"In nether-earth the darkness will show him a light: of mankind, all that are known, none will leave a monument for generations to come to compare with his. The heroes, the wise men, like the new moon, have their waxing and waning. Men will say: "Who has ever ruled with might and with power like him?" As in the dark month, the month of shadows, so without him - there is no light. Oh Gilgamesh, this was the meaning of your dream. You were given kingship, such was your destiny; everlasting life was not your destiny. Because of this do not be sad at heart, do not be grieved or oppressed; he has given you power to bind and to loose, to be the darkness and the light of mankind."

The Shadow Snare

"Trisha" recounts a dream of being alone in a house at night. The trees are scratching against the house, while a shadowy and frightening character attempts to break in. Her childhood was often disrupted by moving each time her mother remarried. She was forced to care for her younger siblings because her mother behaved more like a sister. She lived the mythology of the Survivor, never feeling safe and being labeled a black sheep because of her obvious contempt for her mother.

Two things were at play in undermining her sense of wellness. First was her unrecognized identification with the caregiver, a role model that will have life within us, whether or not we forgive their human failings. Second was her inability to resurrect her beautiful nature, which had been tarnished in her tortured relationship with her mother. In her forties, she still moves a lot, often because of fighting with neighbors. When she manifests illness, it is often glandular as a representation of not being able to process and release toxic feelings.

The shadowy characters that continuously appear in her dreams are the personification of how she projects a sense of ugliness *out there*. Since she spends her life defending its non-existence *in here*, until this disowned energy is recognized, integrated and transformed, her relationships will continue to be conflicted. Truly *owning* one's beautiful nature and *defending* it are two different things and will create very different realities. When we own it, we are just so and at peace. When we have to defend it, we ever fight to *believe* it.

Dreams of trees portray how the key to wellness begins at the root. That is why tree dreams often point us toward our family roots. Her expectations of what a mother should have been *scratch* against her house (inner architecture). The reality of what she experienced created a gulf that is unbridgeable without acceptance and forgiveness. Her mythology requires she confront the beast that hides in the forest of her beliefs.

Once she can resurrect its unrecognized power, she will discover its rejuvenating power. Her intruder dreams always take place at night; a sign that what is stalking her is unacknowledged. Since everything in the dream is an aspect of her, if she can wrestle with the *disowned monster,* she will actually discover it will resurrect her beauty.

In the story of Gilgamesh, the characters are brought together in a type of initiation, which begins with conflict, but leads to transformation and integration. First on the scene is Enkidu, the wild and *second self* of Gilgamesh. Enkidu's story resembles how our organic and vital nature dons the mask of conformity to become the ego. When Gilgamesh dons animal skins and looks like a wild man, we see how we must return to our roots to resurrect our vital nature.

Like Percival, the characters follow strange visions or inspiration to find their way forward. Enkidu is coaxed out of hiding in the same way we must coax our vital nature forward. At the same time, we see how some aspect of the psyche begins to "trap" our wild nature in the character of the Trapper. Later, we must confront, question and integrate all aspects to discover the lost part of our beautiful nature.

The Trapper is terrified by the *wild man* he meets at the watering hole, and sets out to destroy him. Hunters kill wild animals for sustenance, while trappers catch game, usually for clothing. The Trapper personifies our projection-making tendencies, or how vital aspects of our nature are trapped. At the same time, we replay and project this unknown costume upon others. Meeting the Trapper embodies the mechanism that will shape and trap our personality in its growth. *"Face to face they met because the herds of wild game had strayed into the Trapper's territory. And in time, the Trapper's face altered; became anew."*

Our instinctual nature can be trapped by conformity: *"Enkidu tried to follow, but his body was bound as though with a cord. His knees gave way when he started to run; his swiftness was gone. Enkidu had grown weak because wisdom was in him and the thoughts of man were in his heart."* To become the unique creature nature intended for us to be, we need to return to authenticity.

Additionally, the characters come up against Humbaba who they believe must be destroyed. The elements lost within will always appear first, as a threat. This repressed energy can be sent underground to fund the idea of the boogeyman *out there,* although it holds the power of all we fear *in here.*

The situations we face are *charged* when our response shows more emotion and inner turmoil than the situation warranted. *Charge* is a clue to observe emerging energy for what it might teach us about ourselves.

Gilgamesh must wrestle against the wild and instinctive character of Enkidu, and during puberty we also wrestle with our instincts to fit in. The characters remain connected through their dreams, and in the same way, the instinctual realm portrayed by Enkidu's birthplace inspires our dreams. Once we leave our unconscious watering hole, we can become trapped in the Forest of our beliefs. Just as Enkidu is told to enter the Forest first, any unconscious material rising from our dreams emerges from the primordial id before it can be accessed by consciousness.

Gilgamesh appears fixated on experiencing existence from an immortal perspective. He embodies the initiation that allows the Self to become the gravitational center. He acts as a guide when he tells Enkidu: *"Only touch my garment and you will not fear death so that the limpness may leave your arm, and the weakness may leave your hand."* Through dreams, we explore life differently to move beyond defensive fear programming. As the purveyor of dreams that guide the ego, the Self is seeking a deeper and more authentic interaction with life.

The Self and ego are believed to shadow each other at the first level of initiation, and we see this in the first meeting of the heroes. At the same time, the Self must integrate the *wild man* traits of the id that the ego rejected. The bubbling energy of instinct reveals our *real* nature more than the ego could ever imagine. Without it, we may float aimlessly in the river of conformity.

Gilgamesh meets Enkidu *"as something mysterious coming out of the woods. Let him look as into mirrors - Give a second self to him. Like bulls, they held together as rushing wind met rushing wind. Heart to heart and against, yet they held fast and shattered the doorpost of the holy gate. The wall shook with this fateful act."* Whenever a transformation occurs within the psyche, the foundation shakes in a way that will shatter the defensive structures, which hold us back.

In dreams, the Shadow manifests as something which feels frightening or overpowering. Whether it is emotion or aggression, dreams reflect the power the *disowned* holds over us, simply because it remains *foreign.*

As an example, it is common for a woman moving through puberty or menopause to dream about some type of Beast, King Kong creature or a powerful, frightening and wild character overpowering or kissing her. Usually represented as a male or animal, this character is opposite to everything she is, and reflects the evolutionary power *her body temporarily holds over her.* It may be the first time she experiences something activated that feels beyond her control. This type of dream ushers in the initiation of the monumental stages of her femininity. It only overpowers and frightens her until she integrates it.

Anytime we deny latent power, it is projected outwardly. We find those who really get our goat from the beginning will somehow manage to become our best friends. Gilgamesh and Enkidu demonstrate how we immediately wrestle with the oppositional energy, only to celebrate later, the ways in which we are alike. The two heroes grapple with each other until they are united.

We use each other as a ballast to define our differences or unique characteristics. This attraction/repulsion fixation creates dynamic movement and growth from stagnation in the same way positive and negative forces generate life. During the courtship dance leading to matrimony we often find ourselves trying to change *loathsome* qualities in our mates. Later, we recognize these same qualities and call them *endearing*. How is it possible that something which repels us immediately can become our attraction?

Love and hate are variations of emotion in the same way we recognize up/down and hot/cold. They are not so much opposites as they are degrees of *one* idea. We can't know one without knowledge of the other. In the story of Cain and Abel, we see how family members and spouses usually perform the most brutal or emotionally charged types of murder. The passion applied in *shutting down* fear will be in proportion to how strongly we are trying to subdue it.

Reflected in how strongly we need to defend something, or how intently we are fixated on avoiding it, we can find the *measure* of our repression.

To overcome being a Victim, we stop and question *what* we are defending. Chances are *that thing* we are protecting has never truly been owned and integrated. The more we feel the need to defend an identity, the farther away we re from simply being it.

As we seek authentic expression in our journey toward empowerment, along the way we must integrate *all* dynamics of who we are. To actualize our destiny, we discover how being civilized is not the true measure of the Self.

The Shadow as Evil *Out There*

Ultimately, Gilgamesh and Enkidu must journey together through the Forest of Fear to resurrect the power that has been trapped in shadow form. They must visit the realm where Enkidu once roamed free as part of the initiation.

Unrecognized power can sometimes take on monstrous proportions as we saw with Fenris, Seth, the Minotaur, the Hydras and now Humbaba. He is the Watchman of the Forest and meeting the monster *face to face* allows us to access the most procreative part of our nature. When we stop blaming the outside world for our condition, we can take responsibility for who we might become. Fear is a signpost that always beckons us toward the path we must take.

Humbaba raised Enkidu and knew his father, calling Enkidu *"a son of a fish."* This exchange mirrors our long and instinctual climb from our biological origins that may be retained in our genetic memory. They are the roots portrayed in dreams of trees. Like the procreative power, which has ensured our survival, it provides tremendous transformative resource on the road to wellness.

"Gilgamesh was made by the gods with wisdom, and will know you are coming before you even arrive. He needs no sleep by day or night, but will have dreamt of your coming before you cross the open plain." As if some part of us *"knows we are coming before we even arrive,"* the most profound aspect of dreams is in how they guide us. As the one who knows within, dreams reveal how some aspect holds a more all inclusive picture of where we are going.

We have traveled to the shores of the unconscious to retrieve the treasure of the guiding Self and recognized how inner and outer clues reveal how some aspect knows us better than we know ourselves. We have explored how characters challenge the ultimate *good* and receive a blessing for doing so. Now we see what happens to characters who challenge the idea of the ultimate *bad*.

The gods will be angry because mythical deities embody conscience or how the foundation for right and wrong is established within the psyche. The ascendancy of the Self onto the psychic landscape always *"puts aside the rules and laws,"* setting the internal city topsy-turvy. When there is a shakedown within the psyche there will be a reverberation across the Forest.

In the opening sequence, the characters of Uruk offer counsel to Gilgamesh. The many characters of our dreams can be viewed as our internal committee or aspects that work together over time, seeking consensus about the direction (we as the hero) are taking. As we enter the work force in adulthood, we may dream of being chased by characters with knives or guns that represent non-integrated, threatening aspects that have emerged within when we don a new persona. Any new situations we face will force us to adopt behavior *before we have the opportunity to integrate* it. These types of dreams reveal how we are being pursued by our need to understand and integrate all aspects of who we are becoming.

While we dream, we are testing our growth and this happens whether or not we remember them. When we face our opponents, we overcome our fear of change. Whatever the mask, these characters always

within. It should be harvested and not destroyed. *"Should not the snared bird return to its nest and the captive man return to his mother's arms?"*

Humbaba describes his creation and his latent power: *"You...you will raise me. It was Enlil who made me Keeper of this Forest. Free me Gilgamesh! You will be my master and I will be your servant. As for my trees that I have grown, they shall be yours. I will cut them down and build your palace."* Enlil is the part of conscience, which funds the power of this imposter. When accessed, we discover the power is ours. Like the Jinni emerging later from this region, Gilgamesh doesn't know whether he can trust the power, or whether it should be stuffed back into the bottle. Yet, he sees it as his own home, *"Now that I have discovered your dwelling, I will enter your house!"*

How does something horrifying become glorious? Humbaba is the beast that blocks our hidden treasure as gatekeeper to our subconscious net. At the same time, he is the Battering Ram that can destroy it.

If the Shadow could describe how it is an illusion, it is captured in Humbaba's words: *"A mother who would have brought me into the world, I did not know one. A father who would have raised me - I did not know one. The mountain begat me - You, you will raise me."* He is not organically created, but grew from the Mountain of beliefs.

In *Women Who Run With the Wolves*, Clarissa Pinkola Estes writes: "There is a saying from medieval times that if you are in a descent, and pursued by a great power – and if this power is able to snag your shadow, then you too shall become a power in your own right." The Mountain, the Shadow or Humbaba, all mask the powerful reservoir, which offers itself to us. Like Luke Skywalker, who unmasks Darth Vader to discover his father, we can unmask the fearful enemy and in doing so, we recognize a valuable part of *ourselves*.

Gilgamesh was provided the wind as his protection and the wind is another symbol of movement within consciousness. The whirlwind in many cultures represents the divine as it manifests on earth. In dreams, the wind portrays how the hidden can mysteriously stir within us in a type of airing out. To dream of a tornado, signifies urges and emotions that have the potential to overwhelm us. In a sense, we will be picked up and placed into another context, releasing us of our controlling tendencies.

Ninsun, like the Lady of the Lake, is an aspect of the Great Mother. Instead of bestowing a sword to cut through illusions, she entrusts Enkidu with the care of her son. *"Mighty Enkidu, you who came not from my womb, I have now adopted you; you are my other child like the foundlings they bring to the temple. Serve Gilgamesh as a foundling serves the temple..."*

She placed an amulet of stones around his neck. This metaphorical symbol reveals how all that is earthy is also sacred. At the same time, all that is earthy is guided by something greater. Through initiation, Enkidu as ego becomes the custodian of the Self.

Ninsun asks Enkidu to return her son safely to her. *I bestow this guiding Self to you, treat it well and learn from it on your journey. All I ask is that you return it when you are finished. This mirror, this image of what you are growing into, may you see its reflection as all that you might become.*

The Healing Journey

Life has a strange way of reflecting back our inner condition. As we move toward wholeness, we become more observant in approaching our experiences with an open mind. If we are angry, we meet a world that is angry. If we only know pain, we find ways to validate it. This is something we fail to realize as *Victims*.

We can wake up each day to a chariot ride where experience comes to us as a gift. This gift allows us to grow, find authentic expression and discover fulfillment. If emotional pain is all we can draw from our experiences, then who is the next Humbaba or Battering Ram who must come to break our structure, to free us from the illusion of always being attacked?

If we believe in a devil *out there*, we will never learn to approach experience for what it may teach us. Our encounters are oftentimes a mirror and the coming together of like kind. Based on our experiences we ask ourselves: What is *this idea of me* I am defending? What *part of you* frightens me? Standing upon the middle ground between these two questions, we experience growth.

When we find ourselves being the Victim, we can change our experiences by truly listening to what we say to another as what we are attempting to say to ourselves. *Have we left those we have met in a better condition than how we found them?* If the answer is no, we acknowledge that we are projecting, dumping or participating in a drama of recreating emotional pain.

Approaching the Forest of Fear to reclaim the energy usurped in Shadow form, we are questioned many times. From conscience and gatekeeper, *"What is the Country of the Living to you?"* At the threshold of our initiation into a deeper interaction with life: *"Couldn't you have just married a wife and satisfied yourself with her voluptuousness? Why did you come here?"* From the reptilian creatures, who bar the way to the underworld: *"The entire journey must be taken in darkness. Only then, will you find light."*

From the Sybil who asks us to strike a balance between searching and coming home: *"Where are you hurrying to? You will never find that life for which you are looking...fill your belly with good things; day and night, night and day, dance and be merry, feast and rejoice. Let your clothes be fresh, bathe yourself in water, cherish the little child that holds your hand, and make your wife happy in your embrace; for this too, is the lot of man."*

Gilgamesh traveled the world and saw great things. He went places no others had gone. While he bathed in the cool water of a well, a serpent rose up to eat his coveted plant of immortality. This "lord of the tree of life," knows the mystery of our connection to the deeper roots of life. Immortality releases us from shackles of certainty; nothing in nature is destroyed, only transformed.

"Oh Gilgamesh, this was the meaning of your dream. He has given you power to bind and to loose, to be the darkness and the light of mankind." Knowledge of good and evil are illusions that keep us from discovery. We reclaim immortality when we discover how we are continuously dying away to be reborn.

"In nether-earth the darkness will show him a light." We sometimes need to walk through darkness to find this light.

Two of the world's greatest poets come from this region: Jelaluddin Balkhi (Rumi) was born in 1207 in Afghanistan, when it was part of the Persian Empire:

> *"People are going back and forth across the doorsill*
> *where the two world's touch.*
> *The door is round and open.*
> *Don't go back to sleep.*
> *Daylight, full of small dancing particles*
> *and the one great turning, our souls*
> *are dancing with you, without feet, they dance.*
> Rumi
> *(Afghanistan)*

We "cross the doorsill" where two worlds touch each time we awaken from our dreams. We can awaken to the door that is "round and open" by discovering *the waking power of our dreams.*

Kahlil Gibran was born in Lebanon in 1883:

> *"And when you have reached the mountain top,*
> *then you shall begin to climb".*
> *The Prophet*, Kahlil Gibran
> *(Lebanon)*

From the Mountain of Wider Awareness, we can look below and see a great tapestry; it allows us to discover the intricate way our lives are woven together.

Chapter Eight
Nachiketas and the Consuming Fire

Stories of Ancient India
The Unknown Self and the Purveyor of Dreams

"Light
devoured darkness.
I was alone
inside.
Shedding
the visible dark,
I
was Your target
O Lord of Caves."

Light, Allama Prabhu (*India*)

Dreams are always exploring the opposite of what we believe to be true about ourselves. A man dreams of a woman to explore his sensitivity, while a woman dreams of a man to connect with her ability to move fearlessly through the world. He integrates aspects that would not be considered masculine, while she integrates qualities that we would not consider feminine. Dreaming of dominating another in a sexual way, regardless of the sexes or characters involved, usually occurs when we are exploring being more assertive or dominant in daily life. Surprisingly, conflict at work is usually fodder for this type of dream.

Transposing Issues in Dreams

The transposition of the Self into its opposite characteristics shows how the purveyor of dreams juxtaposes the hidden to unleash the potential of the Unknown Self. "Julian" dreams of being at a college and walks down a hallway. Dreaming of being in school represents learning something new, and the hallway suggests a place of transition. The symbolism of his dream included going to the film department and meeting a secretary wearing glasses. Photography, the secretary and

197

glasses are all indicative of documenting, capturing or the attempt to see something more clearly. Since he meets a woman, his sensitivity is explored under scrutiny. Every aspect of this dream represents Julian.

"After I turn right, I look to the left side of the corridor and there are two doors with frosted windows. The first door is closed, but the second one is the supervisor's office. It is open just a bit, but it seems like a private meeting and I don't want to interrupt."

"Jackie" too, dreams of going right to enter a church when she sees a playground to the left. When a client describes the direction of going *left* or *right* in a dream, I see it as a red flag to explore. The *left* reveals the unknown path and because it is mentioned, suggests going against conformity and/or the boundaries established by "thou shalt." When we go *right*, we are doing what is considered to be acceptable. I always lead the dreamer down the path to the left. It usually presents the road less travelled, a pathway to wellness and something meaningful.

Julian's images of frosted glass, private meetings and closed doors portray *his* inner architecture. Even the supervisor is a representation of Julian's gatekeeper. Going right suggests the tried and true. Not interrupting, he moves away from a breakthrough and doesn't upset the status quo.

His dream portrays an attempt at transformation. It shows how he is attempting to get a better *view* of his feelings and sensitivity, symbolized by the woman and all the picture capturing symbols and blockages.

Jackie too, sees a playground to the left side of the church, yet avoids exploring a lighter side to her spirituality by going *right*. Dreams are always exploring the unknown path that will reveal the Unknown Self. Through various characters and settings, we explore emerging aspects, while processing and eliminating the outworn.

The Mythology of Sleep spins an adventure to *wake the sleeping hero* to actualize destiny. The Warrior's daily mythology hides weakness through conquest and mastery designed to increase confidence. Dreams of being chased or stalked are those aspects, which remain non-integrated. The internal committee convenes to decide whether an emerging aspect fits within our growing sense of Self. The waking power of the Warrior's dream arsenal however, arouses the hero to confront weakness. We can discover a more balanced interaction with the world around us when we observe our dreams as a way of introducing us to the Unknown Self.

The Survivor cannot see how power is wasted in always seeking approval and lives a mythology of inner famine. The famine is not real and this disowned and wasted energy simply funds hyper-nervous tension.

We may dream of murky or turbulent water and reptiles stirring below the surface. This is because our inner setting remains murky and therefore, frightening. Dreams of food reveal our attempts at finding sustenance and self-worth. Choppy water and landslides may leave us feeling unsettled. These types of dreams actually reinvigorate the inner landscape so we may wake up and discover the treasure of our organic nature.

The Negotiator is unable to recognize innate unavailability or the downward spiral of trading feelings for medication. We may dream of aggressive animals, aliens and creatures that attack and eat at us, while our feelings remain arrested. We experience something *out there* bringing blood (feelings) to the surface because the ability to do so is foreign to our nature.

The Protector is unable to see the drama of a lifestyle where liberty is traded for bondage. We dream of missing an important event or losing a purse or wallet because some aspect of the psyche knows we are a *no-show* with a lost identity. As the Unknown Self makes its presence felt, it can upset the illusions we live by. We may believe we are a picture of unconditional love, while we dream of domestic animals that *cannot* be controlled. Its message is always the same: *we are living a lie.*

The Zealot doesn't recognize the closet of repressed ideas at the root of strange fixations, where criticism turned inward is unwittingly traded for dis-ease. We may dream that *we* are a Humbaba monster, or self-arresting devil. All we fear and repress appears in dreams or finds its way into experiential reality to be processed. We may search for a treasure in a church as the key to finding and releasing the hold of "thou shalt."

The Victim approaches all interaction as a one-sided dialogue to reinforce fear and trades optimism for a belief in evil. We may dream of a type of slow motion portrayal that will reveal how *we* create our experiences. When "Patricia's" house tipped where she walked, it fell in slow motion around her, providing her with the opportunity to see the correlation between her *beliefs* and experience. In the illusion of living, the Unknown Self leads us to confront our fears, although dreams hold the power to *wake us* and set us free.

The Unknown Self can track us in our contradictions playing the part of the Trickster in our Freudian slips. Forced to get naked or relieve ourselves in public, we acknowledge the *natural* way we might reveal ourselves. Dreams unfold differently when there is no longer anything to take away An enigmatic Guide, Wise Man or Wise Woman seasoned enough to *just be* represents what is guiding us at the same time it reflects who we are becoming. All aspects of who we are then awaken to the chariot ride through life. In the moment, we discover the joy of living.

Atman and the Unknown Self

India is a diverse country with many languages, religious sects and ethnicities. Its ancient region, which included modern Pakistan, presents an area, which has embraced many cultures through the ages, although they have held fast to their social system and traditions. Their primary religion, Hinduism or *eternal law*, is one of the oldest and most complex philosophical systems. Having no single founder, it is the third largest religion after Christianity and Islam.

Just as we approach all characters in a dream as our reflection, Hinduism and the exploration of Atman is a way of activating this type of awareness in daily life. As we explore the stories emerging from this region, we can approach a perspective usually reserved for dreaming. Clients come to appreciate how every aspect of a dream is meant to teach them something about themselves. In the same way, when we can come to observe our connection to what unfolds during the day, we can appreciate our experiences more deeply.

At the core of Hinduism and Buddhism is a way to overcome suffering, and the dissatisfaction, which stems from perpetual need. Need is an illusion that can only block our ability to discover. In the last chapter we observed the energy of our disowned vital nature as the Shadow. In this chapter we turn toward the *fire* to recognize the creative principle at work in the experiences we face.

The stories emerging from this region present the idea of *cause* and *effect*. Experience can become a chain reaction of how our beliefs come to shape the present. A change in perspective allows us to cultivate the essence of what we will experience. The joy of discovery can be usurped by a fire that consumes out of insatiable need. Suffering is simply the distance we travel from understanding how life attempts to unmask us. Our pathway to wholeness requires we stop fighting how experience *wakes us up*. Life doesn't happen to us; it happens because of us.

At the threshold of perception, we can release our attachments and expectations that can leave us feeling lost and dissatisfied. By walking a path of joy we carry with us everywhere, we can learn from the unique situations that manifest to keep us growing. All we meet *out there* can teach us much about what is happening *in here*. When we open to how life peels away the layers that will reveal our destiny, we can embrace the joy of discovery. When *in here* and *out there* have no boundaries, we activate the boundless perspective of the Unknown Self.

There is a creative, sustaining and renewing element driving life. The combination of a creative and destructive principle is found in the Norse stories of the Great Hunt, in Roman myths of Pluto, in the Judeo-Christian story of Job, in the American Indian Thunder Beings, and in the Chinese I Ching, where *Increase* inevitably transforms into *Decrease*. The Roman deity, Pluto is the destructive god of the underworld who also guards the precious mineral wealth that can be extracted from the underbelly of the earth. In the same way, our *underworld* is a place of continual resurrection.

Shiva the destroyer is one of the three faces of the *One*, called Brahman. In the form of *Brahma* it manifests as the creative principle. As *Vishnu* it operates as the preserver and as *Shiva*, it portrays life's destructive manifestation that leads to eventual renewal. The Trimurti, which means "having three forms," describes India's main divinities and is the term used to describe Brahman in his three manifestations.

Akka Mahadevi, a devotee of Shiva, whom she referred to as "Lord white as jasmine," lived during the twelfth century in Karnataka, a region on the southwest coast of India. Her poetry reveals an evolutionary aspect wearing the destructive mask of Shiva. She said: "Till you've earned knowledge of good and evil... *lust's body, site of rage, ambush of greed, house of passion, fence of pride, mask of envy*...Until you know and lose this knowing, you've no way of knowing...my Lord white as jasmine." Her words capture a pure perspective untainted by the past. Recognizing the purity and harmony of change is to embrace it.

We must sometimes confront and overthrow the protector of our underworld on a pathway that *appears* as suffering. Difficulty can break our protective shell so we can be reborn into a deeper level of interaction. What we protect can be removed when we simply allow life to *change its face*, knowing how nature coaxes all things to fulfill their unique nature.

Personified in the stories of India, we can explore the garrison that separates us from seeing how we come to block our growth. To earn the knowledge of good and evil is to transcend its distinctions.

Devi, Devils and Divinities

The Sanskrit word *Devi* means goddess, which is at the root of many Indo-European names for the Great Mother. *Deva* is the name for a god, where the word *devil* and *divinity* both derive from this word. The Czech name for the Moon-goddess, Devana and the Latin Diana also evolved from the Sanskrit word Devi. The German word "gott," which translates as good eventually became the English word used today for god.

Old English *divell* is a derivative of divus, divi or other names for gods. In this way, the idea of devil can be traced back to the same concept for god.

Leviathan, the monster of the Hebrew texts and the inspiration for the later character of the devil, derives from a blending of the myths of the Canaanite Baal and Babylonian Marduk, who both confronted a sea monster. Snake worshipping cults, like the Sumerian Ningizzida, "lord of the Tree of Life," or the Great Serpent, Nehushtan, established by Moses were very popular and rivaled the spiritual ideologies which emerged later.

In the Hebrew book, Second Kings 18 we read: "he broke in pieces the brazen serpent that Moses had made...called Nehushtan." Moses was a Levite and both Aaron and Moses, who descended from the tribe of Levi, worshipped the snake as an image of healing, as did most cultures during this period.

As Jesuit and Christian priests accompanied explorers into remote regions of the world, undoubtedly they discovered the worship of something other than what they were taught to believe. These aboriginal snakes, Devi and fertility goddesses laid the foundation for the mythology of evil. In the Trimurti of Hinduism, we can appreciate the way what appears destructive on the earth is simply an aspect of renewal. A prerequisite on a pathway of joy is the rational understanding of how the natural world is fundamentally regenerative.

Monsters and evil snakes are oftentimes simply the political, spiritual or wartime enemies of ancient epics and sectarian rivals. Yet, these same symbols appear in dreams in an effort to lead us toward wellness. Unmasking any *taboo* will always reveal its essential healing power. The many faces of Brahman reveal how what might be called good and evil are simply the various masks of the creation, destruction and re-manifestation occurring at all levels of life.

The History of India

The sub-continent of India is about the same size as Europe and includes Pakistan, Nepal, Bangladesh and Bhutan. Its history begins with the civilizations that gathered along the two great river valleys of the Indus and Ganges systems. Agriculture developed around 3000BC, but like the cultures in the Americas and China, the people of this region were unaffected by the civilizations that flourished around them. They would remain an independent area, existing alongside of and outlasting their Mesopotamian and Egyptian neighbors.

The Aryans who brought the Vedas to India came from the steppes above modern Iran. The word Aryan is used as a linguistic term to describe the family of languages from which most European languages are descended. In Sanskrit, the sacred and literary language of India, *arya* means noble. The Portuguese would later use the word *caste* to describe the social organization established by the Aryans who classified groups of people into classes. One was born into a caste because of *karma*, or the good and bad behavior conducted in a prior life.

These classes included a warrior-aristocracy class called *Kshatriyas*, the priestly or *Brahman* class and the ordinary peasants, called *vaishyas*. While caste movement was possible between these groups, this was impossible for the native aboriginal class called *dasa*, which meant slave.

These non-Aryans were given the name *shudras*, which meant unclean or untouchable. They were identified as a group of people who were not allowed to study or hear the Vedic teachings. This is a social organization with deep roots that continued into modern times. Mahatma Gandhi instigated reforms in the 1930's and although this system has been drastically modified, it has not been altogether eliminated.

In India, there are numerous deities although they are all considered as aspects of the One: *Brahman*. In ancient times, Agni, god of fire was the most important god and only through his sacrificial flames, could one reach the realm of the gods. Laying the roots for the story of Nachiketas, we see how we can sacrifice *the illusion of living* by throwing all that is unnecessary into the fire, knowing if it is necessary, it will endure.

Varuna, god of the heavens controlled order and justice while Indra, the warrior god slew the dragon each year to release the heavenly waters of the monsoon. We see similar nature deities emerging from the myths of ancient China.

In 400BC, India had a population of 25 million, representing one quarter of the world's population at that time. The worship of the pre-Aryan god Shiva may represent the oldest know cult. Like the Minoans and Egyptians, the pre-Aryans also worshipped a religion centered on a mother-goddess and bull. Today the bull survives as Nandi.

The Rise of Buddhism

While Hinduism promoted charity and kindness, it also reflected an inherent contradiction, upholding the caste system that didn't allow the lowest class to participate. These untouchables had achieved a class allotted by fate. The doctrine of reincarnation denied them access to the Vedic teaching. Buddha's form of enlightenment promoted universal compassion and a teaching beyond this type of judgment. He sought to share this teaching with others.

By following the wandering and starving ascetics who meditated upon personal salvation, Buddha ate a decent meal and meditated on the plight of humanity. Beneath the Bodhi tree, he was *enlightened* with a solution to end the suffering of mankind. Instead of pure asceticism, he promoted the Middle Way. The Eightfold Path encouraged one to know the truth, say nothing to hurt others, free the mind of evil, practice meditation, respect life, control all thoughts, work for the good of others and to resist evil. He also established the Four Noble Truths: misery is universal; the cause of misery is desire, overcome desire and follow the Middle Way. As Buddha or *the enlightened one*, he taught a goal of reaching *nirvana*: a condition beyond desire.

As a reformation of Hinduism, which presented Atman as the universal soul attached to individuals, Buddhism did not recognize a soul at all. Anything which would resemble the *real me* is an illusion that manifests as a state created by ego. The idea of *me* is a fluid and changing center of thought born of sensation and urges. It changes as new thoughts, feelings and urges arise.

Buddha recognized how taking the self so seriously fed its endless, insatiable need, which became an impediment and shackle. Like a dog constantly seeking to be stroked and fed, the ego is a distraction that interferes with the ability to appreciate the beautiful harmony of *what is*. Buddha saw this egocentric shackle at the root of suffering.

Just as Constantine was the promoter for Christianity across the Roman Empire, the Indian emperor, Maurya Asoka in 232BC initiated the adoption of Buddhism throughout Asia.

In China, an Indian Buddhist name Bodhidarma introduced spontaneous enlightenment called Ch'an or *Zen* as it would later be called in Japan. Although Buddhism had reached Japan by the fifth century AD, it was during the thirteenth century that Zen, a form of Buddhism became widely popular.

The goal of Zen is to achieve a moment-to-moment awareness. It promotes the use of a *koan* or paradoxical riddle to shock one into sudden enlightenment. As an example, one may meditate on the question, "Where is your place of birth?" The answer might be: "This morning I ate rice and now I am hungry again." In this way, Zen is a way of discovering who one really is beyond habitual thought programming. Like dreaming, it seeks freedom from conceptual or representational thinking and trains the mind to move away from absolutes.

There is no one side of ourselves we can say remains unchanging. Inner and outer experience is always separated by a threshold, although this threshold is non-existent during dreaming. All of experience changes us, but our dreams have a way of activating our growth without the need to fight against the boundaries we erect in daily life. The ideas that come from the East actively explore how one might cultivate this perspective daily.

Suffering and Joy

Buddhism and Hinduism explore suffering as an illusion or a misunderstanding created by our attachment to *a specific outcome*. We can bang against a closed door, never realizing how something more meaningful awaits us if we only let go.

In the story of Nachiketas we find similarities in the story of Job from Hebrew legend. Job had a large family and was a wealthy man. He was pious and eager to help others. Well respected in his community, it was said that even Yahweh recognized his goodness. Several angels were present when Yahweh made the comment of how pleased he was with Job.

Angels first appear in the Epic of Gilgamesh, which describes how mortals in the underworld are clothed like birds with wings for their garments. These mythological bird symbols of conscience have a special predisposition for stirring up trouble when we grow disinterested or complacent in our journey.

One of the angels argued it was only because Job's life was pleasurable that he was pious. If he could be tested by way of suffering, and have his family, possessions and health taken away, the angel assured Yahweh that Job would lose his piety. Yahweh instructed the angel to take power over Job and to do what he would to test him. He was told Job must not be harmed physically.

What ensued was the torture of Job where he lost his possessions, sons and daughters. Job was grief stricken, but he declared he had come into the world naked and would leave that way. He blessed the Creator and his faith remained steadfast.

Reminiscent of Odin's ravens, the angel returned from inspecting the earth, and Yahweh commented on Job's piety, even while he was tortured without cause. The angel replied it was only because he was not harmed *physically* that he remained pious. If he could be stricken, he would surely lose his faith. Yahweh allowed Job to be infested with boils. When his wife saw his horrifying condition she told him to speak out against his god. Job replied: "just as I receive the good, so should I receive the bad."

Several men came to visit Job out of sympathy. They questioned what he had done to deserve Yahweh's wrath. Job argued continuously that he had done nothing wrong. He grew desperate over the injustice of it all and his friends interpreted his anger as the source of all his troubles. They argued, one after another why Job should just admit his behavior was vain and impious since Yahweh does not arbitrarily punish anyone except those who deserve it. Nothing Job said would dissuade them, and both sides reached an impasse.

Job upheld his faith in Yahweh, although he wished he could have the opportunity to plead his case. "If only I had the indictment that my adversary has written!" The use of satan as the Hebrew word for adversary in this statement set the stage for what would later evolve into the mythology of evil. When they all grew quiet, the youngest of the group said: "Why do you contend against Him, saying, 'He will answer none of my words?' For Yahweh speaks in one way; and in two ways, although people do not perceive it. In a dream, in a vision of the night, when deep sleep falls on mortals, while they slumber on their beds, then He opens their ears."

Ultimately the Creator appeared in a whirlwind and spoke of His powers to control everything in a way that is similar to how Vishnu revealed his Universal Form to Arjuna in the Bhagavad-Gita. After Arjuna saw how *Brahman is everything*, both awesome and terrifying, Vishnu said: "Time I am, the great destroyer of the worlds." Yahweh also told Job: "Whatsoever is under the whole heaven is Mine." He spoke of the power more potent than one could imagine. He also asked: "Who put wisdom inside of you and who gives understanding to the mind?"

Similarly Arjuna is told how one can enter into the mysteries of understanding life from the omniscient perspective reserved for dreaming. Both Job and Arjuna apologize for their mortal ignorance. Yet, both are told an omniscient understanding is quite possible. This timeless and boundless awareness accessed during dreaming can be activated when approach life from the same willingness to learn form it.

Regardless of whether we own or disown the creative principle, which is symbolized in many mythologies as *fire*, there appears to be a renewing element at work in life. Lightning ignites a forest fire that burns away the larger growth in preparation for new life, and all we can know for certain is that nature has its own way of doing things. Yet, nature's profound power to renew itself stirs us in the same way.

It is both frightening and reassuring to believe there is whimsical entity causing the events that unfold around us. We ward off change by building defensive structures and complain when the walls crash around us to set us free. This is a common dream theme that teaches us about our defenses.

The story of Job reveals how those who are open to the idea of change do not suffer as deeply as those who fight against it. We hold within a creative fire that burns in different ways. It can consume us as the fire of *destruction* in the way we use life up ever seeking something to fulfill us. Unable to understand life on its terms, we gratify ourselves for being empty or unfulfilled.

In the stories of the East, the pursuit of pleasure is believed to be a trap. Whatever *that thing* might be which will bring pleasure is forever changing, and will never be satiated. Pleasure can be associated with many things, although what makes the process of seeking pleasure a trap is the idea *satisfaction is fleeting*. In both dreams and in life, we see how unhappiness is simply the hunger pain for change. It is better to allow difficulty to guide us toward authenticity, rather than fight against the light growing in the darkness.

Perpetual joy can be found in a change of perspective. Pleasure associated with *something* has an *attachment to an outcome*. It is transitory and insatiable by nature, rising from expectation. We find how we are attached to an outcome if not having "it" leads to disappointment.

The Dove's Egg

There once was a farmer who had a large tree in front of his house. In the branches above, lived a dove. One day, the dove left her nest and egg to go in search of food. While she was away, the farmer's wife climbed the tree and stole the egg. When the dove returned to her nest to find the egg missing, she looked below and knew it must have been the farmer's wife. She saw her in the garden below and began crying.

"Please give me back my egg," the dove said. The farmer's wife played ignorant. "What egg? I do not have your egg." The dove was heartbroken and went to find help. On the way, she saw a pig.

"Why are you crying, little dove?" The pig asked.

"Oh Pig, could you please use your nose to dig up the yams of the farmer's wife, who stole my egg?"

"No, not I," the pig grunted and wandered away.

She then met a hunter, who asked: "Why are you crying little bird?" The dove replied: "Will you shoot an arrow at the pig, who wouldn't dig up the yams of the farmer's wife, who stole my egg?"

"This is none of my business. Why would I do that?" The hunter walked away.

The dove was crying as she flew above a rat in the field below. The rat asked why she was crying and she said: "Will you gnaw the bowstring of the hunter, who wouldn't shoot the pig, who wouldn't dig up the yams of the farmer's wife, who stole my egg?"

"Certainly not," and the rat scampered into the field.

Next, she met a cat who asked why she was crying. "Will you catch the rat, who wouldn't gnaw the bowstring of the hunter, who wouldn't shoot the pig, who wouldn't dig up the yams of the farmer's wife, who stole my egg?" The cat simply ignored her.

The dove continued to cry and soon a dog came by. The dog asked why she cried so pitifully. "Will you bite the cat, who wouldn't catch the rat, who wouldn't gnaw the bowstring of the hunter, who wouldn't shoot the pig, who wouldn't dig up the yams of the farmer's wife, who stole my egg?"

"No, not I," said the dog and it ran down the street. Soon the dove's wails attracted the attention of an old man with a long, gray beard.

"Why are you crying little bird," he asked.

"Sir, will you beat the dog, who wouldn't bite the cat, who wouldn't catch the rat, who wouldn't gnaw the bowstring of the hunter, who wouldn't shoot the pig, who wouldn't dig up the yams of the farmer's wife, who stole my egg?" The old man didn't want any part of it, and continued on his way.

The dove then asked the fire to burn the white beard of the old man but the fire wouldn't do it. She asked the water to put out the fire because it wouldn't burn the beard of the old man, who refused to beat the dog, who wouldn't bite the cat, who wouldn't catch the rat, who wouldn't gnaw the bowstring of the hunter, who wouldn't shoot the pig, who wouldn't dig up the yams of the farmer's wife, who stole the egg. The water too, was unwilling to help.

Not long afterwards, the dove met an elephant and asked if he would stir up the water, that refused to put out the fire that wouldn't burn the beard...but the elephant refused.

A black ant heard her cries and asked her what was troubling her.

"O little ant! I know you can help me. Will you go into the elephant's trunk and bite him for not stirring up the water which refused to put out the fire, that wouldn't burn the beard of the old man, who refused to beat the dog, who wouldn't bite the cat, who wouldn't catch the rat, who wouldn't gnaw the bowstring of the hunter, who wouldn't shoot the pig, who wouldn't dig up the yams of the farmer's wife, who stole my egg."

"Why not? Here I go," the ant crawled inside the elephant's trunk and bit it very hard in the softest place. This made the elephant dash into the water where he unwittingly stirred it up with his trunk. The water splashed and accidentally threatened to put out the fire that drew back and burned the white beard of the old man. He kicked the dog, who ran after the running cat and bit her in all of the excitement. The cat landed on top the rat, who gnawed the bowstring of the hunter's bow as it tried to hold on with its teeth. The hunter tied on a new string and tested it by accidentally shooting an arrow at the pig's snout. The pig went and dug up all the yams of the farmer's wife in an attempt to quench its pain. Upon seeing her garden destroyed, the farmer's wife realized immediately she must carefully put the dove's egg back into the nest.

This story is a metaphor for our responsibility to the chain reaction which ties all of life together. Even non-action has a consequence because at some level, there is meaning in how we come together. Many people can approach the same event, although each will interpret it differently. Everything we experience is shaped by the mythology of our beliefs.

Gopal Bhar Cures a Dreamer

Gopal Bhar lived next door to a poor couple, who were incorrigible dreamers. One day, Gopal overheard them vying with each other about their daydreams. The husband said: "When I get some money, I am going to buy a cow."

His wife said: "Then I will milk the cow. We will need lots of pots to catch the milk. I will need to buy some tomorrow." The next day, she went out and bought pots.

When she returned, the husband asked what she had bought. "Oh, pots. One for milk, one for buttermilk, one for butter and one for cream."

"That's great," he said, "but why did you buy the fifth one?"

"I bought that one to carry some of our extra milk over to my sister."

"What! Carry milk to your sister? How long have you been doing that? Without even telling me or asking my permission?" In a fit of rage, he grabbed the pots and smashed them all.

"You stupid woman! I work and sweat all day to buy a cow, and you give away the milk to your sister! I will kill you first!" He threw the pieces of the broken pots at his wife. Gopal thought this was going too far and he walked over to their house.

He asked innocently: "Now what is the matter? Why are you throwing things?"

"This woman is giving away the milk from our cow to her sister!"

"Your cow?" Gopal asked.

"Yes, the cow I'm going to buy when I have enough money."

"Oh, that one! You don't have a cow yet, do you?" asked Gopal.

The man said: "Just wait, I am going to get one."

"Oh really! Now I know what's happening to my vegetable garden!" said Gopal, picking up a stick and thrashing his neighbor.

"Stop! Stop! Why are you beating me?"

"Your cow! It has been eating all of the beans and cucumbers in my garden and you're letting it!"

"What beans, what cucumbers? Where is your vegetable garden?"

"The one I'm going to plant! I've been planning it for months, and now your cow is destroying it!"

The neighbor suddenly saw what he was doing and they all had a good laugh.

This story demonstrates how the *illusion of living* can become a lifestyle. Projection initiates a chain of reaction set in motion by desire rather than experience. Desire can take us so deeply into the future that we wander away from what experience may teach us.

As we step back to explore how we create our experiences, we make changes within and the outer world mysteriously changes. Being responsible for our condition, our only goal is the freedom to grow. We can unleash the joy which comes from discovering how life is a process that *awakens us to our destiny*. This requires we become a traveler, comfortable in not knowing the destination.

The Fire of Nachiketas

Nachiketas, a young boy, observed how his father made sacrifices and performed rituals. His anxiety about what happens after death made him give away all that he had. As he saw the gifts his father was sacrificing, his heart was filled with respect and devotion, but he pondered: "Unblessed, surely, is the place where he may go, if he is sacrificing cows that have given their milk and are barren."

Wondering whether his father truly meant to give *everything* away, the boy asked: "To whom are you going to give me, father?" His father ignored his foolish question until Nachiketas asked the same question several times.

"Would you sacrifice *me* to Death as well?" Angrily, his father said he would. Nachiketas pondered this idea and decided if it were true, then he should meet Yama, Lord of Death.

210

Nachiketas went to the abode of Yama and came to rest on his doorstep. He waited three nights, hoping to meet the Lord of Death. Yama was told that was a Brahmin lad waiting as a guest on his doorstep. When Yama appeared, he was embarrassed by his neglect in leaving the boy waiting, and said: "Nachiketas, since you have been waiting here for three nights, you should demand three boons from me."

Nachiketas first asked that his father might be set at ease about his disappearance and that he would greet him on his return happily. This was granted. Nachiketas then asked about what happens after death. "Please tell me about this mystery. This is the second boon I desire."

Death said: "This question is deep and difficult. Choose another gift, Nachiketas! Do not be hard. Do not compel me to explain."

Nachiketas replied: "Death! What explanation can be as good as yours? What gift compares with that?"

Death said: "Take sons and grandsons, all long-lived, cattle and horses, elephants and gold, take a great kingdom. Anything but this; wealth, long life, Nachiketas! Empire, anything whatever; satisfy the heart's desire. Pleasures beyond human reach, fine women with carriages, their musical instruments; mount beyond dreams; enjoy. But do not ask what lies beyond death."

Nachiketas was unwavering: "Destroyer of man! These things pass. Joy ends enjoyment, the longest life is short. Keep those horses, keep singing and dancing, keep it all for yourself. Wealth cannot satisfy. But please, Master of All, I will not change my gift. Say where man goes after death; end all that discussion. This, which you have made so mysterious, is the only gift I will take."

Death responded: "The wise, through meditation, discover in the mouth of the cavern, deeper in the cavern, that Self, that ancient Self, difficult to imagine. It is more difficult to understand how one can pass beyond joy and sorrow. One, who comprehends this, distinguishes the body from the Self, goes to the source and attains joy, lives for ever in that joy. I think, Nachiketas! Your gates of joy are already open."

Nachiketas remained curious: "What lies beyond right and wrong, beyond cause and effect, beyond past and future?"

After attempting to persuade Nachiketas to take treasures instead of being told the answer, Nachiketas in unwavering. Death said: "It is a word – and that word is Ohm. The Self knows all, is not born, does not die, and is not the effect of any cause; is eternal, self-existent, imperishable and ancient. The Self is lesser than the least, greater than the greatest, lives in all hearts. When senses are at rest, free from desire, it mounts beyond sorrow. Though sitting, it travels; though sleeping it is everywhere. Who but I, Death, can understand what is beyond happiness and sorrow? Self rides in the chariot of the body, the firm-footed charioteer, discursive mind its reins. Senses are the horses, objects of desire are the roads. When Self is joined to body, mind, and sense, only *It* enjoys. The wise, by meditating upon the all-pervading Self, understand waking and sleeping and go beyond sorrow."

Death continued: "The Fire is the basis of this universe. It is abiding in a cave, hidden within our secret being." Death then told him what bricks to use for the sacrifice and how to assemble them into an alter.

Nachiketas asked: "Where shall I find that joy beyond all words? Does the Self reflect another's light or shine of Itself?"

Death replied: "Neither sun, moon, stars, fire nor lightning lights It. When It shines, everything begins to shine. Everything in the world reflects this light. Those whose minds are always out of control cannot know this that I have said. Otherwise, how could they know the what, the why or the where of it?"

"This Fire that leads to heaven is your second gift, Nachiketas! It shall be named after you."

The Fire of Creation

Julian, in the second cycle of his dream, is in a parking lot with friends in a van. In the first cycle, going right, the glasses, photographs and closed door meetings all portrayed the crisis created by his inability to deviate from the status quo. The van is filled with boxes and they sort through them. The parking lot reflects how he is in a holding pattern, while what takes place in the van embodies the internal committee sorting through the ideas he protects.

Baggage and boxes are a common dream theme of assessing what we hold on to, while the *van* represents forward movement, in this case, associated with what we *carry*. These types of dreams are common because the psyche is ever reminding us that where we are going will be directly affected by what we carry with us.

He then dreams of driving to work where he parks his car. He climbs a hill as if knowing growth is solitary and uphill labor. He enters a warehouse for garbage recycling and asks a worker to help him find a way out, portraying another aspect of sorting through the past and searching for direction. He describes how they are at work in a building near the water, and how the water seeps across the floor. Where the first part of the dream reflects the fire of creation or thought patterns, its opposite symbol (water) rises to the surface as a symbol of disintegration and release. Walls always come down. If nature can teach us anything, it is it's relentlessness in overcoming anything that would block its forward progress.

The final cycle portrays him walking with an older man. He embodies the Wise One archetype who often appears as a guide at the threshold of transformation. Whatever message these characters present should be heeded. Together, they search for a way out of a room, filled with yellow legal size paper.

Yellow in a dream is a message to slow down, while the reference to legal pads can portray the rules and constraints he lives by. He is amazed to see notes *he* has written in *green writing* scattered on the ground. The "aha" for Julian comes when he recognizes his contribution to what he discovers. The green writing suggests healing and renewal, finding a more grounded (less legal) and natural way of being.

The landscape grows soggy as the dream continues to suggest how the waters of renewal are rising. He walks in mud up to his knees as another representation of being slowed down to discover a more grounded way of interacting with the world.

The Healing Journey

Julian's dream cycle captures the weight of the intellect, which can trap us in our growth. He encounters many people in his dream, although the Wise One is coaching him to slow down enough to become a witness to how his thoughts must be recycled or regenerated to keep him growing. This dream sequence is an excellent example of how the *Mythology of Sleep* wakes us to our power to create experiences.

When we reach toward that inner creative fire, "abiding in a cave, hidden within our secret being," we open to a pathway of fulfillment. This fire can also generate *the illusion of living* when we live the mythology of a Consumer, ever driven to fill our emptiness. When we turn back and take stock of what is within, the fire becomes a light that shines upon our pathway.

Symbolically, the fire is a sacrificial flame where we can trade the known to romance the unknown. We lay down the bricks and kneel upon the alter of all we have known. The light reveals our *real* face and we are content in knowing how life leads us. We listen to our thoughts, scattered like notes to no one in particular and yet, so important to what unfolds before us. We see the snapshots of our beliefs, created before we knew we could be more. We remember how far we ran away to find the four corners of the world, only to find ourselves alone, unloved and hungry.

Focused *out there* for continual reassurance we are good, we need this constant reassurance even while we cannot actually hear it. We may feel inferior, insufficient, and afraid to feel, confused by the ambiguity of love, unable to see the gifts we may share with others, afraid of everything, and left feeling victimized by life. The part of ourselves, which keeps us from actualizing our real nature, we sacrifice to the fire.

Nachiketas was told: "*Self rides in the chariot of the body, the firm-footed charioteer, discursive mind its reins. Senses are the horses, objects of desire are the roads. When Self is joined to body, mind, and sense, only It enjoys.*" In the carriage ride through life, the Self takes the reigns when inner and outer clues merge together. It is all meaningful and it is all good. Synchronicity is no longer a chance happening, but a way of life. The doorsill separating the inner and outer world is an illusion.

When we reign in the mind, we can observe whether we are responsive to life or reactive to it. All of experience attempts to heal us by making us whole; dreams and daily life cannot be separated because both are meant to teach us about ourselves. Whatever blocks our journey toward authentic empowerment, we throw into the flames. All that is real and worth keeping cannot be destroyed. All that is real and worth keeping is fortified.

We throw our darkness into the flames so evil is no longer our illusion. "*Light devoured darkness. I was alone inside. Shedding the visible dark, I was Your target O Lord of Caves.*" Even the most *complex* experiences are meant to peel away the mask that would hide our *simple* face. It is simple because when we stop trying, we find we are simply *doing.*

"*Till you've earned knowledge of good and evil... lust's body, site of rage, ambush of greed, house of passion, fence of pride, mask of envy...Until you know and lose this knowing, you've no way of knowing...*" To earn knowledge of good and evil is to see how they are one. We open to the purity of what unfolds, without judgment, and discover a powerful peacefulness in existence.

"*The wise, by meditating upon the self-dependent, all-pervading Self, understand waking and sleeping and go beyond sorrow.*" To understand waking and sleeping is to see how growth occurs through both. The great tapestry is a doorway to our boundless journey of enlightenment.

As we reclaim the wisdom of the Unknown Self, we discover the treasure of our destiny. "*When it shines, everything begins to shine. Everything in the world reflects this light.*" We need only stoke the fire and keep it burning. We discover how the pathway of joy is illuminated by this light.

When we look for the divine, we will find it is an inward journey. Observing experience bathed beneath a light that shines from within, we recognize life's unity expressed in a thousand different forms. Unmasking an ambivalent deity, we find the root of our suffering within. The myths we live by are merely the distance we travel to escape this knowing.

Chapter Nine
The Thread Running Through the Way

Tales of Ancient China
Balancing Opposites in the River of Change

"Do you not see
that you and I
are as the branches of one tree?

With your rejoicing
comes my laughter;
With your sadness
starts my tears."
Tsu Yeh (China)

We turn to the philosophy of ancient China to explore how the idea of opposites can be viewed as *one phenomenon* that is *changing*. During dreaming, we explore the idea of something *out there* to learn about what *we* are repressing. The self-knowledge that is activated in dreams can be amplified when we apply this perspective to daily life.

The ancient Taoist polished the *mysterious mirror* to keep it without blemish. We too, can grow through experience if we are aware of how we project the past upon it when not open to change. Everything in our dream is a reflection of us and so, we carry this pure perspective back into daily life. Turning back, "we do not contend and nothing contends with us." Turning back, we open to the great river.

We have also explored how dreams present the opposite of what we believe to be true. In my book, *The Mind's Mirror: Dream Dictionary and Translation Guide*, I compiled over a thousand symbols that can help in dream interpretation and show how dream act as a mirror. A woman may dream of a sexual encounter with a male and believe she is exploring her sexuality. The dream is actually waking the dominant or assertive part of her own nature, associated with whatever *role* this male character plays in her dream.

We may dream about an intruder and feel afraid we are being invaded or at risk of robbery. The dream is not a message about taking precautions, but is actually a message about being *too reclusive* and the need to open up. We may need to become more open so others aren't *intruding* into our life.

When we dream of going to school in our underwear, we feel embarrassed and humiliated. The dream is actually waking us to how we may have donned an unnatural costume. We need to remove it to reveal our more natural and intimate self. During the day, we may have opened up in a way that felt uncomfortable and didn't realize it. The experience becomes fodder for the exploration of who we are as we move to actualize our destiny.

We may dream of going on a vacation and are unable to find an outfit, make-up, luggage, wallet or purse. We observe the dream as a message about paying extra attention to our valuables, when it is actually suggesting how we might discard insecurity and our focus on the *non essentials* that trap us in the river of change.

As we fall out of step with life, we cover and *paint* ourselves with an unnatural mask. We dream of a landslide and therefore, become fearful of impending danger, when the dream is actually exploring the necessity of shifting our foundation so we can experience a more fulfilling existence.

If we were to approach each encounter with the same *mysterious mirror*, we would open to a world which is always meeting us halfway to guide us. The natural world has a special predisposition for shaking things up so renewal can occur. *How* we encounter the world will determine the type of events that ensue.

Confucius taught: *"When meeting another of contrary character, one would do well to examine themselves."* Difficulty *out there* always comes *out of nowhere*, but nature shows us how the energy released was always *inherent* in the things that crashed together.

The difference between Eastern and Western philosophy can be summarized in how both approach life. Where the West always strove to understand the nature of being or *things* as they *exist* in time, the East was content to observe the *transient* aspect of what is in an endless state of *becoming*.

As a Warrior, we discover how the drive to actualize the Self can lead to isolation. We are guided to swim closer to those we care about. As a Survivor, we find how a lack of Self can lead to inner famine. Life leads us to swim alone awhile to discover *our* way. As a Negotiator, we hide sadness with humor or intellectual puzzles, while barely noticing how our boat has run aground. Life brings forward the deluge meant to set us free.

As a Protector, we are so busy watching where our partner is swimming that we fail to see the rapids up ahead. The free fall through the cascading water releases us from the things we cling to.

Overly Zealous about good and evil, we discover how too many rules can make us miss the point about life: *it is our home.* In an effort to awaken us to the real value of life, it can be threatened. As a Victim, we allow the fear of what *may* transpire to avoid discovering what may *be.* Grace stalks us in an effort to show us life's beauty.

We can approach fulfillment as an ever illusive goal, using instant gratification to offset a lack of real fulfillment. When our growth is stunted in a way that even our dreams go unheeded, illness manifests as a *time out.* Whatever the journey, we can be certain it holds relevance for us.

"Know contentment and you are rich;
When you are lost,
fall back into the great river."

The Mythology of *Dis-ease*

"Kelly" has a problem saying no. She finds herself in situations where she feels *guilted* into doing things. Her anger is palpable when she describes her frustration, although she does little to establish boundaries based on her needs.

Like Trisha who dreams of the intruder, Kelly's health issues are glandular, as a representation of her inability to process *toxic* feelings. What the mind can't process in daily life or through dreams, the body finds ways of bringing to the surface for elimination. When Trisha learned to *accept* her mother's shortcomings, *she* experienced wellness. Once Kelly found the proper *relationship* to a sense of acceptable selfishness, her illness also abated.

"Jane" has migraine headaches and visual disturbances. She describes how she was diagnosed with fibromyalgia several years ago. Many illnesses of this type occur with the onset of menstrual changes due to hormonal fluctuations. This coincides with a time when women can experience life-changes as children become independent.

We may experience emotional changes that feel like depression because of hormones. The medications for auto-immune disease present their own complications and toxicity. I have seen people cured of fibromyalgia, lupus and multiple sclerosis symptoms through anti-depressants or change in diet. Artificial sweeteners, soy and hormones injected into meat can disrupt the normal flow of hormones, but that is

217

something rarely discussed. Instead, the pharmaceutical industry gives us medicine to heal us of our *dis-ease.*

In Chinese medicine, which dates back to 2500BC, the liver is connected to the eye. When menstruation is abnormal, we can develop anemia or a deficiency of vital nutrients. When we are emotionally distraught, the body is susceptible to an imbalance of neuro-chemicals that can become toxic. The more the body works to balance itself, the more tired we become.

To compensate for our lethargy, we augment our diet with comfort foods like red meat, wine, cheese and chocolate. When our diet changes, everything changes and the liver is unable to process toxic substances fast enough. To cure the headaches brought upon by this onslaught of histamines and phenylethylamines, we ingest large quantities of over the counter painkillers. This exacerbates the problems developing in the liver, leading to more headaches, visual disturbances and arthritic conditions. Eventually we become one of many going through countless tests with no sign of what is really at the root of our illness.

I have observed how a popular liver cleanse of lemon juice, maple syrup and cayenne pepper can actually stop symptoms that mimic lupus, MS, and Rheumatoid Arthritis. Cayenne pepper is used in topical arthritic medications to stop pain signals and the lemon juice flushes the system of toxins. Once the diet is back in check, we find our vitality increases.

Western doctors compartmentalize symptoms and remove organs that are vital in Chinese medicine. The Traditional Chinese Medical practitioner analyzes the entire body, lifestyle and emotional well being of the patient to keep wellness flowing rather than to treat dis-ease.

The circle of symptoms that lead to a type of diagnosis above may have originated with the hormonal change of menopause. In many cultures however, menopause is not a negative condition. Only 10% of Asian women experience the adverse symptoms of menopause, while this figure is 75% in the West. In Japan, menopause is called *konenki. Ko* means renewal and regeneration. *Nen* means years, and *ki* means season or energy. In Japan, menopause is described as a time of a woman's *rebirth.* In the West, menopause translates as the *stopping* of something a woman has experienced her entire life.

Many indigenous cultures believe a woman accesses her profound spiritual powers or the Wise One archetype when her body is no longer used to produce life. Instead, this energy offers inspiration so she may become a spiritual leader in society. Our relationship to the body's changes will determine the type of relationship we have with the body. When *the changes* lead us to become more introspective, we often grow.

The ancient Chinese philosophers knew: "All things in the universe have a purpose; is it right that the human journey should be different?" Because nature ever strives to become stronger, we must assume all we experience has a similar purpose.

Western medicine treats illness through medications that alleviate symptoms. Eastern medicine approaches illness from a sense of wellness and balance. Chinese philosophy is based on the assumption that no single aspect of life can be understood except in its relationship to its place in the whole. Human beings were viewed as a microcosm of the processes observed in the universe. Every living thing abides by the same powers of regeneration and renewal observed in nature.

Western medicine would view the body as a machine and the doctor as a mechanic. An individual is seen by many specialists with little attention paid to the entire person, or to the environment in which they thrive. In Chinese medicine, the doctor behaves more like a gardener, cultivating wellness and balance to prevent the development of *dis-ease*.

In the second century BC, the *Nei Jing*, a medical classic, presented the following advice: "Maintaining order rather than correcting disorder is the ultimate principle of wisdom. To cure disease after it has appeared is like digging a well when one already feels thirsty or forging weapons after the war has begun." Everything that happens in nature has a purpose and human beings are not simply placed on the sidelines. In ancient China, positive and negative had no more relevance than what is found at the molecular level. Like the Medicine Men of the Americas, if a person demonstrates illness then the *entire* lifestyle is examined to determine where an imbalance has occurred.

If big business thrives on remedies then the result will be propaganda that ensures a constant demand for their products. When we are facing an illness, the best medicine is usually found by turning within.

At the same time, nature brings forth natural remedies at certain times of the year. When allergies are prevalent, sour citrus fruits abound, which alleviate the production of histamines. Plagued by phlegm during winter, drying fruits like pomegranates and pumpkin seeds spring up as a cure. By observing these natural processes, the philosophy of Taoism was born. Traditional Chinese Medicine was its offshoot as a way of respecting the wisdom of nature in curing illness.

Nature is a Teacher

The newest branch of science explores how all individual systems within the universe are exchanging energy, revealing what the ancient Taoist called the "thread running through the way." In fact, the similarities between modern physics and the original ideas of Taoism led Neils Bohr, a pioneer of quantum mechanics to use the circular Yin and Yang image on his coat of arms when knighted by the Danish King.

As we transcend our study of individual structures or things to observe the thread of interconnectivity existing at all levels of life, an uncanny wisdom emerges from long ago. One of the oldest works of literature, the *I Ching*, comes to us from ancient China and states: "Something and nothing produce each other." We see this demonstrated in the imploding singularity of the Big Bang, fifteen billion years ago. As this implosion reached critical mass, life is believed to have been generated from a point of nothingness. What began as unified symmetry in an incredibly hot universe broke down into the four known forces.

Something and nothing produce each other when energy becomes mass, or mass becomes energy in particle accelerator laboratories. These experiments help cosmologists understand the first few seconds of our early universe.

Kelly discovered how something and nothing produce *dis-ease* when *something* eats at us, while we do *nothing* about it. Jane may one day explore how *nothing* or a fear of being useless can become *something* like a condition that brings an extra dose of attention and love. In the river of life, nature always attempts to awaken us to wellness.

When Einstein penetrated the secrets of the molecular world, he observed, "Nature does not distinguish between mass and energy, but observes them to be one and the same." His work transformed our understanding of the natural world, revealing our tendency to compartmentalize every aspect, as if each might exist independently. We now realize that there are no isolated building blocks, only the intricate relationship of how each part is an *observable* variation of a larger whole.

We may idealize a world of harmony, although nature reveals how conflict or opposition becomes the driving force of evolution. Our image of a perfect world would reduce it to one of stagnation and degeneration. Explosions of life occur in the traffic accidents of shifting tectonic plates below the ocean. Renewal takes root in the wake of hurricanes, floods and wild fires. The force driving life toward change is relentless, and it is better to follow where the changes may lead. The ancient Chinese believed nature was a teacher and by studying its ways, knew: *Nothing Bad Happens in Life.*

Without beginning or end, all things flow endlessly as seeds become trees that become seeds again. Great rivers meet the sea, where the water is gathered into clouds, moving across the landscape to return to its source. A pathway of wellness requires we remain open and overcome our

220

need to classify life in terms of good and bad. What we may not understand today, is often revealed tomorrow.

Whether we realize it or not, we remain tied to the subtle mechanisms of rebirth observed in nature. Conflict arises when we fail to acknowledge the need for continual change in our lives. If we ward off change during the day, the psyche finds growth and renewal through dreams. As the body seeks continual balance, we sometimes learn more about *the art of living* when we can no longer take it for granted.

The ancient Tao te Ching states: "We shiver when cold and sweat when hot; we do nothing and it happens naturally." The body is regenerating itself at all levels. All of experience shows us that the process doesn't stop at shoulder level.

The Return to Nature

The ancient Chinese studied the purposeful way nature sought renewal and came to know it as Tao. By following the *way of nature*, they opened to its wisdom to understand the human condition. All of experience presented an opportunity for further growth, and crisis was simply the distance one travelled from the *Way*. In 500 BC, the ancient Chinese philosophers were exploring a *Back to Nature* doctrine based on more ancient ideas. Like the Greeks of the same period who were intellectualizing all of experience, these "natural" philosophers sought to return man to a more natural condition.

There is a profound harmony in the earth's inter-dependent systems. Animals take in energy as food and oxygen, and discard it as heat, carbon dioxide and waste. Bacteria and fungus process the waste back into plants. These plants take in carbon dioxide and use it to build their own substances through photosynthesis, which releases the oxygen within the molecules. The animals breathe in the oxygen and exhale carbon dioxide that returns to nourish the plants.

At the same time that we observe harmony in these self-organizing systems, we also see mating collisions, battles for sustenance, and eruptions reflecting the earth's fundamental transformative power. From the standpoint of regeneration, these processes are the same. Progress will always demand that some things fail, where others succeed. Yet, those that fail are simply being made stronger.

Approaching nature, we see our reflection in life's *mysterious mirror*. At our cellular level, we see the same processes of growth and renewal being transferred in information packets that mirror our social interactions. Two molecules will collide, and both are changed by the *encounter*. The West now accepts concepts like The Uncertainty Principle, which reveals the future as a place of endless possibilities. When we follow the ways of nature, it reveals how we might become more comfortable viewing life in its state of motion, rather than attempting to classify it in terms of stasis.

Where classical science once emphasized order and stability, today we are exploring fluctuations, instability, multiple choices, and limited predictability at all levels of life. It is a world in which we are born, although it is a world that still holds great mystery for us.

The natural world can teach us about crisis and growth. Energy within a system can become overwhelming and natural processes occur to strike a balance. As hot and cold pressure systems collide, thunder and lightning release the bound up energy in the atmosphere. In the same way, two individuals who are *hoarding* the same type of energy may clash together so *bound up* energy can be released.

In the natural world, diverging energy will slip into temporary chaos, until both can reorganize to function at a higher level. Conflict too, presents us with this same opportunity to move to a higher state of being. Chaos, the unknown, and the possibilities presented to us will always lead to growth. Perhaps that is why no matter the difficulty, everything always works out.

When we observe how all living things are dependent upon each other, we let go of the illusion of structure to observe the nature of the *flow* itself. This flow was called *Tao*, or the Hindu concept of *Brahman*. It is the ancient Egyptian idea of *maat*, or how we can do little to change what is happening *out there* until we understand what is going on *in here*.

This flow is embodied in the Native American's description of *the great unifying life force* that flows in and through all things. It underlies Aristotle's idea of an *organizing principle* and the substances used by nature that tie us to our environment and the people we meet. This energy has propelled us through our existence, and yet we fail to understand how its fundamental essence is about *change* and not punishment.

The ancient Chinese approached difficulty as opportunity, and employed a perspective called *Crossing the Great Water*. The Taoist philosopher, Lao Tzu was often depicted riding a water buffalo as an image of moving through the river of change with ease. In dreams, we cross the great water to become fearless in testing the depths of our mysterious nature.

Vehicle dreams that involve the threat of sinking below the water commonly involve being with a parent. As we try on the motivational behavior of our role models, we often discover *their way* is not *our way*. The threat of choppy seas or *going below the surface* allows us to find our way back into the great river.

Nature teaches us that by bringing two separate entities (our parents) together, we were given the opportunity to become a *better* version of what had gone before. We were never meant to be like them.

In civilization too, *Crossing the Great Water* is how we might move fearlessly to understand the unfamiliar. In a dialogue of truth, Lao Tzu would say: "The wise meet all opposition with a quiet and open mind; then all opposition disappears." Chinese philosophy teaches us how overcoming others demonstrates force, although when we *overcome ourselves* we become strong.

Weather changes because a cold and warm front approach each other. Immediately their encounter creates a circular dance...a turning. "You have noticed that everything the Indian does is in a circle," Black Elk would say. "That is because the Power of the World always works in circles." If a leaf is floating on the river and it encounters an obstacle, the leaf will begin to spin in a circle. Beyond the leaf and the obstacle is another force which seeks continual movement. This can be viewed as the great river of life.

The History of Ancient China

Since its beginning, China has been a nation relatively isolated from the rest of the world. What makes China stand out in comparison to other civilizations is the longevity of a culture which has endured longer than any other. Like most civilizations, agriculture developed along the fertile valleys of the Yellow, Yangtze and Hsi Rivers. It wasn't until the early part of the twentieth century that China discarded her ancient past for the Socialist ideas of the nineteenth century German philosopher, Karl Marx in the form of Communism.

Its discernable history begins with a tribe called the Shang, who in 1700BC conquered the Yellow River valley using chariots. They succumbed to the Chou tribe from the West during the eleventh century BC, developing as a proud civilization that viewed the rest of the world as barbarians. During the late second century BC, the Ch'in tribe formed China's first empire. Its first emperor, Shih-Huang-Ti unified the country, standardized Chinese script, and completed the Great Wall that crossed the countryside as a fortified structure of nearly 3000 miles. Although this dynasty only endured for fifteen years, the Ch'in gave China its name and established its unique identity.

During the Shang and Chou periods, Chinese society was divided into the landowning nobility and the common people or peasants who made up its majority. Only the nobility belonged to a family and therefore, had ancestors who were worshiped as gods. The peasants were left to worship nature deities. Following the wisdom of nature and emulating its ways, the ancient Chinese would develop the nature oriented philosophy called Taoism.

Once Buddhism became an offshoot of Hinduism, it was brought to China, and was infused with the original ideas of Taoism. Like the idea of *Crossing the Great Water*, Prajna paramita was the "wisdom for crossing to the other shore." This other shore was a transition of awareness and a change of perspective. In the same way the *Tao te Ching* describes the mutability of Tao, Madhyamika Shastra described the void: "It cannot be called void or not void..."

Legend describes a ruler, Fu Hsi who ruled during the third millennium BC. He looked upward and contemplated the images of heaven, and looked downward to contemplate its manifestation on the earth. On the back of a tortoise shell, he discovered the arrangement of the sixty-four principles and eight trigrams that define the order of change in the cosmos. These basic ideas gave birth to the world's most ancient work of literature in a philosophical text called the *I Ching* or *Book of Changes*. From these initial characters carved onto shells and bones, the original Chinese language of pictographs emerged.

The Bubbling of Te

"Not the call, but the flight of the wild duck,
leads the flock to fly and follow."

While modern Asia may have developed into a culture which has more of an emphasis on the group rather than the individual, the philosophers of ancient times were focused on individualistic growth. Called *te*, it resembles our idea of individuation. They believed it was not the pull of conformity, but instinct that guided each creature toward actualization, just as the duck follows its own drive for flight and not the call of other ducks.

Even while we walk with others, we must still discover our unique pathway. Long before the ideas of Darwin and evolution in the West, the ancient Chinese explored how life moved toward purposeful growth and regeneration in its pursuit of a better way.

Te is a word that captures nature's drive for growth active within each individual. Mencius taught: "Te is the bubbling of instinct, excited by the prospect of your coming to be real." This Chinese word resembles our idea of the Self or the inspiration and guidance which emerges to lead us to actualize our destiny.

"Success is a pathway of self completion and the seed is always within you." Like the seed that will eventually become a great oak, we hold a design within, which is being cultivated by all we experience.

All we need to self actualize is already within us; we need only turn inward and empower it. When we can begin to see unhappiness as the hunger pain for authenticity, we can move with life to allow it to orchestrate the flowering of real nature. We take our place in the larger fabric without losing our connection to the Self. Where other philosophies negate the world of experience or the idea of the Self, the ancient Chinese actively learned from experience to understand *both*.

"The truth is not a sign that points at something beyond itself; *it just is.*" With nature as our teacher, we can overcome the idea of opposites and absolutes. Life is always in a state of becoming. At the molecular level, opposite forces generate life and we too, can meet difficulty by emulating the wisdom of nature. In this last chapter, we explore *the art of living,* something that was an art form in ancient China.

Yin and Yang

"Things cannot exhaust themselves.
This is the image before transition.
Once the power has been exhausted, it must become yielding."
The I Ching

Energy cannot be exhausted. What is unobservable in one manifestation is gathering somewhere in another form. We understand forces in terms of pushing and pulling phenomena. The pushing force that leads all things toward actualization was called Yang. Like electricity, a force *pushes* a current through metal. This force, however, is also the result of *pulling* fields, called Yin. Yang is productive, while Yin is receptive.

Both electricity and gravity are the result of pushing and pulling phenomena. The work of Einstein revealed how the natural world is not what it appears to be. The successive movement, or pushing and pulling behavior is how the ancient Chinese understood Yin and Yang; they "reveal the two modes of the one," or Tao.

Change is the outcome of natural energy as it moves through various stages of opposition, harmony, and dissolution. Although energy dissolves, it is never destroyed. It merely changes form.

Nature, in its creative form or Yang, explores diversity by bringing opposites together. At the same time a constant movement of the yielding, or Yin, takes form in life's pursuit of balance.

When we defend ourselves against creative change, we are forced to become open or yielding. Floating along yielding to our beliefs, events will force us to embrace creative change. When either is overly demonstrated, the other emerges to strike a balance. "Inherent in each is the seed of what will become its opposite."

In the *I Ching* or *Book of Changes*, the cosmos is described as moving toward manifestation in an "oscillating expression of its negative and positive nature." This resembles the West's models of a Super String or Membrane Theory. Both unify the forces in a similar theory of oscillating behavior, where phenomena may appear different, but is reduced to unity at a fundamental level. From the combination of the Creative (Yang) and the Receptive (Yin) emerge "the ten thousand things." Similarly, the positive and negative forces at the root of the atom become the building blocks of the many manifestations that we observe.

The *Tao te Ching* states: "Hold to the wisdom of antiquity to discover the thread running through the way." What is most profound about exploring ancient Chinese philosophy is the fact that in 500BC they were resurrecting a *more ancient* philosophy. As Western science is validating the basic ideas of Taoism, the medical community is also appreciating the ancient Chinese approach to wellness. Acupuncture cures many conditions that continue to stump Western medicine.

The changing energy of life is filled with vitality and newness at every level. Whatever transpires around us is necessary. Tao is this spontaneous expression in its many forms. To be in harmony with Tao is to participate fully with life. One does not lead with expectation but follows with excitement.

The Yang principle is positive, active, creative, masculine and brings day, heat and light. The Yin is negative, passive, receptive, feminine, and responds to Yang, as it's opposite. Even without the light of Yang, we experience night, cold and darkness and are received into Yin. Just as light can only be recognized in relation to the objects that receive it, without Yin, Yang is not actualized; without Yang, Yin is not actualized. Productive power and receptivity are always necessary for sustained growth. They area not so much opposites as they are variations in approach that mimic nature.

Yin and Yang literally meant the dark and sunny side of a hill. While it is the same hill, there is a natural ebbing and flowing of phenomena *that has the effect of changing its appearance*. Once darkness has reached its peak, it dissolves beneath the growing light. Once the light grows to its zenith, darkness rushes in again. In the great circle of life all things return to their beginnings.

Like the plant that loses its leaves during autumn to regenerate, while we sleep, we are returned to our vital center. When difficulty emerges we turn within for regeneration and open to nature's way of renewal.

The Thread Running Through the Way

*"We can appreciate
the changes observed
in the world around us,
while remaining wholly unaware
of our own mutability."*
Hu-ch'iu Tzu

The *Book of Changes* presents 64 principles of transformation based on eight phenomena observed in nature. Each principle is constructed of eight primary forces, called Pa Kua. *Pa* means eight and *Kua* means suspending or hanging. These primary principles can also be viewed as the Chinese Pantheon since each is associated with one of eight family members.

Each captures nature's movement toward renewal and offers a type of virtue to be emulated. By doing so, we become rooted without being stiff and develop a strength which need not be proven. We meet life at the threshold of perception an open to its teaching.

Ch'ien The Creative

Ch'ien is a snapshot of nature at the apex of creativity, symbolizing the power of Yang as it drives life to become. Embodied in the mythology of the *Warrior*, we demonstrate our creative power and actualize our destiny. This vital life energy leads the natural world toward the survival of the strong. At our best, we demonstrate strength, power and persistence, although Ch'ien suggests a power that is poised, gentle and confident, not intimidating and despotic. When we are *just so*, like all living things of the earth, we stop *trying* and find we are simply *doing*. To conquer the weak so we can mask our insecurities and shortcomings is not power, but an inferiority complex.

All cultures celebrated the life giving power of the sun and it was the first deity to emerge in many mythologies. Without the sun, very few things on the earth could survive. In the same way that summer's power gives way to decline during autumn, Odin experienced the boundaries of power that become *unnatural*. Like autumn, the excess of power gives way to a time of turning inward, where regeneration can begin.

In the Sumerian myth, the sun deity Shamash helps Gilgamesh to discover his destiny. At the same time, he questions him as to why he should seek it. In Judaic stories, Jacob wrestles with Yahweh, and receives a blessing for doing so. As we wrestle against the pull of conformity to actualize our nature, we discover why life only meets us halfway. The other half of the journey allows us to find *our way.* The ancient Chinese taught: "failure and success come to test the depth and nature of our sincerity." If it is real, it will endure.

At the apex of summer, the earth begins to turn back and "all things turn back with it. Turning back is how the way moves. Know when to stop and you will meet with no danger."

Ch'ien is the essence of how the *fertilized* is given form; our thoughts today are growing to become our circumstances tomorrow. If there is nothing to be taken away, "we meet with no danger." We open to the Creative principle to recognize how its root is within.

Inspired by the regressive movement of autumn and winter, the Masters respected even those times, when one appeared to be turned back. "The Way goes round and round and does not weary. Being great, it is described as receding. Receding, it is described as far away. Being far away, it is described as turning back."

By turning within and wrestling ourselves free from our internal prisons, we discover *the way forward.*

Just as powerful Yang is only actualized by the receptivity of Yin, we can only succeed through win/win situations that serve all parties. Caught up in the vision of what the future may require, we may lose sight of the present and exhaust ourselves into a time of turning inward.

K'un the Receptive Earth

During the winter of K'un, the ancient Chinese observed the laws of conservation. The rivers that would sustain the population in the coming year were conserved as ice sculptures on the hillsides. Branches that were stripped of foliage were now encased in ice for added protection. All things of the earth appeared to be sleeping, although an incredible amount of energy was recognized to be gathering below.

K'un offered a lesson about the potential power of the unseen. Our perception makes distinctions in the natural world which are not necessarily there. Each person is a complex network of cells, but we recognize them in only one form. Complete openness without the prejudice allows us to feel our connection to everything around us.

228

As all signs of the *Creative* recede below the *Earth* at the onset of winter's incubation, nature demonstrates a movement toward balance and harmony, which the Egyptians called *maat*. As we turn inward, we are given the opportunity to cultivate the roots that will lead us into the springtime of tomorrow. We merely strive to be real and success will come naturally.

Like a tree, we remain steadfast in our unbroken contact with the germinating power of life. Similarly, beneath the snowy landscape, the seeds of a future landscape are taking form.

The *Survivor* lives the mythology of discovering how composing the inner terrain allows the outer world to mysteriously change. Where Ch'ien is how we *actualize* our potential, K'un is the energy that spins our dreams and embodies the guidance that takes shape *within*.

Representing the Earth, K'un is life's nurturing energy that portrays what may be called our feminine ability to look inward to find our footing in the world. This feminine side of the psyche connects us to the natural realm of instinct. Just as Yin and Yang are dependent upon each other, we strike a balance where our creative, masculine or self-sufficient power can be *effectively* actualized by heeding our inner direction. Receptive to our inner processes, we find when we conquer others we use force, but *when we conquer ourselves, we become strong*.

As the potential power of the unseen that looms on tomorrow's horizon, we know the shortest day of the year means that each day will begin to grow longer. In the darkness, when the sun has traveled its greatest distance from us, we can be certain a new sunrise awaits us.

Li the Clinging Fire

The principle of Li or Fire reveals spring's early growth bursting through the earth. Li suggested a time of clarity and intelligence, where all of life follows an inborn pattern of development. Li is dependent and attached to the illuminating energy of the surrounding Yang. This sense of movement in harmony with the creative principle can best be described as spring fever. More than at any other time, we feel a deep connection to the changing seasons and a sense of rebirth.

Fire, like passion, has a synergistic connection to whatever keeps it burning. It captures the self-actualizing principle that connects all living things to an *inborn* sense of direction. As the gift of Prometheus, who gave Fire to humans, or Raven, who stole the sunlight from Manmaker, unlike Earth, Air and Water, Fire is the one element, which connects us to the divine.

229

When we discover how the fire within is fundamentally connected to what unfolds, we discover our omniscient ability to see our way forward.

Light gives definition to all we see and it is a phenomenon, which we know little about other than how its movement defines the basic laws of our universe. In every way, it is fundamental to life, as we know it. We observe its physical properties as particles, but also watch as it behaves like waves. In prisms and in the laws of physics, light offers more than meets the eye.

There is a synergistic aspect of life as it moves in its endless flow of variation and interdependency. Li captures both, the idea of observable order, and how it becomes the organic field of relationships that ties all things together. In a cross section of the earth, or in the circles of a tree stump, we see the observable order of what has passed. Within the seed and in our cellular structure and DNA, we see the outline of an order that will come to be.

Li is the Clinging or synergistic aspect of life, and reminds us to open to the Creative drive that rises *in here* to discover how it is being shaped by events *out there*. At the same time, all that takes shape *in here* will give rise to what unfolds *out there*. It cannot be separated.

Fire is dependent upon whatever it uses to keep burning. Approaching experience, we do not fight the very thing that gives us life. Li is a model for how we might move harmoniously with the changes, no matter where they may lead. Fire can reflect our desire to consume and destroy, although it is also symbolic of our celestial heritage that allows us to transform. Like the Phoenix, or mythical bird that rises from the ashes, all events coach us to renew ourselves from the residue of the past.

For many centuries, the wisdom of the ancient Greeks was lost to civilization. When it was rediscovered during the middle ages, we find the springtime of Western thought and the lantern that would lead humanity forward. The Age of Reason reflects the cyclical movement of civilization each time we return to nature for answers as to why we have become lost.

When ideas become prisons, we are always brought back to earth. The Negotiator discovers the need for balance in all of our passions, balancing a passion of the mind with our passionate feelings. Intelligence without an appreciation for life will always burn itself out.

By allowing the color and texture of experience to permeate our being, we activate the synergistic intelligence of our real nature or te, and discover how events emerge to unleash it.

The clinging and attachment movement portrayed by Li requires full participation with life and not just detached curiosity. No longer observing life with intellectual objectivity, we burn away the shackles that disconnect us from what unfolds.

Feelings make life valuable, and Li suggests that we discover what intelligence alone, cannot reveal. To have a mind disconnected from heart is to live a life searching for meaning, when meaning is unfolding all around us. As the Fire returns light to our footsteps, it reminds us of how we remain intrinsically connected to all we see.

Ken the Mountain of Keeping Still

In ancient China, the Mountain was respected for its ability to remain steadfast. The Masters coached great leaders to establish order in ancient society by emulating how Mountains established order. Firm in our power, one can remain still, and become a model of "tranquility in disturbance." No matter where we are traveling, the Mountain remains stationary on the horizon. It can offer a pathway when it appears to block our way. Forced to climb upward, we have the opportunity to see life from a different perspective.

The virtue suggested by the Mountain was called Keeping Still. The Master said: "Composure straightens out one's inner life; righteousness will square one's external life." In this way, the Mountain offers us a lesson about sameness as we connect with our real nature, and move ever deeper into the changing landscape.

Ken, the *Mountain* portrays the boundary between actual experiences and projected past beliefs. It is something that can only be recognized when *keeping still* and not taking defensive action. In the *Protector* and the myths of ancient Rome, we see the ways in which we conquer from fear and the illusion that something *may* happen. The *Romanitas* that keeps us from seeing the truth about our defensive posture and projection tendencies requires we stop to become present and observant in the moment.

Beneath the Mountain, we also discover the mechanisms of the *subconscious* net. In Ken, we keep still to meditate, transcending the noise of the mind *in here,* and life's distractions *out there.* We do not negate the world; we are looking for "the doorsill where the two worlds touch." We travel below the surface to let go of how we project a past which no longer serves us. Defense mechanisms built to keep the truth inaccessible may eventually become our prisons.

Our need to project past experience upon each event can cause a type of resistance, or turbulence in the great river of life. "Be open, that is all. When one comprehends nature and understands the transformations, one lifts the character to the level of the miraculous."

Whether we travel to the height of the Mountain to gain a wider perspective, or as a place of meditation, Ken is the last opportunity to understand experience before what is left of the Creative must be relegated to the past.

We see how the hero is given extraordinary power by climbing a Mountain. Moses climbs its heights to hear the words of Yahweh and Gilgamesh asks the Mountain to inspire his dreams. When we are told something over, and over, we come to believe it so strongly that hearing any opposite suggestion will fall on deaf ears. "The Mountain is the beginning and end." It is the barrier and gateway where we can unleash potential power. As the air grows thinner, we are disoriented enough to become still and receptive.

By keeping still, we observe the world from the perspective reserved for dreaming: everything is meant to teach us about ourselves. We do not deny the world, but trade reaction for perception. By taking responsibility for our past and the part it plays in creating the present, we move toward a life of self-sufficiency, independence and authentic power.

Aeneas seeks his destiny in the underworld below a Mountain. He meets the hideous and snarling creatures who have become the confusion of inner turmoil. Below the subconscious net, we enter a place that allows us to retrieve our conditioning tapes. They may play mindlessly, but they are actually keeping us a prisoner.

The *mysterious mirror* is a way to remember how a perspective without blemish ensures purity in a way that we meet with only favorable events.

Like Aeneas, we separate our branch of the World Tree from our parent's trunk. At the threshold of perception there is only newness and discovery.

When our perception is clear, we have the opportunity to move forward and claim our destiny.

The Mountain can become the hardened perspective which keeps us a prisoner to the past or the heights that we climb to obtain a wider view. "Do not climb the Mountain to hear the words of the Masters; climb them to seek what they sought." Each journey is unique, and it will mean something different to each individual.

Evolution requires that we participate with life and not mystify it. At the heart of Ken is the idea that by bringing composure to the inner terrain, we will discover its tranquility reflected in the outer world.

K'an the Abysmal Water

The Masters observed how Water demonstrated great power in its ability to overcome all obstacles in its path. When it approaches a barrier, it appears still and yet, continues to grow in volume and energy. It takes no aggressive action but remains even, suggesting a temperament where power grows from stillness.

Water has always symbolized the mysterious reservoir that holds the treasure of human potential. Whether it is Mimir's well, where Odin finds the secrets of the future, beneath the sea that held the coveted plant of immortality for Gilgamesh, or within the mysterious waters guarded by the Lady of the Lake, there is always a treasure to be retrieved by delving beneath the surface.

Water represents all that remains mysterious to us, and the Masters called this element the Abysmal or Profound. Symbolizing danger, within these depths are also the frightening things which remain unseen. Home of the great sea monsters, Leviathans or sea serpents, we discover ancient images that were often the deities of nearby enemies. Whenever something remains nonintegrated or opposed, it can only be given over to the dark depths as something to be feared.

We are composed primarily of this element and it is imperative to our survival. We think of our planet as being Earth, but from a spaceship, we might call it Planet Ocean. Resembling the composition of the human body, 70% of the Earth's surface is covered in water. Whether erecting Neolithic alters of worship or building agrarian civilizations in river valleys, Water has always been a central element of our existence.

The work of Dr. Masuru Emoto shows how water responds in much the same way as human emotions. He detected a response where the harmonic vibrations of music reflected beautiful symmetry in its crystal formations. On the other hand, frozen water observed within a negative environment demonstrated chaotic and irregular crystal formations. He measured this phenomenon in tap and spring water from around the world, and discovered water in a natural environment reflected symmetry more than the water processed in treatment facilities.

Dreams embody integration and change, while water always reflects how we feel about the changes. Water can overwhelm and threaten us, and how it behaves suggests the ways in which we are currently approaching change in our lives. It can be calm and smooth or turbulent and murky as a reflection of our inner landscape. Perhaps that is why the image of water continues to suggest the wellspring of what lies hidden below the depths of the unconscious. It remains an extremely potent symbol of our unrecognized potential for growth.

As the elixir of life, it can symbolize the healing process that can bring about renewal. In many myths, Water is home to the great shape-shifter, masking the truth about our regenerative and pro-creative powers. What remains untapped in our unconscious can lend itself to the shape shifting mechanism of projection, where we observe the world as a way of validating our beliefs. When we *cross the great water* to look back from another shore, we take responsibility for the situations we create.

K'an the Abysmal yet, meaningful symbol of Water is associated with late autumn. It reflects the opposite of Li or Fire or our synergistic connection within and how it unfolds as experience. K'an reveals the power of our center which emerges when everything around us is disintegrating. Warding off change, we are sometimes swept away by the Abysmal current, to be returned to the great river of life.

As we see nature in its decaying form, the world grows darker. The Creative energy recedes around us, and we must turn inward to find the light that will lead us forward. If we hold too tightly to a center that does not serve us, the great river will lead us into a deluge of change.

"The town can be changed, but the Well cannot be changed." We can build our homes anywhere, but we take our inner *wellspring* wherever we go. As the source of our inspiration, dreams and intuition, we must access its unfathomable depths and "discover the Well before we are thirsty."

"Concerned with what is inside and not what is seen outside, one abandons the 'that' to lay hold of the 'this.'" The difference between "that" and "this" is ownership. "This" resides in the Abysmal Water and becomes the image of accessing the depths our mysterious nature. We could live our entire lives and still never exhaust the resources inside of us.

When we are trapped in a transformative process, inspiration rises through dreams, intuition or events to reveal the *way through*. Synchronicity removes the barrier separating the inner and outer landscape. Without our connection to this guiding source within, we may float aimlessly in the river of life.

Therapists explore dreams to uncover symbols that can re-empower a client in crisis. Bringing the inner and outer together, the Masters spoke of *ming* as destiny in the sense of the path, but also how the pathway leads one to self-actualize. "In the Great Circle, there is no separation." Ming is the unified awareness achieved when *me in here* and *that out there* are indistinguishable.

In the Abysmal Waters of K'an, just like the unconscious, there is a riddle or a paradox to be solved. Something vital is seeking expression in the only way it can. Dreaming is a type of initiation which calls us deeper into the Waters of the unknown. We discover the source of our dreams as the residence of "the one who knows within." The idea of danger associated with the Abysmal represents crisis, only when we fail to heed life's message that we are on the wrong path.

We can fill a container with seawater but we cannot call what we have captured, the sea. Our Holy Grail reveals how the intangible nature of change refuses to be contained within our logical structures. Life is a flowing, changing and ceaseless phenomenon meant to orchestrate innovation and renewal. When the Abysmal Water destroys our tower, we find our deeper connection to life.

Chen the Arousing Thunder

Since *Thunder* appeared when the seasons change, it embodied the shocking elements that arouse the *Creative* out of dormancy. In early spring, the Creative is aroused to bring life to the sleeping Earth of winter. As this creative power stirs to become the principle of Chen or Thunder, the seeds are ignited with the electrical energy of life. Chen was understood to be arousing and shocking, inspiring movement and growth from a state of slumber. In the archetype of Trickster, we discover a similar mechanism that leads us away from absolutes.

When a cold front moves in, the wind builds in momentum, stirring the dark clouds gathering along the eastern horizon. Out of nowhere, a flash of lightning explodes in brilliant color as Thunder Birds, Feathered Serpents and Dragons scratch their long talons against the sky. Although the lightning illuminates the scenery of a distant horizon, we feel the reverberation of the Thunder deep within our bones.

"How admirable, he who thinks not that life is fleeting,
when he hears the sound of thunder."

Lightning redistributes unbalanced energy within the atmosphere, finding its most direct pathway to the earth. When thunder and lightning emerge, nature shows us its rejuvenating power. More importantly, it is a sure sign the climate is about to change.

In virtually all myths, Thunder was personified as characters who ushered in the changing seasons. It is a time when warm and cold fronts collide, transforming the atmosphere and ultimately the landscape. Whether in the Great Hunt of Norse mythology that laid the seeds for our Yule time festivals and Halloween rituals, or the Heyoka and Trickster who did outrageous things that went against tradition, fear wakes us from our slumber so we can be rejuvenated.

The ancient Chinese observed how energy being depleted was gathering somewhere else. In the discharge of lightning of a changing sky, nature always moves to redistribute unbalanced or bound up energy. Any power locked in a closet will come forward as nature strives for balance.

We too, require balance, and natural processes move to renew us in similar ways. Inherent in the Trickster of our Freudian slips, we are awakened from unconscious hibernation to discover the truth of what we attempt to keep hidden. Released from stagnation, shocking events allow us to escape into a higher order. Whether the earth is aroused during the storms of spring, or whether we awaken to the myths we live by, Chen sets the stage to allow the Creative to be reborn.

Sun the Gentle Wind

The Wind is another phenomenon that appears when the atmosphere is changing. Although it is invisible, it is given form in the swaying trees, and in those things supple enough to be moved by it. We may not see the greater force that moves life, but can observe it in the shape of how events unfold.

Like bamboo, laughing and bending when the winds of change set in, the ancient Chinese observed how the Gentle Wind taught one how to remain pliable enough to be led. Just as the seed pods rely on the Wind for regeneration, the idea of following life is another virtue on the pathway to actualizing destiny.

The most common celebrations of ancient times revolved around the harvest festivals of autumn. Perhaps it was out of fear and reverence as the days grew darker, and the natural world began to die away. It was an important time however, because what was done in earnest during this time, laid the foundation for future harvests. Autumn portrays how even in the darkest times, there is nothing to fear.

The Wind allows for the gentle effects of autumn to return the seeds to the earth. Like the regenerative power of sleep, the trees may appear lifeless, although the creative aspect of life is ever active in its unseen form. As autumn comes, we see the gentle effects of the Wind as it removes the seeds of the future from the outer husk or protective covering of the past. Just as leaves are tugged from the branches during autumn, the Victim discovers how to let go of the past to grow to meet the future.

All of the evolutionary forces bring about change and the Wind accomplishes its work slowly, but persistently. In the majestic mountains carved by the Wind, we see how what is removed will reveal the core essence of our nature. "All of life will not change you; it evolves as a way to unmask you." The germinating power of life appears in the same silence where a thousand seeds are becoming the landscape of spring.

In the Sumerian story of Gilgamesh, the mighty Winds come to the hero's aid when he goes into the Cedar Forest to wrestle evil Humbaba. As the Victim releases the idea of evil *out there* they can discover a more real power *in here*. Resurrecting this power, even in sleep, nature always urges our authenticity forward.

In the mountain of awareness, the Shadow is the side of us that we raised unwittingly each time we denied our growing power to be real. Since we refuse to acknowledge this power as being our own, it often takes on the face of our enemy. Because it is not recognized as good, it is given over to the dark side to be classified as evil.

We may hide from our unacknowledged inner life, but our efforts are no match for the Winds of renewal. "To discover the future potential of something, we must come to terms with what must pass." In dreams, the Wind is a symbol of the movement of consciousness, and suggests how the hidden continues to stir within. To dream of a tornado, signifies urges and emotions that have the potential to overwhelm us. In a sense, we are picked up and placed into another context. We are released of our need for control, which can only keep us rooted to the past.

The Jinn offers his powers to Aladdin when he is released from the lamp, and similarly, Humbaba tells Gilgamesh how he will serve him. When we meet the Shadow through our conflicts with others, we have the opportunity to tap a tremendous power that can make us whole and integrated.

The Wind reminds us to remain pliant in the river of change. If we cannot change the direction of the wind, then we must only adjust our sails and let it guide us.

Tui the Joyous Lake

Inspired by a sense of peacefulness reflected in the *Joyous Lake*, the ancient Chinese observed how satisfaction and dissatisfaction moved like ripples upon the surface of a lake. Satisfaction offset a desire for the endless change that can arise from being discontent, while dissatisfaction became the hunger pain that prodded one toward necessary change.

The Lake offers a place to relax with family and friends. Along its shores, we discover the art of tranquility and watch life's reflection upon its shimmering surface. A gust of wind may disturb its surface momentarily, although it remains anchored to its depths and always evens out.

The ancient Taoist emulated the behavior of the Lake as another way of achieving tranquility in disturbance. Regardless of the changes, we can make our heart like a lake to discover how the path always opens before us.

"Make your heart like a lake
with a calm, still surface
and great depths of kindness."

At the onset of summer, Tui or the Joyous Lake embodied how the landscape becomes a joyful celebration of fertility and exploding color. Like the path of Joy in Hindu philosophy, Tui offers a lesson about removing judgment and an attachment to a specific outcome to find the pleasure of discovering life on its own terms. We do not lead with expectation but follow with excitement, expressing wonderment in the unfolding moment.

Consumed by need, we can sometimes find ourselves in cycles of expectation and ultimate disappointment. Masking the emptiness of our lack of fulfillment, we resort to instant gratification and discover only fleeting satisfaction.

Adopting the innocence of a child, we experience true joy by being open to the world we are growing into. We allow events to pull us forward from the center of our te. Making "the heart like a lake," we reach deep inside and discover a wellspring within. Once tapped, all we seek from others transforms into our unique way of giving.

"Is not the action of nature like the stretching of a bow?
The high, it pulls down; the low, it lifts up;
It takes from what is in excess
In order to make good of what is deficient.
Who can take what they have in excess and offer it to others?"

We search for reassurance in the ways we are alike, although our te is revealed in the ways in which we are different. Tui or the Joyous Lake represents how a sense of fulfillment becomes an evolutionary mechanism. Dissatisfaction or unhappiness is merely a hunger pain that prods us toward necessary change. At the same time, satisfaction can sometimes keep us trapped on the shores of the great river. To balance satisfaction and dissatisfaction is to release them. "Be open, that is all."

As children, we threw stones into the Lake to observe how it moved in circular waves that rippled outward toward the shore. We could have thrown a rectangular block into the water, and the waves still moved in perfect circles. This is because the *fabric* of water is not what it appears to be: its horizontal movement is an illusion and its molecules spin vertically. The molecules remain stationary as the water crests in waves. It is merely energy, which is moving through the medium of water molecules. As a lesson from the lake, we find our center and hold to it. To feel life's energy moving through us in this way brings joy.

Moving with the flowing energy of life, we witness how we live, interact, play and learn all at the same time. We are part of the great bow that stretches across an endless space to release us like arrows into the path of our destiny. Our ability to remain pliable ensures that we stretch with the motion of life. The great waters of the Lake run deep because it remains connected to the greater river of life.

Everything Flows and Nothing Abides

"I have one thread that ties it all together."

Standing at the bank of a river, Confucius commented: "everything flows on and on like this river, without pause, day and night." We have a tendency to fight this perpetual flow, while we hold fast to the familiar.

Well aware of the changes taking place around us, we sometimes forget about our own mutability. When we are stuck, we need only tap the wisdom of our dreams. Appreciating the wisdom of our dreams, we learn to recognize how events lead us forward in similar ways.

Comparative mythology reveals a common thread that weaves an ancient wisdom into a unified message of wellness. Perhaps we once shared a type of inspiration that continues to shape our dreams. Wherever we look in life, we see its strange symmetries and design that reveals a type of thread "that ties it all together."

Circumstances break us free from what no longer serves us; we are stripped of the unnecessary that may come to block the necessary. The harder we cling to the illusion of living, the longer and more difficult the struggle. However, when the dust settles, we usually discover the purpose for the change.

Life has a way of always reflecting the things that *we* need to learn. We study climate change in an effort to sustain nature, yet we are learning a lesson about *sustaining ourselves*. Everything in life is meant to wake us to "the thread running through the way."

The Art of Living

*"Success is a pathway of self-completion
And the seed is always within you."*

"When one is at ease with themselves, one is near Nature. This is to let Nature take its own course. When you are just so, you are not defending anything. When *this* and *that* have no opposites, you discover life's very axis."

Transcending the idea of opposites, we discover our unity with everything around us. The art of living requires that we keep our mysterious mirror polished "to keep it without blemish" and learn to live without preconceptions or without *dumping* our stuff on others.

We spend one third of our lives asleep, where we are led toward a time of turning inward to unleash the judgments we cling to. Just like the mythical hero, we approach the mysterious reservoir within and solve the puzzles that will reveal who we are. These clues can move us beyond a state of crisis and actually allow us to discover greater meaning in life.

Dreams reveal a guiding source which is always active, but rarely accessed. When we pay closer attention to our dreams, growth can be accelerated.

We are the hero who climbs mountains, traverses forests and enters strange underworlds as places of trials and initiation. We transcend the mountains of our beliefs and escape the Trapper to be renewed. Within this landscape, we discover the truth about ourselves. To be "just so," we need only be more vigilant and less reactive.

*"While carrying on with life in your head,
can you embrace its mystery and not let go?"*

The whirlwind appears in our ancient stories and stirs things up to reveal our power to create and destroy. Anytime our towers are toppled, we discover how they became prisons. Although we may meet others in emotionally charged encounters, we might recognize the truth of the Winds of change *that stir within.*

The ancients approached autumn with apprehension and reverence. It is a time which teaches us that what we call bad is not necessarily bad; it is a time of letting go. Through illness, we often discover wellness; through conflict with others, we often discover ourselves.

In the mirror of those we meet, we observe how we are brought together propitiously. This is not a mystical event; life simply has a way of bringing like things together to balance and redistribute bound up energy.

240

We are always exchanging energy with our environment, and as part of nature's tapestry, we are subject to its economies.

The Chinese masters would teach us: "Propitious means that we attract the things we need." Like a trapped log in a river that encounters a spinning leaf, if two things are stuck and doing similar things, it is only a matter of time before they meet in the great river of life. We meet with no danger as long as we remain open to the teaching.

"Those who go against the way end up being called unlucky."

We are gathered together with great energy, but split open with equal vitality. Because the emotional intensity of the encounter is so profound, we know the meeting was propitious. "The wise meet all opposition with a quiet and open mind; then all opposition naturally disappears." Opposition disappears when no one is defending anything.

As our dreams demonstrate, we access an omniscient awareness while we sleep. During the day, we move away from the idea that this is possible. Yet, the more we pay attention to our inner clues, the more we see how these clues validate our pathway. Believing the power to create is under the control of anything else will leave us victimized on the banks of the river.

The natural world teaches us how the Wind gives movement to all that is stationary. Forms stir and shadows are created, although they are merely the reflections of how we come to block the light. We need only look around to separate what is real from the illusion of living. We take hold of the *this* and discard the *that*. Only then, can we take ownership of *this* or the evolving mystery of our real nature.

Perhaps when we were planters and more dependent upon nature for sustenance, we respected the natural processes which guided us. We still experience a sense of rebirth during spring, and the gentle tugging of what comes to pass during autumn as the way is prepared for another cycle. Life removes what is no longer necessary and we must bury what no longer serves us for the rebirth that will occur next year.

There are times when we feel this connection and celebrate and a time to turn inward to contemplate. In keeping still, we meditate and are inspired to create anew. There are times when we push forward with small, yet penetrating efforts. We express gratitude in our magnificent display of creativity and turn within where we are ignited with inspiration anew.

In ancient China, evolution and growth were recognized as oppositional energy that broke through stagnation to keep the universe unobstructed and free flowing. Something rises; it will fall. Something falls; it will rise. It is simply nature's way. The only constant we can be sure of is that in time, all things will change. In the circular dance of life, we also find that in time, everything turns back.

The *Book of Changes* says: "If one stands still at the end, disorder arises as the way comes to an end." The *old way* may come to an end, but the Way moves ever onward. Disorder merely completes a course that begins moving toward order.

In civilization too, opposition takes the form of conflicting ideologies that separate us. At the same time crisis churns the dormant waters of stagnation. The natural world is driven to eliminate any obstacles that would impede its movement toward growth. If we followed its ways, our way might be easier.

We thrive in a universe which generates energy and innovation *through collision*. It is purposeful, and the pathway is always necessary. Eventually we discover nature has been committed to our success since the beginning.

Who Knows What is Good and What is Bad?

Once upon a time an old farmer lost his best stallion. His neighbor came around that evening to express his condolences but the old farmer just said: "Who knows what is good and what is bad?" The next day the stallion returned, bringing with him three wild mares. The neighbor rushed round to celebrate but the old farmer simply said: "Who knows what is good and what is bad?" The following day the farmer's son fell from one of the wild mares while trying to break her in and injured his leg. The neighbor turned up to make sure all was well but the old farmer said: "Who knows what is good and what is bad?" The next day the army came to conscript the farmer's son to fight in the war, but finding him an invalid, left him with his father. The neighbor thought to himself: "Who knows what is good and what is bad?"

In life, there are periods where we climb and periods where we fall. "The climb is hard and steady, but the fall is quick and inexorable." Life is a flowing river where we identify its direction and can submit to its current. It is easier to fall or to flow than to climb. If we tap the momentum of how life is leading us forward, we can "fall backward into contentment and suffer no disgrace; know when to stop and we will meet with no danger. To know contentment, we are rich."

The Wisdom of Dreams

The *Mythology of Sleep* unfolds as an adventure of self-discovery, full of symbols that reveal our evolutionary journey. Beyond the darkness we keep, something emerges within the psyche to shine its light upon the ways we might continue to grow.

Whether we view mythology's transformative landscape and sacred symbols, or the common language we speak only in our dreams, if we could awaken into a world without boundaries, we would discover life *has no* boundaries. Through nature's chains of sustenance and swirling elements, life moves back and forth to orchestrate a landscape of change.

We thrive in a world of endless possibilities and the intangible nature of change refuses to be contained within our logical structures. Life is a flowing and ceaseless phenomenon meant to orchestrate renewal. We spend our lives building the belief structures which are disassembled while we sleep. When we cling too tightly, the deluge returns us back into the great river.

The processes driving life may be nothing more than evolutionary checks and balances. Nature shows no favoritism; it promotes harmony, while honoring differences.

It is just so.

In a global world, markets are overcoming ideologies because even business trends follow *natural* cycles. *"Black cat, white cat, all that matters is that it catches mice. Who knows what is good and what is bad?"*

As we Cross the Great Water to look back upon our ancient and shared heritage we see the roots of inspiration that continues to guide us. If our dreams can teach us anything, it is that our boundaries are an illusion: "If you understand nature's symmetries, you will use no counting rods." Without counting rods, we experience a life without limitations.

"In the old days our people had no education. All their wisdom and knowledge came to them from dreams. They tested their dreams and in that way learned their own strength." When we test our dreams, we discover profound meaning in life.

There is an ancient story that the rainbow is a promise of our well-being. This may well be true, because as it arks across the sky, it reveals the round way of things we may never see.

Made in the USA
Coppell, TX
08 December 2023

25602533R00152